JUSTICE, DEMOCRACY AND THE JURY

Justice, Democracy and the Jury

JAMES GOBERT
Professor of Law, University of Essex

Routledge
Taylor & Francis Group
LONDON AND NEW YORK

First published 1997 by Dartmouth and Ashgate Publishing

Reissued 2018 by Routledge
2 Park Square, Milton Park, Abingdon, Oxon, OX14 4RN
52 Vanderbilt Avenue, New York, NY 10017

Routledge is an imprint of the Taylor & Francis Group, an informa business

A Library of Congress record exists under LC control number:

Typeset by Manton Typesetters, 5-7 Eastfield Road, Louth, Lincolnshire

ISBN 13: 978-0-367-02666-0 (hbk)
ISBN 13: 978-0-429-39843-8 (ebk)

Contents

Preface

While writing this book I was visited by a Japanese judge who was based in London for the year. Japan was considering whether to reinstitute its jury system, which had been abolished after the Second World War, and my visitor had been sent to England to study its merits and report back to his judicial colleagues in Japan. It was while gathering information for his report that he had come to talk to me.

I was envious. Japan was in a position to do precisely what I wanted to do – to study the jury from an *a priori* vantage point, unaffected by the latest decision. Inevitably, the verdict in sensationalized cases will engender controversy. As this book was being written, the *cause célèbre* in the United States was the acquittal of O.J. Simpson for murder; in the previous year it was that of Lorraine Bobbitt, who was found not guilty of malicious wounding after having cut off her husband's penis while he was asleep. The jury verdicts in Britain have been no less controversial: three Liverpool women who trashed a British Aerospace factory because it manufactured fighter planes bound for Indonesia; two political dissidents who helped a Soviet spy to escape from Wormwood Scrubs prison; and a woman who killed the alleged rapist of her daughter following the decision of the Crown Prosecution Service not to bring formal charges against the man – all found not guilty. Questionable convictions, generally referred to as miscarriages of justice, raise similar questions about the ability of 'the gang of twelve' to reach a correct verdict.

Throughout its history the jury has been at the eye of a storm. Whichever way it decides a controversial case – whether by acquitting, convicting or being unable to agree (or 'hanging') – some group or another seems to be offended. In the real world the esteem in which the jury is held tends to rise and fall with each new verdict. In such ever-shifting tides one cannot justify the preservation of the jury system by citing the latest case. What is required is a principled justification – one that transcends individual cases and the public mood of the moment. For countries, such as Japan, Russia and Spain to name but a few, which have recently considered, or are considering, the adoption of a jury system, it is not a matter of mere academic interest. Even within the Anglo-American system, where the institution of the jury is supported by centuries of history, a better reasoned response to charges of perversity is demanded than a citation to the jury's historical pedigree.

About a dozen years ago, when I was a law professor at the University of Tennessee, I received a summons for jury service. My initial reaction was one of surprise, because I had assumed that lawyers, such as myself, would be ineligible. My reaction after checking the statute books and discovering that I was, indeed, eligible, was to seize an opportunity rarely afforded lawyers – to see the jury from the inside. It was an eye-opening experience. On the juries on which I served were men and women from all walks of life. They were of different races, different religions and different ethnic backgrounds. Their educational attainments ranged from nuclear physicists with multiple doctorates to high school drop-outs. If I and my fellow jurors were a family, it would have been possible to discern three generations, from fresh-faced high school graduates who had yet to find their first job to wizened retirees whose working days had long since passed. At a social function it might have been seen as a bizarre mix. For a jury it was not atypical.

Somehow or other, all the generational, cultural and class differences managed to be bridged. In the end it was what united us rather than what divided us that was important. What united us was our common pursuit of the right verdict in the case on which we had been brought together. Moreover, this odd collection of individuals was somehow able to function effectively as a group. All of our members contributed to the deliberations and all played a meaningful role in the decision-making process. What most impressed me was the seriousness of purpose with which my fellow jurors approached their task. Contrary to anecdotal stories (probably disseminated by frustrated lawyers who had just lost a case), none of the jurors was in a hurry to go home; all were prepared to put in as much time as it would take to reach the right verdict. We argued and argued, but in the end reached a verdict with which we could all feel satisfied. As an academic, I was struck by how jury service had both a levelling effect (in the sense that gender, class, education and income were irrelevant to one's role as a juror) and an elevating effect (in the sense that persons who were not used to wrestling with knotty problems managed to rise to the intellectual challenge). As a juror, I was pleased with both the process and the outcome. However, I knew deep in my lawyer's heart that the verdicts which I and my colleagues had returned would not necessarily meet with judicial approval even though the judge had to accept them. In several instances we had bent the rules to reach what we saw as the just result in the case.

My experience as a juror made me want to learn more about the jury and what made it work. In this book I plan to look at the jury from a number of perspectives – legal, historical, political, psychological and philosophical.

Most books on the jury tend to be directed at a narrow audience. A lawyer writes a jury primer for other lawyers; a psychologist conducts mock jury experiments and publishes the results in journals that only psychologists are likely to read. Neither lawyer nor psychologist may be familiar with the writings of political theorists or philosophers who have addressed the same issues albeit in different guises. What is needed is a discourse about the jury that cuts across artificial academic lines. My somewhat grandiose objective is to bring together the lessons to be gleaned from the various disciplines which have studied jury-related issues in an attempt to gain a deeper, richer and fuller understanding of the jury and its potential.

I am not a psychologist, philosopher or political scientist by trade, and my efforts to discuss these topics may appear simplistic to those whose familiarity with the respective literature far outstrips my own. I accept the merits in such criticisms. I have unrepentantly drawn on disciplines in which I am not as well versed as I would wish to be. If the discussion of legal principles is somewhat more sophisticated, it reflects my own background, as well as the fact that the jury is, in origin and in its most common guise, a distinctly legal institution. Even in this regard, however, those who are seeking a compendium of the law as it bears on the jury will be disappointed. My goal is not to set out a learned treatise on 'the law of the jury' nor 'the jury and the law'. Also, although this book looks at both the British and American jury systems, its pretensions of being a comparative study extend no further. There are numerous forms that the jury might take: in some countries, for example, the jury consists of a mix of judges and lay assessors. A comparative study of the various approaches would no doubt be a fascinating exercise but it would lead me too far afield from my chosen focus. I am less concerned with variations and more with the core concept of the jury as a body of ordinary citizens, drawn at random from the community, which is brought together to hear evidence and decide a particular controversy then. That I have used the Anglo-American jury as my model is explained both by the fact that it embodies the systems with which I am most familiar, and the fact that Great Britain is the birthplace of the modern jury and the United States the locus where the overwhelming majority of jury trials today take place.

This book is written with professional, academic and lay audiences in mind. Academics are more fastidious about citation form than the other intended audiences. Because the book is aimed at both a British and American market, I have adopted the citation protocol for court decisions which will be most familiar to readers in those respective countries who seek to trace the references to case law. George Bernard Shaw once remarked that Britain and America are two countries divided by a common language, and I have learned first-hand the truth of this observation. I was educated in the United

States and taught and practised law there as well. For the last decade I have been teaching law in Britain, I have learned through experience that terms that mean one thing in the US may carry a quite different meaning in Britain. Language is a barrier, and no doubt there will be occasions when I use an American term that has a somewhat different connotation in Britain, or vice versa. I can only ask the reader's indulgence.

There are many individuals, far too many to mention, who have graciously read all or part of this book. I particularly wish to thank Albert Weale and Sheldon Leader for reigning in my political and philosophical forays when they threatened to become too undisciplined, David Sanders for enlightening me on political theory and the dangers of post-modernism, Peter Luther for deepening my understanding of the jury's history and Janet Dine, Carolyn Hamilton, and Bob Watt for attempting to keep my legal analysis free from error. They may not have succeeded completely but the book is better for their efforts. I am also indebted to the members of the Political Theory Group at the University of Essex for their comments on aspects of the book that I presented at various workshops. I have not adopted all of their suggestions but they have all been valuable in assisting me to think through and formulate my own ideas. I would also be remiss if I did not acknowledge the many friends and strangers alike who were kind enough to share with me their own jury experiences. These were, as was perhaps to be expected, not of one piece, but all helped to further my understanding of the jury. Finally, I would like to thank the University of Essex and its Law Department for their generous support of my research, and the British Academy, for providing me with a grant under their Research Leave Scheme and thereby allowing this project to be brought to fruition.

James Gobert
University of Essex

1 Justice and the Jury

The dilemma for states which purport to subscribe to the rule of law is how to reconcile the requirements of the law with the demands of justice. The view which equates justice with law or sees justice implicit in law (Hobbes, 1914, ch. 30) is too simplistic. Obviously, society wants its laws to be just, and no legislature consciously sets out to enact a law which it knows is unjust (or so we would prefer to think). Nonetheless, many examples of unwise and unjust laws can be found. Even more commonplace are instances where the strict application of a just law to the facts of an individual case can lead to an unjust result. A just law, unjustly administered by police and prosecutors, presents yet a further danger. To avoid the latter, the legal system increasingly puts its faith in the objectivity provided by uniform rules and procedures. While these may help to guard against arbitrary decision-making, they may be powerless to prevent the injustice that can flow from laws that are themselves unjust or the application of just laws to inappropriate fact situations. Indeed, uniform procedures may inadvertently abet these kinds of injustice.

It does not follow that the state should go to the opposite extreme and issue a directive that justice be done in all cases without regard for law. If judges (or whoever was charged with adjudicating disputes) were to be left on their own to achieve the just result in each case, different decision-makers might reach different conclusions in similar fact situations. Yet not to treat like cases alike may itself violate a cardinal principle of justice. Thus rules of general application, enforced in a non-discriminatory manner, may be an integral part of justice. On the other hand, universally applicable rules and rational procedures do not by themselves guarantee just outcomes: strict adherence to legal rule can sometimes lead to results which would be widely regarded as unjust. The challenge is to achieve justice in the individual case while keeping faith with the rule of law. When there is tension between the two, however, which must yield? Who decides this question? Who should decide? This chapter, as well as Chapters 2 and 3, will examine the role of the jury, both in theory and in practice, with regard to these matters.

The discussion will centre primarily on trials in serious criminal cases, for several reasons. First is the practical point that the inquiry is intended to span the Anglo-American jury experience. However, in modern-day Britain, jury trials in civil cases are a rarity.[1] Even more rare is a jury trial in a case involving a minor criminal offence, jurisdiction in such cases largely having been transferred to juryless magistrates' courts (see Chapter 4). Serious criminal cases provide the primary common ground for an analysis of the role of juries in both the English and American criminal justice systems. Restricting the focus to such cases, however, suits my purposes. It is in these trials, where a conviction may mean an extended loss of liberty, and, in the United States, the possible loss of life, that moral culpability becomes a legitimate matter of legal concern and the case for jury decision-making becomes most compelling. One can be a supporter of the jury system without incurring the obligation to defend the proposition that juries are the *only* appropriate method for deciding *all* legal controversies. In the world of commerce, moral assessments may have to take a back seat to the security of contract, and, if this is so, the moral sentiment of the community which a jury brings to bear is of lesser relevance. In contrast, a criminal conviction for those serious crimes that at one time were known as *malum in se*, or wrong in themselves, is inescapably a judgement about moral blameworthiness. This judgement is the jury's responsibility, and it is no accident that it is in the criminal courts that the jury's powers have traditionally been the most far-reaching and unencumbered.[2] Although the British and American legal systems are dissimilar in many respects (for one thing, in the United States there is a written Constitution, and judges are able to strike down legislative enactments that violate its provisions whereas, in the United Kingdom, parliament occupies a more centrist and powerful position, and judges are inclined to defer to its authority), they share the common feature of entrusting the decision in serious criminal cases to twelve randomly selected men and women from the community – the jury.

The Conventional View of the Jury's Role

The conventional view of the jury's role is that it is engaged in a two-stage process. The first stage requires the jurors to determine the facts; in the second stage, the jury applies the law to those facts. The jury's determination of the facts is based on the evidence presented in court (as opposed to any independent knowledge that the jurors might have or might glean from the newspapers or other such sources). The law which the jury is to apply is that set out in the judge's directions.

The law, broadly conceived, consists of general rules of behaviour, promulgated pursuant to lawful authority, which govern those who live in the relevant jurisdiction. These rules restrict individual choice in respect of conduct which is prohibited. H.L.A. Hart offers a more refined vision, distinguishing between what he calls primary and secondary rules (Hart, 1961, ch. 5). Primary rules are rules of obligation, directed to the people, which inform them of what they can and cannot do.[3] Secondary rules, in contrast, are directed to officials. Among the most important secondary rules are rules of change, which enable officials to amend the law, rules of adjudication, which provide guidance to those responsible for resolving disputes and rules of recognition, which direct decision-makers where to look in their search for primary rules.

It is possible to gain a measure of understanding of the jury's role, as conventionally seen, through Hart's concept of law. The criminal law consists of primary rules of obligation. When there has been a violation of one of these rules, a legal prosecution will be brought so that there can be an official determination of whether the person charged with committing that violation did in fact do so. In the Anglo-American criminal justice systems, the responsibility for this determination has been assigned to the jury. Although a jury is composed of twelve individuals randomly selected from the community, as a collective body, the jurors become an official organ of the state and, like other official bodies, will be guided by secondary rules. The rule of adjudication which governs the jury's proceedings instructs it to apply the law to the facts of the case. The relevant rule of recognition states that the law is to be found in the directions of the trial judge. The judge is perforce bound by a different rule of recognition which tells him or her to look at the enactments of the legislature and the decisions of higher courts to discover the law which is to be conveyed to the jury.

One of Hart's sternest critics has been Ronald Dworkin. Like Hart, Dworkin accepts the value of rules in the routine case. But where Hart is prepared to see the judge exercise discretion in cases where no clear rule applies, Dworkin asserts that there are non-rule standards – principles – which inform a judge's decision-making in such cases (Dworkin, 1986). Dworkin's analysis focuses on how *judges* decide *hard cases*. However, the idea of non-rule standards is a powerful one which also provides insight into how juries decide cases. For the jury a hard case is not that described by Dworkin – one where the rules of law seem to have run out – but rather one where the rule of law which seems to be applicable would lead to a verdict which conflicts with the jurors' sense of justice. To avoid the unjust result the jurors have to look, as does the Dworkinian judge, beyond the law to non-rule standards. Jurors and judges do not necessarily apply the same non-rule standards, but both are pushed to extend the scope of their inquiry beyond the four corners of the law.

The number of true hard cases may be only a small fraction of the criminal cases decided by juries.[4] Their infrequency, however, does not detract from their significance; indeed, precisely the opposite. Hard cases provide a critical insight into the justification for the jury's very existence. There may, in any event, be more hard cases than is commonly estimated. Many never reach trial because the government agencies responsible for bringing a formal prosecution, anticipating an adverse jury verdict, prefer to have an unenforced law on the books (because of its presumed deterrent effect) than a law that has been rejected by a string of juries.

The term 'hard cases' is also somewhat misleading when applied to jury trials. It suggests two discrete categories of case when the reality is more likely to be a continuum. At one end may be the straightforward case where the law is clear and leads to a result that reasonable persons would accept as just and where, therefore, there is no tension between law and justice. At the opposite extreme is the case where the applicable rule of law would produce a result which would be widely condemned as unjust. In between, however, are a plethora of cases where the law tugs in one direction and considerations of justice in another. Such cases present the jury with a dilemma. Examining how it resolves that dilemma will further our understanding of the jury's true role within the criminal justice system.

First, however, it might be observed that even the conventional description of the jury's role in terms of determining the facts and applying the law is more complex than its simple statement might suggest. Modern jurors, unlike their ancestors, are not chosen because of their first-hand knowledge of the facts.[5] Today's jurors must deduce the facts from the evidence, and they are beset by many obstacles in their efforts to do so (Frank, 1963). In a criminal trial, first the prosecution and then the defence will present its case. The testimony of two witnesses which bears on the same point may, as a result, be separated by days or even weeks. Within each side's case, moreover, evidence is not presented holistically but piecemeal. The order of the witnesses may not accord with the temporal sequence of events, and any given witness's testimony may relate only to a singular, and sometimes minor, aspect of the case. The jurors have to weave the disconnected pieces of information provided by the witnesses into a coherent whole – a challenge which is further complicated by the fact that it is not uncommon for witnesses to disagree. None of the witnesses, moreover, may be deliberately lying. Often two persons who see the same event have different recollections of it. Psychologists tell us that memories are faulty, and become more so the longer the interval between the event and the recounting of it (Loftus, 1979). Many months may intervene between the crime and the trial. Human beings are also suggestible. A subconscious tendency to identify with the party who has called a witness to testify may incline the witness to see 'the truth' in terms favourable to that side. In addition, nervousness, induced partly by the occasion, partly by the unfamiliar surroundings of the courtroom, and partly by cross-examination techniques designed to trip up the witness, can result in testimony that does not necessarily come across as what the witness intended. Furthermore, language contains its own limitations, and some witnesses may be relatively inarticulate. The jury's task is to assess the testimony of each witness (taking into account such factors as the witness's opportunity to observe, motivation to lie and general demeanour), piece together the credible evidence and, from that, construct an accurate picture of events.

The jury suffers from additional handicaps in its efforts to determine the facts. Sometimes it is not presented with all the relevant information. At one point in English history parties were not permitted to testify in their own behalf.[6] This prohibition is no longer in force, but often a defendant will make a tactical decision not to testify because evidence that would otherwise be inadmissible, such as the defendant's criminal record, will be a permissible subject of cross-examination. In some instances, witnesses may not appear in court because the best efforts to locate them have failed. Indeed, the jury may never even learn of the existence of such witnesses. The knowledge of those witnesses who do testify may also not be presented in full. The scope of a witness's testimony will be shaped by the questioning of the lawyers and constricted by rules of evidence. So, for instance, the giving of opinions and the recounting of what others have said is generally not allowed (Tapper, 1995), although this evidence is of a sort that people routinely take into account in making decisions in their own lives. The reason that it is kept from the jurors is because of a judicial fear that they will give it more weight than it deserves. Whether or not this fear is well-founded, it complicates the jury's efforts to construct an accurate picture of the facts.

The second half of the jury's task, that of applying law to fact, is no easier. It requires that the jurors both understand what it is that the law requires and be able to apply its provisions correctly. To appreciate the difficulty of asking the jury to grasp the nuances of the law, one need only take note of the fact that it is not uncommon for eminent judges to disagree among themselves as to the meaning of a statute.[7] The crash course in the law provided to the jurors by the trial judge may not only be inadequate, but may raise more questions than it answers. Judicial directions are usually crafted with the goal of stating the law accurately rather than making it comprehensible to the jurors. When a judge's directions stray from the approved language of precedents, the judge increases the risk of committing reversible error.[8] That the judge's motivation is a desire to assist the jury in its understanding of the law provides no protection against a reversal. A jury, confronted by judicial directions couched in arcane language, may request clarification, but is likely to be met by a repetition of the original instruction or a restatement in jargon that is no more illuminating. Even assuming that the jurors understand the law, they must be able to apply it. Judges often disagree among themselves on the scope of a law's applicability.[9] The requisite degree of fit between fact and law which the jury must find to exist is also difficult to pin down, and the mere statement that the proof must establish guilt beyond a reasonable doubt leaves unanswered the question of where the boundary lies between a reasonable doubt and the fact that absolute certainty is an illusion.

The indeterminacy of both fact and law, on the other hand, does enable the jury to introduce value judgements into the deliberation process without feeling guilty about doing so. Roscoe Pound was undoubtedly correct when he observed that the jury had the power to determine the facts in such a way as to lead to a different result from that which the legal rule, strictly applied, would require (Pound, 1966, p. 66). Whereas Pound gave little in the way of concrete example, Thomas Green provides numerous illustrations in his comprehensive historical study of the English jury (Green, 1985). In one case, a jury of inquest had established that a husband had come home at midday to find his wife in bed with another man, whom he then proceeded to kill. The trial jury, on the other hand, found that the victim had entered the defendant's home at night, rather than during the day, and, as a trespasser rather than as an invited guest of the defendant's wife. Furthermore, the trial jury found that the victim had attacked the defendant with a knife, and that the defendant, finding his escape blocked, had in desperation seized his hatchet and struck the victim a fatal blow. One might wonder at this revisionist account of events but the explanation lies in the limitations imposed by the then prevailing law of self-defence. By its findings of fact the trial jury was able to afford the defendant a defence of self-defence that would not otherwise have been available. Similarly, Green reports cases in which a jury determined that a defendant had been personally attacked although the evidence clearly indicated that it was a close relative who had been attacked (ibid., pp. 42–3). Again, the jury's purpose seems to have been to bring the facts within the legal strictures of self-defence.

Kalven and Zeisel (1966) offer a more refined version of Pound's thesis that the 'facts found [are] found in order to reach the result and are by no means necessarily the facts of the actual case' (Pound, 1966, p. 66). They suggest that juries resolve factual ambiguities to accord with their view of the equities of a case (Kalven and Zeisel, 1966, p. 165). In Kalven and Zeisel's scheme, factual ambiguity liberates jurors to introduce value judgements into the decision-making process. Jurors do not, as Pound seems to imply, simply reason from back to front, constructing a factual picture that allows them to reach the verdict that they desire. If Kalven and Zeisel are correct – and, unlike Pound, they offer a wealth of empirical evidence to support their position – then the phenomenon of verdicts contrary to the actual facts would not be as prevalent as Pound's thesis might suggest. Nonetheless, Kalven and Zeisel would not disagree with Pound that jurors are able to justify an acquittal by choosing not to believe the prosecution's witnesses, or by filling in gaps in the proof to fit with the desired outcome. Without having to go so far as to maintain that there is no such thing as objective reality (see Mungham and Bankowski, 1976) and that one's perspective of facts and events is predetermined by one's experiences and values, it can be said that jurors are required to interpret evidence and to decide what inferences are to be drawn from the testimony. The leeway involved in this process allows the jurors to bring the facts to which the law is to be applied into line with their conception of what would constitute a just result in light of the totality of the circumstances. On the other hand, by invoking their law-applying authority the jury can justify what might seem to be a questionable acquittal by finding that the prosecution's proof does not rise to the level of 'beyond a reasonable doubt' (Kalven and Zeisel, 1966, ch. 14). This non-mathematical legal formulation of the requisite burden of proof lends itself to adjustments that permit a jury to return the verdict that it considers appropriate (Kerr, 1994; Uviller, 1990).

Clues to a Different Role

The conventional description of the jury's role in terms of finding the facts and applying the law is not so much inaccurate as incomplete. It may fairly well capture what the jury does in the case where the facts are straightforward, the law is unambiguous, and the result yielded by the application of the law is uncontroversial. It is less satisfactory in describing the jury's role in trials where law and justice appear to pull in different directions. In the latter cases the legal system looks to the jury to resolve the tension and to ensure that no injustice occurs.

Indications that the jury has such a responsibility may be gleaned from a number of practices which do not accord with the traditional account of the jury's role. Many would assert that the jury's superiority to the judge lies in its capacity to determine the facts. When it comes to the interpretation and application of legal rules, however, the law-trained judge has the obvious advantage. If this is so obvious, one might well ask why the jury's role does not end with the determination of the facts. Could not the jury simply report its findings of fact to the judge, who would then apply the law to them? Such a bifurcated procedure would seem to offer the optimal blend between the jury's ability to discern the facts and the judge's expertise in applying the law. It would avoid the types of error that can result from the jury's misinterpretation or misapplication of legal doctrine. It would also have the ancillary benefit of providing an appellate court with the jury's statement of the facts as found by the jury.

Notwithstanding these advantages, a modern jury is not restricted to reporting the facts to the judge. On the contrary, in criminal cases, the trend has been away from the use of the 'special verdict'[10] – a procedure which required a jury to respond to a series of questions, the answers to which enabled the court to enter a legal order. Under the special verdict procedure, the judge applies the law to the facts. In returning a general verdict, the jury applies the law to the facts and announces only a result – that the defendant is guilty or not guilty.[11] The general verdict contains no explanations, no reasons, not even a statement of the jury's understanding of the facts. In England, Fox's Libel Act 1792, although addressing the specific controversies surrounding prosecutions for seditious libel, stated that in these trials, '*as in criminal cases generally*', a jury could not be required to return a special verdict. A particular jury might choose to do so, but a judge could not order it to do so. In *Bourne* the Court of Appeal stated that special verdicts were to be employed only in exceptional cases.[12] In the United States, also, the special verdict has fallen into disfavour. In *United States* v. *Spock*[13] the trial judge had instructed the jury both to return a general verdict and to answer ten specific questions. The appellate court disapproved the latter inquiry, holding that it infringed upon the jury's right to return a general verdict.

One might also reflect on the role of the jury in a trial where the facts are not in dispute. The prosecution presents its evidence-in-chief. The defence does not examine the state's witnesses and offers none of its own. Where, in such circumstances, the prosecution's evidence has not reached a certain threshold level, a judge may dismiss the charges or find no case to answer. In the converse situation, however, where the evidence of guilt is overwhelming, the judge is not permitted to enter a verdict of guilty. The case must still be sent to the jury for its decision.

Finally, an appellate court is not permitted to overturn a jury acquittal which appears to be contrary to the evidence or based on a misconstruction of the law. Although a wrongful conviction may be reversed, an apparently wrongful acquittal cannot be deprived of its authoritativeness. Nor, as will be seen in Chapter 2, may jurors be punished for such a verdict. The only other decisions which enjoy a comparable stature in the law are those of the highest court in the land. On the rare occasion where an appellate court does review a case in which a jury has acquitted, its purpose is limited to determining whether the trial court erred in its legal rulings or directions. The objective is not to cast doubt on the jury's verdict but to correct the judge's error before it becomes imbedded in the law. The jury's verdict remains sacrosanct.

The relationship between judge and jury, the fact that jurors are not restricted to a fact-finding role and the finality of an acquittal all point to the conclusion that there is more to the jury's role than the courts normally imply. It is not merely a question of choosing whether a judge or jury is better qualified to determine the facts and to apply law to fact. The jury introduces, and is expected to introduce, dimensions to the decision-making process which go beyond what the court can provide. What more, then, does the legal system – and, indeed, society – seek from its juries?

A Four-stage Process of Adjudication

The jury's role, as we have seen, is traditionally depicted as involving two stages. The first involves the determination of the facts; the second, the application of the law to those facts. The conventional view is that the verdict represents (and should represent) the law as applied to the facts – nothing more, nothing less. The thesis to be presented here is that the jury's responsibility extends beyond the mechanical application of legal rules. A jury must become engaged not only with issues of fact and law, but also with issues of justice. The jury bears the responsibility for protecting an accused from an unjust conviction. Its ultimate goal is a just verdict, 'all things considered'.[14]

A jury's deliberations proceed through a four-stage process, although this is a somewhat crude chronology. First, the jury ascertains the facts. Second, it applies the law to those facts. So far the description might seem in accord with the conventional account of the jury's role. It is, but the reason that the jury seeks to determine the correct legal outcome is because an important component of justice is the right not to be convicted when one has not violated the law. The converse proposition – that a defendant found to have violated the law must be convicted – does not follow. Justice is a more encompassing concept, and the jury needs to satisfy itself that the guilty verdict that might be produced by a strict application of law to fact would not perpetrate an injustice. At the third stage of the adjudication process the jury will consider the defendant's moral culpability and any explanations, excuses or justifications which he or she might wish to submit. The jury may well be persuaded, for valid reasons, that, under the circumstances of the case, a conviction would be unjust despite proof that the defendant committed the acts attributed to him. If so, the jury may again return a verdict of not guilty. Finally, even if the jury concludes that the defendant is factually, legally and morally culpable, it may decide that there are additional aspects of the case that need to be taken into account if justice, all things considered, is to be achieved.[15] This is the fourth and final stage of the adjudication process.

The first-stage determination of the facts is often crucial, since what would be a just result in one set of facts might be unjust if the facts were to be slightly altered: who struck the first-blow, for example, may be the critical issue in determining whether a defendant is entitled to a claim of self-defence. In respect to the facts the jury's task is to construct an account of events that best fits the credible evidence. A jury's collective perception of the facts is likely to be more accurate than that of any single individual, including a judge. Indeed, many would maintain that it is this superior ability that justifies the jury system in the first place. The reasons why a jury is better able to determine the facts will be examined more closely in Chapter 3 but, for now, it is sufficient to note the importance of this stage of the deliberations. Accurate fact determination may be a necessary, even if not a sufficient, condition if the jury is to reach a just verdict.[16]

While the jury is undoubtedly an effective body for discovering the facts, its more important function is to safeguard the rights of the accused. In the second stage, where the jury applies law to fact, it protects the defendant's legal rights. By so doing the jury satisfies the requirements of what might be called legal justice or 'justice under law'. It is unjust to deny any person rights to which he or she is entitled by law. In the Anglo-American criminal justice systems, those accused of a crime are entitled to their liberty until such time as their violation of the law is proven beyond reasonable doubt. It is the jury's duty to protect that right. If the jurors determine a reasonable doubt regarding guilt exists, they must return a verdict of not guilty.

It is not just a defendant's legal rights that a jury is charged with protecting. It does not follow from the premise that justice includes the protection of an accused's legal rights that justice will be served by a rigid adherence to the law. If the jury determines that the defendant has violated the law, it will proceed to a third stage in which it considers the defendant's moral blameworthiness and whether he or she is deserving of punishment. The law tacitly invites this inquiry. The requirement of *mens rea* focuses the jury's attention on the defendant's mental state.[17] In a strict legal sense motive is irrelevant to *mens rea* (see Hitchler, 1931); a good motive cannot undo the illegality of an illegal act, and a bad motive will not convert an act that is lawful into one that is criminal. Nevertheless, questions of mental state and motive are not easily separated in a juror's mind, and the two in turn become intertwined with the more general issue of moral blameworthiness. It would be a poor reflection on the perspicacity of judges if they were not aware of this merger. Justice Robert Jackson of the US Supreme Court indicated that not only were trial judges aware of it, but that they encouraged it:

> [C]ourts of various jurisdictions, and for the purposes of different offenses, have devised working formulae, if not scientific ones, for the instruction of juries around such terms as 'felonious intent,' 'criminal intent,' 'malice aforethought,' guilty knowledge,' 'fraudulent intent,' wilfulness,' 'scienter' to denote guilty knowledge or '*mens rea*,' to signify an evil purpose or mental culpability. By use or combination of these various tokens, they have sought to protect those who were not blameworthy in mind from conviction of infamous common-law crimes.[18]

Most criminal defendants can be divided into one of two camps. In the first there are those defendants who claim that they did not commit the criminal acts attributed to them. In these cases the jury's finding of fact will usually determine the outcome. If the jury decides that it was the defendant who committed the offence, it will almost always convict, and the defendant's disingenuousness in denying the offence will count against any claim of justification that might otherwise have been advanced.

The second category of defendant comprises those who concede that they may have violated the law but maintain that they do not deserve to be convicted. Their basic position can be expressed as 'Yes, I did it, but ...'. Most individuals who run foul of the law do not see themselves as criminals. The Oxford Jury Project found that 70 per cent of defendants who pleaded not guilty admitted to being involved in something that might be regarded as criminal but denied that their involvement was malicious or intentional (McCabe and Purves, 1972). Such defendants would assert that their actions were appropriate (or at least not inappropriate) under the circumstances. They believe that, if the jurors had been in their position, they might well have reacted similarly. They therefore invite the jurors to step into their shoes and to see events through their eyes. They place before the jury not only their conduct but their character and ask the jurors to decide whether they have behaved in a blameworthy manner, and whether they are deserving of criminal sanction. They ask, in effect, that the jury judge them not by the formal rules of the law, but as autonomous and responsible moral agents (Huigens, 1995).

That the jury, in this third stage of the adjudication process, considers a defendant's reasons for acting does not mean that the jury has to apply a subjective test of criminal liability set by the accused. This would reduce the criminal law to a shambles, as every defendant would become a law unto him or herself. The jury is not required to accept the legitimacy of the premises under which the defendant's actions made sense to him or her. The jurors will accept the defendant's position only when they are persuaded that the defendant's actions are not deserving of condemnation. But when will a jury be so persuaded? The claims that are most likely to succeed are those where the attempted vindication of the defendant's conduct is based on principle. Acts of civil disobedience in protest of an alleged unjust law or government policy are often claimed to have been motivated by higher moral principles. Another situation where a jury might acquit is if it is convinced that a defendant's crime was the product of forces for which the defendant should not be held responsible. A classic example is the out-of-work single mother, cut off from state benefits, who steals to feed her starving family. This is not to say that a jury will accept social determinism as an across-the-board defence, but rather that there are situations where fair-minded persons will be prepared to concede that, in comparable circumstances, they too might well have acted in the same way.

If the jury determines that the defendant has not violated the law or that the defendant is not morally blameworthy, even though he or she may have violated the law, justice demands an acquittal. But can there be situations where the jury determines that the defendant is factually, legally, and morally culpable yet decides not to convict? The fourth and final stage of the deliberation process involves the jury's search for the just verdict, all things considered. Here the jury is not so much attempting to vindicate a right of the defendant as to balance a wide range of factors, both legal and extra-legal, which it deems to be worthy of proper consideration regardless of what the strict rules of the law might be. It is extremely difficult to pin down the considerations that may enter into the jury's thinking but a few empirical examples may help to illustrate the point. The Chicago Jury Project discovered that juries are prone to acquit when persuaded that the defendant (or his or her family) has suffered enough already, particularly if the defendant has expressed genuine remorse (Kalven and Zeisel, 1966, ch. 20). Mercy, which is a matter of grace, should not be confused with justice, which is a matter of right, but the merciful decision may be seen by the jurors as the most just outcome, all things considered. If the defendant's conduct is generally acceptable, albeit illegal, within the community, a jury may also be led to return a verdict of not guilty (ibid., ch. 19). The same result can occur when the jury deems the penalty for the crime to be disproportionate to the gravity of the offence (ibid., ch. 21). In some instances the jury seeks, by its verdict, to take into account the victim's role in bringing about the crime. Improper behaviour by the police or prosecution is another consideration which may enter into the jury's calculations. Although such misconduct is technically irrelevant to a defendant's legal guilt or, indeed, moral blameworthiness, it may nonetheless influence the jury's thinking.

Trial lawyers are not unaware that juries take into account these extra-legal factors and strain to introduce relevant evidence. This evidence, however, is usually irrelevant in the strict legal sense of the term. The result is a frequently repeated charade. The defence introduces evidence relating to a matter that bears on the justice of a conviction. The prosecution objects that the evidence is irrelevant. The trial judge sustains the objection and admonishes the jury to disregard the evidence. However, as common sense would predict and as psychological studies confirm (Casper and Benedict, 1994; Kassin, 1990; but see LSE Jury Project, 1973), the jurors cannot completely shut this information out of their minds. It may enter their deliberations directly, but more probably it will lurk below the surface, influencing the juror's interpretation of the evidence in ways of which they may not even be aware. Thompson, Fong and Rosenhan (1981) discovered that inadmissible evidence was more likely to be considered when in the defendant's favour.

In *The Morality of Law* (1964) Lon Fuller drew a distinction between the morality of duty and the morality of aspiration. If one were to attempt an analogy to the situation of the jury, the obligation of the jury would be to prevent injustice to the accused, and its aspiration would be to achieve justice, all things considered. That the prevention of injustice should take priority accords with values that lie at the heart of the Anglo-American criminal justice system. It is commonplace for courts to observe that it is better that ten guilty defendants go free than that one innocent individual go to jail. The requirement that the prosecution's case be established by proof beyond a reasonable doubt reinforces this prioritization. The avoidance of an unjust conviction of an innocent defendant is institutionally deemed to take precedence over the conviction of the guilty – a fact that too often seems to be lost sight of by the jury's critics. Lord Devlin, a strong defender of the jury system, has gone further and stated that trial by jury is not so much an instrument of getting at the truth as a process to ensure that, to the maximum extent possible, no innocent person is convicted (Kalven and Zeisel, 1966, p. 190). No system is perfect, of course, but both legal burdens of proof and jury decision-making practices combine to give priority to preventing the unjust conviction.

There are also practical reasons why the prevention of injustice should receive priority over the achievement of justice. The jury's options are limited. In a criminal case it is restricted to the verdicts of guilty, not guilty, and conviction of a lesser included offence.[19] These crude alternatives may be insufficient to take into account the myriad dimensions of a complex case. Neither the crime charged nor any lesser included offence may, in the jury's estimation, capture the degree of the defendant's fault. In some instances, the jurors might wish for the defendant to be detained or to receive treatment but not be sent to prison. In others the jury may believe that sanctions against a third party not before the court are necessary to achieve justice, yet finds itself restricted to returning a verdict in respect to the defendant in the dock.

Even if an infinite range of dispositions were available to the jury, it might still be unrealistic to expect the jurors to achieve justice rather than the more modest objective of avoiding injustice. As a matter of logic, to establish that a verdict is 'just' requires a demonstration that the verdict complies with all criteria of justice. If the verdict fails to satisfy any of the criteria, it would lose its claim to this standard of excellence. To meet such a test the jury would first have to construct a model of justice and then measure a proposed verdict against each of its components. This is likely to be well beyond the capability of even the most intelligent and educated jurors. In contrast, it is not necessary to comprehend the full nature of justice in order to recognize a potential injustice. We can recognize the bad without knowing the totality of the good; or, in the words of Lon Fuller, 'we can ... know what is plainly unjust without committing ourselves to declare with finality what perfect justice would be like' (1964, p.12).

This is not in any way intended to discourage the jury's search for justice, all things considered. Whether or not its achievement is likely in practice, it is valuable to have standards of excellence to which one aspires. The goal of achieving justice presents a challenge to the jurors even if its attainment may be difficult or impossible. On those occasions where the jury does manage to produce the truly just verdict, it rises to what Plato might have described as the ideal of the jury – the ideal for Plato being the conceptual embodiment of an entity in its perfect state. The ideal sets the standard and the objective is to approximate that standard to the maximum extent possible. For the jury, the ideal is justice.

To recapitulate, the jury's search is, literally, for truth and justice; truth, in respect to the facts; and justice, in respect to the verdict. The jury's obligation is to prevent injustice to the accused. Justice under law is subsumed within the overall concept of justice but is not identical to it. The jury has also to consider the defendant's moral and other claims to an acquittal. Consequently, the defendant who is legally culpable but morally blameless may be acquitted but so too will the defendant who may have behaved in an immoral but not an illegal manner. Finally, justice, all things considered, provides the ideal to which the jury aspires.

Jury Justice

Although the jury may strive for a Platonic ideal, the justice to which it aspires is not necessarily that which Plato might have contemplated. The justice of the jury is not the justice of philosophers, for jurors are not philosophers nor should they be expected to be. Jurors are also not lawyers and 'jury justice' is not the justice of those who would equate justice with the strict application of legal rules. When juries apply legal rules, they do so in a non-technocratic fashion, with an eye to the equities of the case and the moral blameworthiness of the defendant. Their verdict embodies a common-sense, community judgement as to the most appropriate result on the merits of the case, taking into account all factors, *both legal and extra-legal*, that fair-minded and impartial persons would deem relevant. Jurors intuitively grasp the instrumentalist point that judges often appear at pains to conceal – that, fundamentally the decision which they are called upon to make is whether the accused shall go to prison or remain free in the community – *their community*. The just resolution of a case often turns on factors beyond the simple question of who did what to whom and with what state of mind.

The justice of the jury is a unique blend of community standards, on the one hand, and principles of conventional and universal justice, on the other, with the occasional dollop of mercy added for good measure. From the earliest descriptions of the jury's role two themes emerge. A criminal defendant was said to 'put himself upon his country'. By this was meant that the defendant was to be judged by his countrymen and neighbours and that his conduct was to be evaluated against the moral and ethical standards of their common community. At the same time, juries were exhorted to do their duty 'to God and their consciences'. This suggested that jurors were also expected to consider the defendant's conduct in light of higher, more permanent principles. For their verdict the jurors had ultimately to answer to God.

A distinction is commonly drawn between universal and conventional justice. While universal justice consists of principles that would be accepted by all people, in all places and at all times, conventional justice is culturally specific. Its principles are those which a particular state counts as part of its conception of justice, even though other states might not. The jury itself is an example. A fair and impartial system of dispute resolution that did not employ a jury system could certainly be envisaged; indeed, many advanced societies do not make use of juries. In both Great Britain and the United States, however, jury trial is an integral part of the conventional justice guaranteed to one accused of a serious crime.[20] Standards of both conventional and universal justice will bear on a jury's deliberations.

Where do jurors find the guideposts of justice that are to direct their deliberations? Rarely will a court refer to these in its instructions in any more than a cursory and perfunctory fashion. More often than not the judge will not even tell the jury that it has the responsibility to seek justice, let alone providing it with standards that might enlighten its search. For their part, few jurors will have studied ethics or philosophy. Secluded in the jury room, lacking access to a library, with no advisers to guide them, the jurors are left to draw on whatever internal resources they can bring to bear in determining where justice lies. What resources the jurors in fact draw upon must inevitably remain something of a mystery, as the jury does not provide reasons for its verdict and jurors may be prohibited from revealing the substance of their discussions. Nonetheless most jurors – most people – seem to have a strong sense of right and wrong. But from where does it derive? The answer may lie in biology, sociology or acculturation, or perhaps some combination of these. Whether it is inherent or learned may, in the final analysis, not matter as much as the fact that jurors are prepared to apply their collective sense of right and wrong to the case before them.

The jurors' sensitivity to community values stems from their status as members of the community. The jury is drawn from the state, and usually the locality, in which the crime occurred.[21] The moral and ethical standards of that state and community, and its conventional principles of justice, may be formally taught in the schools (for example, in civics and politics courses) or informally communicated through parents and community leaders. Even in the absence of formal tuition, they would be inescapable, since they permeate the culture. The relevant values and principles will have been absorbed and internalized, usually without the individuals in question being aware of the process by which this occurs. During their deliberations the jurors will instinctively draw on these values and principles and use them as benchmarks in determining where justice lies in the particular case.

The jury's verdict will also be informed by principles of universal justice. As noted, the latter refer to standards that can be said to be common to all people and all societies. They have to them a quality of permanence, timelessness and immutability. Unlike standards of conventional justice, principles of universal justice are not specific to a particular state or culture. They form part of a higher law – what is sometimes called a 'natural law' – that is said to take precedence over human law. Cicero wrote that an unjust law is not law: 'Lex iniustia non est lex' (Cicero, 1928). The demands of positive law must yield to those of the natural law. However, where theory tends to draw a sharp distinction between positive law and natural law, the jury provides a bridge between the two. The defendant on trial is charged with a violation of the state's positive law but, in determining the defendant's culpability, the jurors will also take into account principles of natural law.

Like principles of conventional justice, principles of universal justice may be learned. But whereas the content of conventional justice is apt to be taught in schools, principles of universal justice are more likely to be learned in the home or religious institutions. It is a curious fact that parents who may not themselves lead a particularly moral life are concerned with the proper moral development of their children. Thus a child may be taught that lying and stealing are wrong by parents who are involved in welfare fraud. Whether the parents are thereby attempting to atone for their own failings or trying to encourage their children to lead a more virtuous life is a moot point. The objects of their instruction, their children, will not be concerned with their motivation. For them content is what counts. This learning, moreover, will typically occur at an early stage of a child's development, when the child is too young to question the principles taught. They are simply accepted and internalized. Reinforcement comes in the form of approval of actions which accord with the relevant values and disapproval or outright punishment of actions which do not. A Freudian might explain all this in terms of the development of the child's superego (Freud, 1948); a behavioural psychologist might say that the child has been conditioned (Skinner 1971). No matter who is correct, it is to these instilled values that jurors are able to turn in their search for the just verdict. Just as their parents were prepared to provide moral guidance even though they might themselves have been leading immoral lives, so too jurors will apply their internalized moral standards even though they themselves may not abide by those standards.

Although moral values will permeate a jury's deliberations, an objective observer who watched the deliberations would be more likely to see the jurors engaged in a rational discussion in which morality was rarely mentioned, if at all. Reason is the apparent tool which the jurors employ in their deliberations. Reason, however, is not unrelated to natural law. Cicero referred to natural law as 'the mind and reason of the intelligent man, the standard by which Justice and Injustice are measured' (Cicero, 1928) and Locke wrote of the 'light of nature', which could be discovered 'without the help of another if [one] makes proper use of the faculties he is endowed with by nature' (Locke, 1952). The 'reason', however, which the jurors bring to their deliberations is not the formal reasoning of logicians. It is more of a common sense or practical reason. The idea of 'practical reason' (or wisdom) was conceived and developed by Aristotle. It is concerned with 'particulars', rather than universals, and owes more to experience than formal tuition. The case for practical reason was well made by Miriam Galston (1994) in a passage not intended as a description of jury decision-making but which easily could have been:

> [M]any contemporary theorists ... have rejected the model of demonstrative or syllogistic reasoning based upon universal truths in favor of some form of contextual reasoning process. The catalyst for this development is a growing appreciation of the importance of the particular. This development seems to derive from two basic insights. First, because of their general nature, rules cannot capture the detail, concreteness, and complexity of political life. Political

> and moral rules, even if in some sense 'true', are too abstract to furnish meaningful guidelines for the types of particular decisions that make up everyday life. A wealth of considerations would have to be added to any rule before it could be transformed into a prescription for action. Second, since human nature and circumstances are themselves evolving, general rules describing human affairs must be similarly evolving. As a consequence, the premises of political and moral reasoning cannot be known deductively or theoretically, but must be acquired as part of the practical reasoning process. (Galston, 1994, p. 371)

In applying their practical reason, jurors are guided not only by experience but by conscience, a term commonly used to refer to that part of the human intelligence that enables individuals to distinguish between right and wrong. The source of conscience is unclear. It may be an innate quality, something we are born with, as even young children seem to know instinctively when they have misbehaved. Perhaps some day a 'conscience' gene will be discovered. If there is merit in Jung's concept of a collective unconscious (Jung, 1965), it may turn out that conscience is a facet of that. Or perhaps conscience is the repository of those moral lessons that we are taught at a very young age. That there is such a thing as conscience finds confirmation in the numerous references to it in literature, common speech and even judicial opinions. Its precise source, in the final analysis, is unimportant. What matters is that, when jurors retire to deliberate, they do not leave their consciences at the jury room door. Jurors will instinctively recoil from a verdict which goes against the grain of their conscience. A case may cry out for justice in the sense that it makes an appeal to the jury's collective conscience. As human beings, jurors will not be insensitive to this cry. Judges realize this, and this is why courts speak so freely of 'a verdict according to conscience'. Arguments addressed to the jurors' conscience are directed at the jurors' sense of justice, and vice versa.

Appeals to conscience might have little impact were it not for another distinctly human attribute, which is empathy. Jurors are able to put themselves in the position of someone who is threatened by injustice even though no injustice is threatened to themselves. The jurors identify with the danger to the accused. But why, and what motivates them to act to obviate this danger? It may be a sense of altruism or a commitment to fair play. More selfishly, jurors may see a threat to themselves in the threat to the accused. We are often dependent upon others for our own well-being, and this dependency is particularly marked for the defendant in a criminal trial. But the roles, as the jurors no doubt are subconsciously aware, could some day be reversed. Once the possibility of unjust laws, or unjust arrests, is acknowledged, then any individual could fall prey to an unjust prosecution. Jurors may therefore be prepared to save others from injustice in order to safeguard their own position. By acting to prevent injustice, the jurors acquire a psychological expectation that jurors in their own future hypothetical trial will similarly protect them.[22] Yet the reason why jurors are prepared to prevent an injustice to a criminal defendant even though they themselves are not directly threatened by injustice is, like the source of their sense of right and wrong, ultimately of secondary importance. Whether it is out of self-interest, genuine altruism, or their conception of their role, what counts is that juries do take seriously their responsibility to prevent injustice to an accused.[23]

The reason why a particular juror's conscience may be offended by a proposed verdict may be difficult for the juror to articulate. It may be little more than a visceral reaction whose external manifestation takes the form of a statement that the proposed verdict 'does not feel right to me'. However, the inability to express the reasons for one's uneasiness does not mean that the reasons do not exist; it may simply be that they have failed to penetrate beyond a subconscious level. Conscientious jurors will undoubtedly try to discover the basis of their discontent. This is desirable, for critical reflection serves to guard against intuitions that turn out to be based on prejudice. Nevertheless, in the final analysis it is not essential that jurors fully comprehend the internal logic that underlies their sense that a particular outcome would be unjust. It is sufficient that, after reflection and discussion, they are not dissuaded from that position. It is the innate aversion to the unjust verdict that prevents its occurrence. It may be out of a recognition of the role played by conscience and the jurors' sense of right and wrong, and of justice and injustice, that the legal system does not probe the jury for the reasons behind its verdict. Even as staunch an opponent of the jury as the British academic Glanville Williams had this to say against requiring reasons for a verdict:

> Lord Mansfield's reputed advice to a newly appointed colonial judge – 'Give your decision, because it will probably be right, but do not give your reasons, because they will probably be wrong' – applies to juries. Even an experienced judge often does not arrive at his decision by way of conscious reasoning; what happens is that as he listens to the evidence, he begins to feel the answer in his bones. The purported reasoning in his judgement is rationalisation, an *ex post facto* statement of how he has come to feel. The jury's verdict may be right even though it is not thus verbally rationalised. (Williams, 1963, p. 314)

Whether by chance or design, the freedom from having to explain their verdict liberates jurors to follow their conscience.

Reaching Consensus

Even assuming that the jurors share common standards of justice, is it reasonable to expect them to agree on the standards applicable in a particular case and the weight to be attached to principles that might appear to be competing with each other?[24] An analogy to the work of John Rawls (Rawls, 1972) suggests that, under the right conditions, the answer might be 'yes'. Rawls set out to discover whether agreement could be reached on principles of distributive justice. He hypothesized an 'original position' in which free and rational members of a society came together in a state of equality to hammer out the fundamental terms of their association. Those involved did not know their race, sex, class, economic or social status, or individual capabilities. All such features were hidden behind a 'veil of ignorance'.[25] The challenge was to reach a consensus regarding first principles of justice without knowing how the principles agreed upon would affect the participants personally. Those principles that would be chosen in this initial situation of equality and fairness were deemed by Rawls to be just.

The 'original position' was not intended to provide an historical account of how our conceptions of justice came into being. There is no evidence that there ever was an 'original position'. Even if there were, those in it could hardly have not known their race, gender and other personal characteristics. The value of Rawls' construct is that it provides a vantage point from which the requirements of justice can objectively be considered. Impartial decision-making depends upon the decision-makers keeping separate the merits of the arguments and the impact that any decision might have on their personal lives. Rawls creates impartiality by the counter-factual assumption that the members of his congress know nothing about themselves.[26]

Impartiality on the jury, however, cannot be achieved so simply. In the real world people cannot help but be aware of their personal characteristics. What is important, however, is not whether or not jurors are aware of their personal characteristics or individual circumstances, but that they not allow these to distort the decision-making process. This suggests the desirability of screening prospective jurors. Any bias resulting from a juror's individual situation that might affect the juror's ability to be fair and impartial can, in fact, lead to the juror's being excused from service. But not all biases that might bear on a jury's decisions in a given case may be identifiable at the outset. There is thus much to be said for providing jurors with general training that will allow them to recognize and resist biases that might affect their ability to be fair and impartial. The screening and training of jurors will be further explored in Chapter 6.

Both jurors, and presumably those in the 'original position', should be allowed to carry on their deliberations in an environment which is free from outsiders who might seek to influence them. Rawls again seems to assume the necessary conditions. In the real world the creation of an appropriate environment is the product of concerted effort. The jury conducts its deliberations in a room which is 'off-limits' to others. Not even the judge may intrude; if the jurors wish to speak to the judge they must make a formal request to do so through the bailiff who stands guard outside the jury room to prevent third parties from entering. Once it has retired to deliberate, the jury will usually be kept intact and separated from the outside world.[27] Indeed, in some cases, that of O.J. Simpson being the most recent notable example, the jurors may be sequestered for the duration of the trial.

In both the 'original position' and on the jury, decisions are made by a group, although why Rawls prefers a group whose members are virtual clones of one another is not clear. The advantages of group decision-making on a jury – and these will be discussed in greater detail in subsequent chapters – include the thoroughness of analysis (relevant lines of inquiry are less likely to be overlooked), the synergism of deliberations (the contributions of each member of the group will stimulate the thinking of the others), the dialectics of debate (superior analyses compete with, and displace, inferior analyses) and the communitarian perspective generated in a collective endeavour. Rawls presumably envisaged the same dynamics operating in his 'original position' congress. Thus, both on the jury and in the original position the 'process' expectation is that group deliberation by impartial decision-makers will lead to consensus judgements reflecting shared principles unmarred by the distorting effects of personal interest or bias. In both it is envisaged that the resulting product will be something which can appropriately be described as just.

However, the analogy to the 'original position' should not be overstated. It is a hypothetical construct and there is no indication that Rawls either created it with the jury in mind or intended it to be applied to the jury. Rawls was seeking to derive general principles of distributive justice; the jury's concern is with achieving a just result in the particular case. Rawls was also looking for principles which could be set down and passed on to future generations, as well as being applied to the participants themselves after the veil of ignorance was lifted. The members of a jury, in contrast, do not seek lasting principles, nor do they set down any rules for regulating either their own behaviour or that of a future jury. Juries in future cases are free to make their own determination of what justice requires in the case before them.

The Hierarchy between Law and Justice

The proposition that justice may require a verdict contrary to the law assumes an hierarchical relationship between law and justice that warrants closer examination. Why should the law be subordinated to the interests of justice when there is a conflict between the two?

One way of approaching this question is to ask whether the citizenry would be prepared to live in a state which adhered to the rule of law but had no regard for justice. Let us hypothesize that, whenever the question arose as to whether conduct should be prohibited in this mythical state, the legislature would decide by tossing a coin: heads, the conduct would be legal; tails it would be made illegal. Then, once the question of legality was settled, the law would be rigorously enforced and applied. Every person who violated the law would be prosecuted. No exceptions would be permitted, for the country's unerring commitment to the rule of law would not allow for any.

Would such a state of affairs be long tolerated? This might seem a rhetorical question, for few would defend the system that has been hypothesized. The riposte, however, would be that the fault lies not in adherence to the rule of law but in the arbitrariness of the initial decision of whether or not to make certain conduct criminal and, to some extent this point must be conceded. But, in the real world, some laws are unjust and many just laws can lend themselves to unjust results in certain circumstances. The hypothetical extreme is presented only to highlight the priority that is actually given to justice.

One might ask a related question which probably would be seen as less fanciful. Would a society be prepared to tolerate a limited amount of injustice in order to gain the benefit of living under a rule of law? The problem with this formulation is that it ignores the plight of the individual who is subjected to the injustice. That person will have been treated no less unjustly if his or her case is the exception rather than the norm. Those accused of a crime are in fact rarely concerned with cases other than their own, and understandably so. If they were to be unjustly convicted and sent to prison, the fact that other trials produced a just result would be of scant consolation. Moreover, if an injustice could occur in the case of any given individual, a similar fate could befall other individuals and no one's liberty would be secure. The public would not be prepared to take the risk. It would demand that safeguards be established to prevent injustices from occurring. The jury is, in fact, one of the prime such safeguards.

Language can often sharpen and clarify our understanding of concepts, and the proposed hierarchical relationship between law and justice finds strong linguistic support. We commonly speak of an 'unjust law'. To those who would maintain that justice and law are co-extensive this might appear to be a contradiction in terms. But it is not. When the phrase 'unjust law' is invoked, it is intended not simply to signal the speaker's personal disagreement with the law. It is employed to describe a failure of the law to meet certain principled criteria. Not only individual laws but entire legal systems are sometimes described as unjust. Although not everybody might agree with the substance of the criticism, all would understand the point that was being made. While the phrase 'unjust law' is commonplace, the concept of 'unlawful justice' is virtually unheard of. The phrase grates as much on the mind as on the ear. In ordinary speech justice takes priority.

The phrase 'unjust law' is revealing in another respect. It indicates that justice is the benchmark against which law is evaluated. The equally common formulae of 'justice under law' or 'justice according to law' carry the same implication that justice is the goal and law the means. Justice is likewise the goal of the jury, and just as justice is a suitable standard against which to measure laws, so too is it a suitable standard against which to measure jury verdicts.

Conclusion

The vision of the jury's role which I have sought to advance sees a conviction as more than a factual determination that a defendant committed the alleged acts with the mental state specified by the law. This is a narrow and formalistic conception of guilt. The deeper meaning that I wish to attach to the term includes a dimension of moral fault. It is submitted that, in cases of serious offences, considerations of moral fault have never been far removed from the jury's deliberations. The ultimate question which a jury must decide is whether, given all the facts and circumstances of a case, the defendant on trial is deserving of society's condemnation and punishment. This is not to suggest that juries totally disregard the legality of the defendant's conduct, but rather that the deliberations of a jury are not confined to narrow legal issues. The jury brings, and is expected to bring, the law into line with the community's sense of justice.

Few judges, however, readily acknowledge the point. Yet acceptance of this broader vision of the jury's role provides insight into aspects of the criminal justice system which are otherwise puzzling – its preference for general over special verdicts, the authoritativeness it accords to a jury acquittal, and its unwillingness to require juries to give reasons for their verdicts. This is not the time or place to debate the historical pedigree of the role that I have ascribed to the jury. Legal historians, such as Sir William Holdsworth (1966) and Professor Thomas Green (1985), have traced the jury's development and have concluded that the search for a just verdict is part and parcel of the jury's remit. In any event, I wish only to advance the more modest proposition, which will be supported in the next chapter, that the role which I have attributed to the jury is not lacking in historical support.

The thesis that I wish to present, while to some extent *descriptive*, is to a greater extent *normative*. It is an account of how jurors *ought* to be approaching their task. Chapter 2 will look more closely at the situations where a jury might exercise its power to do justice and explore why this power is not exercised more frequently than it is. Chapter 3 will then tackle the question of why the responsibility for doing justice should be entrusted to juries rather than judges. It will examine the processes at work in jury deliberations – processes that allow society to have confidence in verdicts that in effect demand that they be taken on trust. Subsequent chapters will examine why trial by jury is uniquely suited to a democratic state.

Notes

1 The original limitations on jury trial in civil cases were enacted in 1918 and were intended to be temporary. However, after the reinstatement of jury trials in civil cases for a brief period following the war, such trials were subsequently abandoned on a permanent basis (Administration of Justice Act 1933 s. 6), except for a handful of cases involving libel, slander, malicious prosecution and false imprisonment (see Supreme Court Act 1981 s. 69).

2 In a civil case in the United States, in contrast, a judge can order a new trial if the judge believes that the jury has reached an incorrect verdict. That option is not available following an acquittal in a criminal case.

3 In addition, Hart identifies a class of power conferring rules that enable individuals to do things that they might not otherwise have been able to do, such as writing a will, or entering into a marriage.

4 The percentage of criminal cases decided by juries is itself extremely low. In Britain in 1993 only 3 per cent of criminal cases were heard in Crown Court (where jury trial is available) and only 23 per cent of these cases were heard by a jury (Padfield, 1995, p. 283). The overwhelming majority of criminal cases are heard in magistrates' courts, where jury trial is not available. The percentage of jury trials is also low in the United States, but for a different reason. Most criminal prosecutions there are concluded by a plea bargain pursuit to which the defendant enters a plea of guilty in exchange for some negotiated concession on the part of the prosecutor.

5 The original jurors were individuals with personal knowledge of the facts that gave rise to the controversy. It was this knowledge, rather than the testimony of witnesses, which provided the factual basis on which they reached a decision. See generally Forsyth (1852).

6 See Williams (1963), p. 12. It was not until 1898 that the Criminal Evidence Act allowed the defendant to testify under oath. Id.

7 Compare, for example, *R.* v. *Morris* [1984] AC 320 with *R.* v. *Gomez* [1993] AC 442 (on the meaning of appropriation in theft). See also *Caminetti* v. *United States*, (1917)

242 US 470 (where the Justices on the United States Supreme Court were in sharp disagreement on the meaning of 'immoral' in the Mann Act, which prohibited, *inter alia*, transporting a woman from one state to another for an 'immoral purpose').

8 See *Cage* v. *Louisiana*, 498 US 39 (1990).

9 What constitutes proof of intention in English criminal law provides an example. Compare *DPP* v. *Smith* [1961] AC 290 with *Hyam* v. *DPP* [1975] AC 55 with R. v. *Moloney* [1985] 1 AC 905 with R. v. *Hancock and Shankland* [1986] 1 AC 455.

10 For a history of the special verdict, see Morgan (1923).

11 The exception is the case in which a defendant raises an insanity defence; in these circumstances, the jury may return a verdict of not guilty by reason of insanity.

12 *R.* v. *Bourne* (1952) 36 Cr. App. R. 125.

13 416 F.2d 165 (1st Cir. 1969).

14 The phrase 'all things considered', is restricted to matters that are relevant in the context of the individual case.

15 What might appear as a formalized step-by-step procedure is not so stilted in real life. The first two stages, for example, may be bypassed in a case where the defendant does not dispute the facts but asserts that his actions were justified. In another case the jury's attention may be directed to the alleged injustice of the law or the prosecution, or the conduct of the police. See Chapter 2.

16 The reader might recall, however, Kalven and Zeisel's point that ambiguities in the evidence may liberate the jurors to construct a picture of the facts that allows them to inject their values into the decision-making process.

17 There are, of course, some strict liability crimes, where proof of *mens rea* is not required, but these are not favoured and are usually restricted to regulatory offences. Even here, courts are not averse to reading a *mens rea* requirement into a statute where there is none visible. See, for example, *Sweet* v. *Parsley* [1970] AC 133.

18 *Morissette* v. *United States*, 342 US 246, 252 (1952).

19 There is, in Scotland, the additional verdict of not proven. This verdict, however, is generally to be avoided, for it leaves a cloud over the head of the defendant even though the prosecution has failed to establish its case by proof beyond a reasonable doubt.

20 In the United States the right to jury trial is guaranteed by the Constitution. US Const., amend. VI. In Britain juries are the product of the common law. See generally Halsbury's Laws (4th edn) paras 601 *et. seq.*

21 The exception is in cases where a change of venue is ordered in order to preserve a fair trial.

22 Perhaps in preventing injustice jurors are engaged in a more general reciprocal commitment to protect others when they can do so without personal risk. However, one need not go this far in the present context.

23 It might seem that, under this analysis, jurors should automatically acquit an accused regardless of guilt because they themselves would want to be acquitted, regardless of guilt, if they were to be charged with the same crime. However, jurors also have an interest in ensuring the safety of the community in which they reside and the well-being of their fellow citizens. The overall demands of justice, all things considered, argue against freeing a defendant who will endanger those interests.

24 Jurors, of course, do not have to agree on the reasons for the verdict; they only need agree on the verdict. It is to be expected, however, that in many, if not most, cases there will also be agreement on the rationale.

25 The participants, however, were acquainted with human psychology and different models of social association.

26 Rawls does not deny that the participants in the original position are motivated by a desire to promote their self-interest. They are, but because they do not know where their self-interest lies, they are forced to adopt principles that will maximize their chances of coming to its fruition whatever it should turn out to be.

27 In Britain, this requirement has now been modified by statute. See the Criminal Justice and Public Order Act of 1994.

2 Doing Justice

The preceding chapter introduced the concept of jury justice. This chapter continues the inquiry by examining cases in which juries have exercised their power to do justice, as well as those situations where it would not be inappropriate for them to do so. While these defy neat categorization, it might broadly be said that a jury in a criminal case will judge the law and its sanctions, the substantive merits of the cause and the procedures whereby the defendant was brought to trial. Considerations of social justice may also at times come under a jury's scrutiny, as they perhaps do in civil cases where a jury in effect redistributes the wealth of the society by awarding seemingly exorbitant damages to an individual plaintiff against a large corporation, insurance company or other institutional defendant (Lempert, 1992).[1]

If one were to observe criminal trials on a regular basis, one might see few cases that present any clear-cut issue of justice. Many seem to require only that the jury resolve questions of fact. That these cases are the norm is not surprising. The government does not usually set out to enact unjust laws. Aware that whatever laws it does seek to enforce will ultimately be judged by a jury of the people, the government may also shy away from prosecutions which it anticipates will be perceived as unjust by a jury. Like the sentinel who never is called upon to fire even a warning shot, the looming shadow of the jury casts a restraint on officials who might be tempted to ignore the demands of justice.

Of the cases that do raise issues of justice, there are two main categories. Every now and then there is what might be called the 'grand' case, where law and justice are in open conflict. These generally high-profile cases are the substance of jury lore. The defendants do not deny the criminal acts attributed to them, but assert that their actions were justified by some higher principle. In these cases the defendants ask the jurors to stand up to the government and nullify an unjust law, policy or prosecution. Jury deliberations perforce will focus on questions other than 'whether the defendant did it'.

The second category of case consists of the more ordinary, daily fare of trials which, unlike the 'grand' cases, may not feature in the media or even the law reports. In these cases no great issue of moral or political principle is either raised by the defendant or suggested by the facts. Considerations of fairness and unfairness, justice and injustice, are not at the heart of the deliberations, as in the 'grand case', but at the edges. They form a subtext to the jury's deliberations and are likely to influence the course of the deliberations in subtle ways of which the jurors may not even be aware, such as in their interpretation of the evidence.

It is easy for police and prosecutors to fall into unhealthy routines. Criminal laws are often enforced out of habit and for no other reason than that they are on the statute books. Although changing times may warrant a reconsideration of certain laws, the legislature may have more pressing items on its agenda. Jurors, unaffected by the routine of law enforcement, are able to see these laws through fresh eyes and in a factual context. Within that context a law which is not generally objectionable may work an injustice. That the jury can focus on the justice of the individual case without becoming bogged down in the ramifications of its decision for future cases is one of the great strengths of the jury system. A judge, sitting alone, in the same situation might have no other option but to hold the law in question unconstitutional, with the inevitable upheaval which such a decision would cause (more about the judge's dilemma in Chapter 3). The jury, in contrast, is able to fine-tune the law without rejecting it wholesale.

Justice is often linked to the concept of desert, as in the expression 'just deserts'. While this term is more commonly invoked in reference to punishment than guilt, it is appropriate in both contexts. To say that a conviction would be unjust is to say that the conviction would be undeserved. But when can a conviction be said to be deserved? Those who stress the paramount importance of the enforcement of legal rules maintain that it is when the prosecution has established beyond reasonable doubt that a law has been violated and that the defendant has violated that law. Those who place their emphasis on justice say that it is when the defendant has been shown not only to have violated the law (for it is unjust to deprive those who have not violated the law of their liberty) but also to have behaved in a morally blameworthy manner.

The Justice of the Law

Justice is sometimes coupled with equality, with law being the identified means of achieving both. This theme is encapsulated in the motto over the US Supreme Court building, 'Equal Justice under Law'. Equal justice is a laudable objective in the sense that no one should be above the law and that like cases should be treated alike. However, justice will not be achieved if the law being applied is itself unjust. After the American Civil War 'Jim Crow' laws were used to preserve racially segregated facilities in southern states, and similar legislation was enacted to maintain a system of apartheid in South Africa. Laws in Nazi Germany imposed inhumane hardships on certain people because of – and solely because of – their Jewish ancestry. In cases such as these, where the substantive law is itself unjust, the like treatment of like cases aggravates rather than alleviates the injustice of the law. The jury, as the historian E.P. Thompson has observed, sits in judgement not only of the accused but of the justice and humanity of the law (Thompson, 1980).

Laws which are based on race, gender or ethnic origin are unjust in several different respects. First, complying with them may be impossible. Unlike religion, on perhaps even gender nowadays, individuals cannot change the colour of their skin. Even in respect to religion and gender there is no good reason why a religious conversion or sex change operation should be a precondition to enjoyment of one's civil liberties. Second, laws defined in terms of personal characteristics are also unjust because they condemn an individual on the grounds of who that individual is rather than what he or she has done. If it is unjust to criminalize being of Chinese descent, it would be equally unjust to make it a crime for a person of Chinese descent to engage in an activity, such as operating a laundry, that is itself innocent.[2] The point is that there are certain characteristics – race, gender, religion, and ethnic origin being foremost among them – which simply have no place in the definition of criminal offences.

In some instances, the law criminalizes conduct which the citizenry is unconvinced should have been made criminal in the first place. A statute, for example, may declare that sexual intercourse between minors below the age of eighteen is illegal, but few would see the wisdom of attaching the stigma of criminality, with its portentous social consequences, to two seventeen year olds who had engaged in consensual sex.[3] The American experiment with prohibition provides another example. When prosecutions were brought, juries routinely returned not guilty verdicts, regardless of the strength of the government's case. The refusal of juries to convict indicated their rejection of these unwanted liquor laws as surely as if they had been asked to vote in a referendum. Kalven and Zeisel found a similar reluctance to convict defendants of gaming and gambling offences (Kalven and Zeisel, 1966, ch. 19). In an age where there is a tendency to overcriminalize (Kadish, 1967) and where 'zero tolerance' of lawbreakers appeals to politicians as a way to win votes, jurors have to ask themselves whether the conviction of a defendant charged with a minor or technical offence would serve any constructive purpose.

Retroactively applied laws – those which punish conduct which was not criminal at the time that the conduct occurred – are unjust for a different reason. If citizens cannot know what a future court will declare illegal, it is impossible for them to conform their behaviour to the commands of the law. Retroactive laws can produce an undesirable degree of social paralysis. Nevertheless, the temptation to enact laws that will allow the punishment of those who have behaved in a condemnable fashion is often strong. This was perhaps never more so than after the Second World War when the atrocities perpetrated by the Nazis were revealed. The outrage was understandable and legitimate, but the justice of retroactively criminalizing conduct that may have been legal under the German law of the time was a more complex question.[4] The issue was evaded by charging the Nazis with crimes against humanity, which could be rationalized as always having been part of international law. The interests of justice thus arguably prevailed without the need to resort to *ex post facto* criminalization.

Retroactive laws may be thought to fall under a broader rubric which would preclude the conviction of anyone who has made a good faith effort to comply with the law. Such a principle is applicable when a law is ambiguous on its face. If those required to obey the law cannot understand the meaning of the law, it is unjust to punish them for disobeying it. A prosecution for a violation of a law whose text is inaccessible gives rise to a similar objection. However, this principle cannot be taken too far, for it would encourage ignorance of the law when knowledge is in the public interest. It would be but a short slippery step to the conclusion that each person had to be judged by what he or she *thought* the law proscribed rather than what the law *actually* proscribed, and everyone would then become a law unto themselves. Rebutting an assertion of ignorance of the law would also be problematic. Accordingly, the position taken by the courts is that ignorance of the law is no excuse. There is nothing improper in enforcing a law which is accessible and comprehensible, even if only by one with legal training. However, a citizen who attempts to ascertain the law by consulting a lawyer may be surprised to discover that a good-faith reliance on the lawyer's advice is also not a defence to a criminal prosecution.[5] This is not to say that a jury might not recognize the injustice of a conviction under such circumstances and return a verdict of not guilty. Indeed, the argument here is that this is precisely what the jury should do.

The Justice of Sanctions

In some instances it is not the law but the penalty attached to it that is deemed to be unjust by the jury. It is trite but true that the punishment should fit the crime. A penalty may be disproportionate because of its mode, duration or excessive cruelty. In the United States the eighth amendment to the Constitution prohibits cruel and unusual punishment.[6] In interpreting this provision, the US Supreme Court has stated that what is cruel and unusual is to be determined by 'the evolving standards of decency that mark the progress of a maturing society'.[7] While the constitutional question is reserved for the judiciary, a comparable issue confronts the jury. Sentencing is not usually the jury's prerogative, but conjecture as to the sentence that will be imposed following a conviction may affect a jury's decision to convict. In deciding whether the penalty which it seems as most likely 'fits the crime', the jury will instinctively be guided by 'the evolving standards of decency' that characterize the society. As members of the community, jurors are arguably more in touch with its evolving standards of decency than are the judges (a fact recognized in death penalty cases in the US, where jurors are generally given the responsibility of deciding whether to impose this sentence). Unfortunately, the jurors' task in evaluating potential sentences is complicated by the fact that the judge will rarely inform them of the range of sanctions, let alone the specific sanction, that might be imposed were the defendant to be convicted. For better or for worse, the jurors are left to speculate on this matter.

This was not always so. When the death penalty was common in England, public hangings sensitized prospective jurors to the consequences of a conviction. The appropriateness of this penalty, which could be imposed for minor acts of theft, would often preoccupy the jury as much as the question of whether the defendant had committed the crime charged (Green, 1985). In many cases of theft the jury would acquit outright, while in others it would grossly undervalue the goods stolen in order to bring the crime within the parameters of petty larceny which did not carry the death penalty (Radzinowicz, 1948). It is extremely doubtful that the juries in these cases were deceived as to the true value of the goods or whether the defendant had taken them (although if is possible that the high cost of being wrong made them more cautious of convicting than they might otherwise have been). Nor, presumably, were the juries in these cases opposed to the theft being made criminal. Their objection was rather to punishment that they considered to be disproportionate to the offence. Because, then as now, the jury is not generally consulted in respect to sentence, the only means by which the jurors could save a defendant from the gallows was by refusing to convict. In the eyes of the jurors this 'pious perjury' (Blackstone, 1765, p. 239) was a lesser injustice than the sentencing of a petty offender to death.

Such jury acquittals presented the government with a dilemma: if it wished to keep the death penalty, it had to accept that there would be acquittals despite proof of factual guilt; if it wanted its laws to be effective, it had to modify the sanction. Of course, parliament may have been content to retain the death penalty for its perceived deterrent effect, while not being opposed to jury leniency in appropriate cases. If this was the thinking, it was probably misguided since, if wrongdoers have no reason to fear a conviction, they will not be deterred. By the nineteenth century, the banking industry had grasped the point and was petitioning parliament to make forgery a non-capital offence (Radzinowicz, 1948). Faced with the systematic nullification of the law by its juries, and perhaps influenced also by a growing disenchantment with capital punishment, parliament relented. While the jury verdicts of the time might be characterized as a matter of conscience, parliament's actions were born of a pragmatic recognition that oppressive punishments can be counterproductive.

A more recent illustration of this same phenomenon can be seen in respect to the English law of vehicular homicide. When drivers who caused death were charged with manslaughter, juries would routinely acquit,[8] even if the facts established beyond a reasonable doubt that the defendant was guilty of that crime. The jury's apparent objection was to the penalty. I use the word 'apparent' because, as noted previously, juries were not informed of the sanction that would be imposed following a conviction. Nevertheless, the jurors no doubt reasoned that manslaughter was a serious offence and that the sentence would be commensurate with the seriousness of the crime. An alternative explanation that was sometimes advanced to explain the jury acquittals in these cases was that the jurors identified with the accused – what might be called the 'there but for the grace of God go I' syndrome. This 'identification' hypothesis was shown to be false, however, after parliament enacted the crime of causing death by reckless (now dangerous) driving. This new offence was apparently not perceived by juries in the same light as manslaughter and the reluctance to convict diminished.[9]

Sometimes the harm caused by a defendant's crime is so minor that any penalty may seem disproportionate. The taking of property, the value of which is *de minimis*, is still theft, but the Chicago Jury Project found that juries, perhaps reflecting an indignation that their time should be taken up with such trivialities, would often acquit (Kalven and Zeisel, 1966, ch. 18). The law of theft is usually graded to take into account the value of the property stolen, but this is not the case for the related offences of robbery and burglary. In simple terms, robbery is theft accompanied by violence or threats, while the added element in burglary is the breaking into a dwelling. In effect, robbery and burglary are aggravated forms of theft. Nevertheless, the Chicago Jury Project was also able to identify cases where juries returned a verdict of petty larceny in respect to these more serious crimes because the value of the property which had been taken was slight (ibid.). The juries had effectively created the crimes of petty robbery and petty burglary. In minor cases of assault – pushing and shoving incidents, single-punch fights – juries will also acquit rather than subject the defendant to potential criminal sanctions.

We have noted that juries are forced to speculate on the penalty that will be imposed following a conviction because courts do not tell them of the range of possible sanctions.[10] Even if a court were to do so, the penalties of which the court would inform the jury would be those imposed by law. Jurors, however, may take a broader – and arguably more realistic – view of punishment. They appreciate, for example, that sometimes a conviction can result in the destruction of a career. The salesman who is dependent upon a car to visit customers will suffer far more than the casual motorist if a conviction for a vehicular offence were to result in a mandatory revocation of his driving licence. The law may not distinguish between such a defendant and one whose need for a care is less pressing, but the jury may. Similarly, a recent Home Office survey, reported in the *Sunday Times* (2 March 1997) revealed that juries were more inclined to acquit female defendants with young children than they were males. The explanation appears to be that juries take into account the potentially devastating effect on the family that can occur if the mother is sent to jail.

The Jury and Legislative Reform

Statutes which are alleged to be unjust because of their content or the sanction attached to them will ultimately need to be corrected through legislative channels. Before this occurs, there are likely to be prosecutions under the law in question. If justice is to be achieved in these cases, it will have to be by virtue of the jury's verdict. The situation is particularly acute in the United Kingdom, where the doctrine of parliamentary sovereignty prevents a court from invalidating a properly enacted statute.[11] The court can generally only exert pressure on parliament to amend the law. Aggrieved parties who have exhausted their UK domestic remedies may take their case to the European Court of Justice or the European Court of Human Rights. This, however, can be a quite lengthy process. During the interim before the relevant European court decides the case or the law is amended by parliament, injustices in other cases can be prevented only through jury verdicts. Thus, while the long-term corrective for unjust laws and penalties lies with the judiciary and legislature, in the short term the jury has critical role to play.

Jury verdicts can also hasten the process of legislative reform, as, for example, in England when jury acquittals led to the abolition of the death penalty for common law theft and to the enactment of the offence of causing death by reckless (dangerous) driving. This feature of the jury was highlighted by Lord Russell when he commented that jury verdicts advance the amendment of 'many bad laws which the judges would have administered with professional bigotry' (Forsyth, 1852, p. 432) Underlying Lord Russell's point is the recognition that judges are appointed by the state, paid by the state and dependent upon the state for the security of their post. Even if the judges were not legally obliged to uphold the state's law, they would be psychologically predisposed to do so. Jurors, on the other hand, are not beholden to the state in the same way. They are appointed by the state, but only for a limited duration. They are paid by the state, but not a significant amount. Their future employment is not dependent on the verdict that they return. Consequently, jurors are able to exercise an independence which may lead them to rule against the government in situations where a judge might be more inclined to be deferential. Partly because of their obligation to enforce the Constitution, American judges may be somewhat less obsequious than their English counterparts at whom Lord Russell's jibe was directed, but psychological pressures to uphold the law are still likely to exert a far stronger pull on them than on the jury.

There is another dimension to Lord Russell's comment. The existence of the jury requires judges to try to express their directions in language that makes sense to laypeople. If the judge also appreciates that rules are easier to understand when the reasoning behind them is explained (see Cheng and Holyoak, 1985), the judge may attempt to set out the rationale of the law for the jury's benefit as well. This process forces the judge to reduce the law to its basic elements. When the jargonistic statutory language is stripped away, the unfairness of the law may be revealed. Were it not for the jury, this exposé might never have occurred.

One seemingly unwarranted acquittal may be attributable to factors idiosyncratic to the particular case or the particular jury. A series of acquittals, on the other hand, may reflect a widespread dissatisfaction with the law itself. To the sensitive legislator, such verdicts are an alarm clock, drawing attention to the need to review the law. As the number of acquittals rise, the louder is the alarm which is sounded. When there is a virtual universal disinclination to convict, it may be time to repeal the law. This is what happened in the United States during the era of prohibition, when juries refused to convict defendants charged with violation of prohibition laws, regardless of the strength of the prosecution's case. It is what happened in England when juries refused to send petty thieves to the gallows. In instances such as these, the dissonance between the law on the books and its abrogation in practice threatens to undermine general respect for law and order, and the laws in question are usually discreetly repealed.

Although Lord Russell's point that jury verdicts can accelerate law reform was well taken, jury verdicts can also have the opposite effect. If a legislature believes that juries will protect against injustice, it may see no pressing urgency to amend the law. In cases of mercy killing, for example, the jury's quarrel with the law is partial rather than total. When juries acquit, it is not because they disapprove of the laws against murder and manslaughter but because they do not think that these laws should extend to mercy killing. This situation is somewhat analogous to that in which the jury individualizes the law (see below), the difference being that, in the individualization cases, it is rarely clear whether the legislature envisaged the circumstances with which the jury was confronted or, if it did, whether it intended the law to apply. Since a legislature would have to be fairly oblivious not to be aware of the potential applicability of homicide laws to cases of mercy killing, the decision not to create an exception in such cases can be presumed to be conscious and deliberate. The legislature has therefore staked out its position that such deaths should be treated in the ordinary fashion. By acquitting, a jury rejects that position. However, it would be incorrect to assume that this is an undesired result as far as the legislators are concerned. They may not wish to amend the law out of fear that the creation of an exception might lead to unjustified homicides by those who would hope to exploit that exception, so the law remains intact to provide the strongest possible disincentive to those who might contemplate killing a seriously ill relative for improper motives. The jury is given the responsibility for preventing injustice in the individual case. The legislature not only is aware of, but relies on, that protection.

The Jury in a Resisting Role

It is no coincidence that the juries whose praises have been most loudly sung throughout history returned verdicts that went directly against the prevailing law. Such verdicts demonstrate the power of ordinary citizens, working through the state's own legal system, to neutralize oppressive laws and unjust prosecutions brought by the government.[12]

In the Old Bailey, London's criminal court, hangs a plaque which celebrates the courage and perseverance of the jurors in *Bushell's Case*.[13] The original prosecution in this 1670 case was not of Bushell but of the Quakers Penn and Mead, who were charged with causing an unlawful assembly after a crowd had gathered in Gracechurch Street to hear them preach. The trial was presided over by the Lord Mayor of London, who left the jurors in no doubt that, in his opinion, the defendants were guilty as charged. Nonetheless, the jurors, led by Edward Bushell, pronounced Mead innocent and Penn guilty only of speaking in Gracechurch Street. The Lord Mayor refused to accept this verdict and ordered the jurors to resume their deliberations. When they persisted in their refusal to return a 'proper' verdict (that is, the guilty verdict that the Lord Mayor thought proper), he ordered that they be locked up 'without meat, drink, fire, and tobacco'. Ignoring both entreaties and threats, the jury still refused to convict. Finally, an exasperated Lord Mayor fined the jurors and sentenced them to prison until the fines were paid.

On a writ of *habeas corpus*, the Court of Common Pleas ordered the jurors' release.[14] The Court reasoned that, as long as the jury of attaint[15] existed to test a verdict, jurors could not be fined or imprisoned by a trial judge. Vaughan, CJ, who wrote the opinion of the court, stated that the fact that the jury did not agree with the trial judge did not impugn the integrity of its verdict. Indeed, to punish jurors for not agreeing with the judge would exalt the opinion of the judge over that of the jurors. He further suggested that the jurors might be aware of evidence, not known to the judge, that contradicted the testimony of the witnesses or that the jurors might have cause to suspect the credibility of a witness stemming from their personal knowledge of the witness's character. Since the jury's findings of fact could not be questioned, neither could its application of law to fact, for one could never know the facts to which the jurors purported to apply the law. As the same law applied to different facts can yield different verdicts, it can never be said with confidence that a jury has misapplied the law as long as the jury is responsible for determining the facts.

Vaughan's analysis rested partly on the fact that the jurors of the time were permitted to bring to bear their personal knowledge of the facts, parties and circumstances of a case. Jurors who have personal knowledge of a case are no longer seen as desirable, and the jury of attaint has also passed into history, but Vaughan's basic point remains. The jury must be allowed to return the verdict that it thinks is appropriate, rather than the verdict which the trial judge would prefer. Prior to *Bushell's Case*, judges had long exhorted juries to do their duty 'to God and their consciences' (Green, 1985, p. 139). Vaughan's decision made meaningful this exhortation by liberating the jurors to follow their consciences without fear of reprisal or punishment.

The American counterpart to *Bushell's Case* was the 1735 trial of John Peter Zenger for seditious libel (Alexander, 1963). Zenger was the publisher of a New York newspaper known for its trenchant criticisms of the local English governor. The prevailing English law allocated separate and distinct responsibilities to judge and jury in prosecutions for seditious libel. The jury's responsibility was to determine whether the defendant had in fact published the material in question. It was for the judge to decide whether the published material was libellous as a matter of law.[16] Zenger's lawyer, Andrew Hamilton, conceded that Zenger had published the offending articles, but argued that truth was a defence. In this he was either mistaken or disingenuous; truth was no defence to a charge of seditious libel under the English law of the day (Holdsworth, 1966) – on the contrary, it was commonly said that the greater the truth, the greater the libel (see Altschuler and Deiss, 1994, p. 873). Hamilton's second argument was that the legal and factual issues in seditious libel were inextricably linked because the factual content of a publication determined its legal status,[17] and that both issues were for the jury to decide. Here he was in tune with Vaughan's analysis in *Bushell's Case*. Hamilton's final, and perhaps most telling argument, however, was that Zenger – indeed, all citizens – had an absolute right to criticize the government. He urged the jurors 'to make use of their consciences and understandings in judging of the lives [and] liberties of their fellow subjects' (Alexander, 1963, p. 93). The jury acquitted.

The basis of any jury verdict is, of course, difficult to pin down, as a jury supplies no reasons for its decision. Different jurors, moreover, may have different reasons for reaching the same conclusion. The one thing that is clear in the trials of Penn and Mead in England and Zenger in New York is that the jurors were unlikely to have been confused about the facts. In neither case were the basic facts disputed. With all due deference to Vaughan, CJ, it is also extremely unlikely that either jury had independent evidence that would have led the jurors to believe that witnesses had lied. There is little cause, therefore, for thinking that the jurors concluded that the defendants did not commit the criminal acts attributed to them. Why, then, did they acquit?

Zenger's case, like Bushell's, presents the jury in a resisting mode. The jurors were unable to return a verdict declaring that freedom of speech or of the press protected Zenger's right to print what he wanted in his newspaper any more than the jurors in the trial of Penn and Mead could have pronounced that freedom of religion precluded government interference with the defendant's right to preach. Nor could the juries have declared that the law was being unfairly or discriminatorily applied against the defendants, or that it was not intended to apply to a case such as the one before them. All each jury was legally permitted to do – and what each did – was to return a verdict of not guilty. In so doing, the jurors stood up to the legislature that had enacted the law, the government which had sought to enforce the law and the trial judge who, in each case, had brought intense pressure on the jurors to convict the defendants of having violated the law.

Cases such as these should not be dismissed as historical anomalies. Examples of juror independence and iconoclasm are regularly to be found. In some instances such as when, during the pre-Civil War period in the United States, juries in New England refused to convict those who had assisted runaway slaves to escape from their masters in contravention of the Fugitive Slave Act, there is a virtual systematic nullification of the law (Morris, 1974). More typically, there is an undercurrent of discontent with a law that is brought to the surface by a particularly compelling set of facts.

An example can be seen in the 1985 trial of Clive Ponting, a former British civil servant, who was charged with having violated the Official Secrets Act.[18] His 'crime' consisted of leaking sensitive information to a Labour MP regarding the sinking of an Argentine ship during the Falklands War. The disclosure, however, occurred after the war was over. The trial judge specifically instructed the jury that Ponting's claim that a civil servant had the right to tell parliament when ministers had lied had no basis in law. Nonetheless, the jury acquitted. Why? Perhaps the verdict was a reaction to a perceived heavy-handed attempt by the government to silence its critics. Or perhaps the jurors decided that the disclosure of information that was more embarrassing than threatening to the government, to an MP as opposed to an enemy agent, simply did not fall within the ambit of the Official Secrets Act. Perhaps the jury saw the case in terms of the role of free speech in a democratic society. Less likely, but still not out of the realm of possibility, is that some members of the jury were opposed in principle to the concept of an Official Secrets Act and chose to nullify it in practice. Each of these factors may have carried varying weight in the minds of individual jurors, or different factors may have influenced different jurors. It is of no consequence for jurors are permitted to take alternative paths to the same end point. Individual juror reservations about the justice of the law or its sanctions, the motives of the prosecutor and the merits of the case often combine, reinforcing each other, to produce a not guilty verdict.

Numerous other modern cases could be cited. In 1972 a Harrisburg, Pennsylvania jury acquitted seven anti-Vietnam protesters charged with a dazzling array of conspiratorial offences that ranged from the destruction of heating tunnels in Washington DC to the kidnapping of the then National Security Adviser Henry Kissinger. (Schulman *et al.*, 1973). In Britain in 1994, a jury acquitted Patrick Pottle and Michael Randle, who admitted to helping the Soviet spy, George Blake, escape from Wormwood Scrubs prison. The accuseds, who defended themselves, had appealed to the jury to allow 'common sense and morality' to triumph over legal technicalities. More recently, in July 1996 a Liverpool Crown Court jury acquitted four members of a peace group who were charged with criminal damage for having caused an estimated £1.5 million worth of damage to a fighter jet.[19] The defendants claimed that their actions were justified by the fact that the planes were to be sold to Indonesia, where they might have been used against the people of East Timor.

Trials such as these are often described as 'political'. All criminal trials are 'political' in the sense that a crime, by definition, is a wrong against the state. Most crimes, however, are against the state more as a matter of form than of substance. The actual victim in an assault, homicide or theft, for instance, is a human being, not the state. The pretence that the crime is against the state primarily serves to distinguish a criminal prosecution from a civil suit, signifying that the state must bear the burden of establishing the case against the defendant by proof beyond a reasonable doubt. In what might be called a true 'political crime', on the other hand, the defendant's offence is committed as a protest against government policy or the prosecution is politically motivated.

The jury plays a critical role in true political trials. Both prosecutor and judge are appointed and paid by the state.[20] In the minds of the defendants, their supporters and perhaps the public as well, there may lurk the suspicion that these officials will be biased in favour of their paymasters. The jury provides an assurance that the verdict will represent not the rubber-stamping of a preordained government decision, but the independent judgement of the community. In *Duncan* v. *Louisiana*[21] the US Supreme Court said:

> Providing an accused with the right to be tried by a jury of his peers gave him an inestimable safeguard against the corrupt or overzealous prosecutor and against the compliant, biased, or eccentric judge. ... Beyond this the jury trial provisions ... reflect a fundamental decision about the exercise of official power – a reluctance to entrust plenary powers over the life and liberty of the citizen to one judge or to a group of judges. Fear of unchecked power ... found expression in the criminal law in this insistence upon community participation in the determination of guilt or innocence. (391 US at 155–56)

The Jury in an Individualizing Role

The jury not only judges the justice of the law and its sanctions, but also the justice of the prosecution in the individual case. Justice demands that like cases be treated alike, and that legal rules be applied in a non-discriminatory manner. But this idealistic vision soon encounters a practical obstacle – no two situations, no two people, no two cases will be alike in all respects. Defendants who commit the same crime may differ in terms of mental abilities, physical attributes, and qualities of temperament and character. The circumstances that gave rise to each crime may also vary. Sometimes the law caters for these differences, but more often the law is insufficiently discriminating to take into account the unique human and factual circumstances of a case.

Justice requires that persons and causes be judged on their individual merits. Underlying the criminal law is a premise that human beings are rational and autonomous moral agents who have the capacity to choose between good and evil. Those who lack the ability to choose, such as young children and the insane, are exempted from the law. Those who choose evil are held accountable by the law. Concomitant with the principle of personal accountability is the right of all defendants to be treated with the dignity and respect that their human status implies. Criminal trials are an attempt to apply these abstract principles to concrete real-world situations. Each case must be addressed on its own merits, as if it were the only one that mattered – as indeed it is for the defendant on trial. A defendant should leave the courtroom, whatever the outcome, feeling that he or she has been treated as an individual and not as an item on some criminal justice assembly line. For this to occur, the decision-maker must take account of the unique circumstances of the defendant's case. Justice is thus concerned not only with the equal application of the law but also with its individualization.

Aristotle (1925) was perhaps the first to identify the tension between general rules and individual circumstances. He introduced the concept of 'equity' as a corrective that allowed a law of general applicability to be adjusted to the facts of a particular case. The purpose was to avoid the unjust result which might follow from the mechanical application of a just but general law to an inappropriate set of facts. General proscriptions can never be drawn in a way that will take account of the complex tapestry of real-life events. Laws supply rough guidelines. Equity provides the flexibility for fine-tuning and applying laws in accord with not only their letter, but also their spirit. In the criminal justice system, taking account of the equities of the case is the responsibility of the jury. In such cases the jury verdict is more of an attempt to round out or complete the law than a rejection of it (Scheflin and Van Dyke, 1991; Fletcher, 1988).

In some instances the legislature may have failed to envisage situations for which, had it foreseen them, it might have been prepared to afford a remedy. In other instances the legislature may have foreseen the exceptional case, but preferred to state the law in general terms. A compromise between generality and specificity often needs to be struck. A criminal code which attempted to address every nuance of each law's potential applicability would be too cumbersome to be of practical use. Too much specificity also risks the inadvertent creation of legal loopholes. In addition, some flexibility may be desirable in order to allow the law to be adapted to a changing world. Finally, there may be some types of equitable considerations that, for policy reasons, the legislature might not wish to commit to writing – for example, it might be considered undesirable formally to recognize a defence of economic duress lest it incline the needy towards criminal activity. Nevertheless, justice may demand mercy in the case of the defendant who steals to feed her starving family, and the legislature might not disagree. The task of particularizing the general law, of dispensing mercy where appropriate, and generally of doing justice in the individual case is left to the jury.

Should the jury be seeking the outcome that the legislature would have chosen had it been called upon to decide the specific case? It is difficult enough for a court, which at least has access to legislative debates and committee hearings that may shed light on the legislature's thinking, to answer such a counterfactual question. Even if a jury were privy to this information, however, its responsibility differs fundamentally from that of the legislature. It is not only permissible, but appropriate, for a legislature to take into account considerations of collective social policy,[22] deeming that the overall best interests of society take precedence over the best interests of any individual. For a jury to do likewise would be improper. It is not simply that the jury lacks the necessary information to make decisions about what is in society's best interest, but that this is not its function. It is the decision-maker only in the case before it. It is the defendant on trial whose liberty is at stake. That defendant is entitled to have his or her particular circumstances considered, and rightly looks to the jury for this consideration.

Two recent cases, both of which attracted considerable media attention, illustrate how equitable considerations can affect a jury's verdict. In 1994 in Virginia, Lorena Bobbitt was charged with the malicious wounding of her husband after she cut off his penis while he was asleep. The defence maintained that her action was a response to years of abuse at the hands of her husband, and witnesses recounted how the former United States Marine would hit and humiliate his wife. Mrs Bobbitt testified that her husband would regularly torture and rape her.[23] The prosecution did not so much dispute these facts as argue that two wrongs did not make a right. Nevertheless, the jury found her not guilty.[24]

The verdict in the Bobbitt case echoed that of the Maidstone Crown Court jury in the case of Stephen Owen two years previously.[25] Owen's twelve-year-old son had been run over by Kevin Taylor, an itinerant lorry driver. Taylor had been given an 18-month sentence, of which he had served a year prior to being released. Taylor had shown few public signs of remorse. Sometime after Taylor's release, the grave of Owen's son had been desecrated, although no evidence directly linked Taylor to this incident. The present case arose after Owen had confronted Taylor and shot him, albeit not fatally. He had also wounded Taylor's common law wife, behind whom Taylor had tried to hide. At Owen's trial the judge pointedly told the jury:

> If it should be that the prosecution have proved that [Owen] is guilty of any offence, do not let the understandable emotion of sympathy distract you from the duty you swore in your oath to return a true verdict according to the evidence.

In seemingly direct contravention of this instruction, the jury acquitted. Afterwards, on the courthouse steps, Owen proclaimed, 'Justice has been done. Thank God for the jury.'

In both the Owen and Bobbitt trials there was no question that the defendants had committed the acts attributed to them. Each defendant, however, had a story to put before the jury – a story of their own victimization at the hands of the victim. Each asked the jury to judge both them *and their victims*. Conceding that they had violated the formal rules of the law, each in effect maintained that, whatever the law might say, they did not deserve to be punished. This may never have been stated expressly, but it was the theme that ran through each case.

The two verdicts illustrate how juries compensate for gaps in the law. Both defendants were ordinary citizens whose lives had been disrupted by extraordinary events. Neither crime would have been committed had it not been for the initial provocative acts of the victim. In this sense each crime could be said to have been victim-precipitated (Gobert, 1977). The law of neither jurisdiction, however, recognized such a defence. The law of Virginia did recognize a claim of self-defence, but that defence is beset with limitations. Mrs Bobbitt would have had to have shown that she was under attack or faced with the threat of an imminent attack; that the force employed was in response to that attack; and that the force used was not disproportionate to that of the assailant. Regardless of whether the severing of her husband's penis was a disproportionate response to his abusive behaviour, Mrs Bobbitt would still have to overcome the fact that, at the time of the attack, her husband was asleep and she was in no imminent danger.

Provocation is a recognized defence but will only serve to reduce a charge of murder to manslaughter.[26] Thus neither defendant would have been able to raise a formal defence of provocation since neither was charged with murder. Say, however, that Taylor had died. It might be reasonable to assume that Owen's crime would have been reduced from murder to manslaughter because of Taylor's provocation in causing the death of Owen's son. However, under the then prevailing law, this claim would probably have failed. Owen's shooting of Taylor took place long after the hit-and-run incident and the law proceeds on the assumption that he would have had ample time to regain his self-control.[27] In any event, provocation is only a partial defence, serving to reduce murder to manslaughter. It is doubtful whether Owen would have been satisfied. What he was seeking in the actual case was not mitigation but vindication. He wanted the jurors to endorse his actions, to state that justice, all things considered, required an acquittal. By its verdict in the actual case the jury gave him that endorsement.

Whether or not the juries in the two cases described reached the correct verdict is, in a sense, a peripheral issue. Reasonable minds might differ as to whether the response of each defendant was unduly extreme. The more important point, however, is that in expanding the scope of their vision to take into account matters that were not relevant in the strict legal sense, the jurors were seeking to do justice in the case. That they had to do so outside the boundaries set by the law is an indictment not of the juries but of the law.

Some would say that the proper solution would be to amend the applicable law. Laws and legal defences, however, are established with paradigmatic cases in mind. Take self-defence. X attacks Y; Y responds, using roughly the same amount of force as employed by X; Y is accorded a defence of self-defence. The statement of the rule conceals a number of assumptions that may not accord with reality. One is that X and Y are of roughly equal size and strength and that Y can fend off X's attack using similar force as employed by X. If X assaults Y with his fists, Y can repel the attack with his fists. But what if Y is the diminutive Mrs Bobbitt and X is her burly ex-Marine husband? If Mrs Bobbitt is restricted to using force of the same character as employed by her husband, she would never be able to defend herself. She needed an advantage – a weapon, perhaps, or the element of surprise. But, in law, the use of a deadly weapon to respond to a non-deadly attack is unreasonable, and a response at any time other than at the point of the attack or when the victim is in imminent danger of attack will fall outside the scope of self-defence. Likewise, the assumption underlying the law's treatment of homicide is that time cools passion. For many, such as Stephen Owen, the passage of time has the opposite effect. Brooding over a past injustice – the death of his son – served only to increase his anger and frustration.

It is doubtful that the law could ever be constructed to take into account the innumerable factual variations of real-life cases. A laundry list of factors to be considered would still present themselves in different degrees and combinations. With regard to self-defence, for example, one victim may be marginally weaker than his assailant; another, like Mrs Bobbitt, significantly so. The nature and amount of provocation can range from slight to severe. The defendant may be of stoic temperament or highly excitable, or somewhere in-between. The response chosen will reflect the circumstances of the moment. No statute could hope to take into account the infinite mix of variables; and one that tried would probably be unsuitable for practical use. The legislature is content to provide rough guidance in its laws and to leave their fine-tuning in a particular case to the jury. Usually this division of labour is merely implicit, but on occasion it is formally acknowledged in the relevant statute. Section 3 of the Homicide Act 1957, for example, provides:

> Where on a charge of murder there is evidence on which *the jury* can find that the person charged was provoked (whether by things done or by things said or by both together) to lose his self-control, *the question whether the provocation was enough to make a reasonable man do as he did shall be left to be determined by the jury*; and in determining that question *the jury* shall take into account everything both done and said according to the effect which, *in their opinion*, it would have on a reasonable man. (emphasis added)[28]

Where the law fails to recognize a defence such as victim precipitation, a defendant, in order to place before the jury relevant evidence for its consideration, may be manoeuvred into raising a defence that the law *does* recognize. The technical merits of the defence may be irrelevant. It serves only as a vehicle to allow the introduction of evidence that creates a contextual framework within which to evaluate the defendant's actions. Thus Mrs Bobbitt's defence was insanity, although she was not being treated for mental illness and suffered from no known mental disorder. She did claim amnesia in respect to the incident but, for legal purposes – as any first-year law student could have told her – mere amnesia cannot be equated with insanity. Any attempt to make sense of the verdict from a strictly legal perspective, however, would miss the point. The purpose of Mrs Bobbitt's insanity defence was to allow her to introduce evidence as to how she had been driven to the point of despair by her husband's constant bullying and violence. Her insanity defence also provided a legal peg on which an acquittal could be rationalized by those jurors who might have felt uncomfortable returning a verdict lacking all legal grounding. That juries should have to so rationalize their verdicts is an indictment of a legal system that persists in maintaining that the jury's function extends no further than the strict application of law to fact.

Both Bobbitt and Owen in effect put their victim on trial – a tactic not unfamiliar to lawyers. Percy Foreman, a highly successful American defence attorney, is quoted as having said that the 'best defence in a murder case is the fact that the deceased should have been killed regardless of how it happened' (Smith, 1966). There is little doubt that the jurors thought that Kevin Taylor and John Wayne Bobbitt got what they deserved, even if the moral qualities of a victim are irrelevant in law. Empirical research also confirms that juries take into account the victim's character: the Chicago Jury Project discovered that one of the key features distinguishing cases where the judge would have reached a different verdict from that reached by the jury was the perceived fault of the victim (Kalven and Zeisel, 1966, chs 16, 17). In other words, empathetic jurors were prepared to acquit in circumstances where judges would have dismissed the victim's fault as not relevant.[29] In Britain, McCabe and Purves discovered a similar phenomenon: no matter '[h]ow clearly the judge explained the law, however strenuous his emphasis that in assault cases provocation is no defence, juries ... would predictably acquit a defendant who acted, *not in self-defence*, but under a degree of provocation' (McCabe and Purves, 1972, p. 32).

There is a view that verdicts such as those returned in the Owen and Bobbitt cases will encourage aggrieved individuals to extract private revenge with the expectation that a jury will approve their actions (see, for example, *Sunday Telegraph*, 24 May 1992). This thesis underestimates the sophistication of the jury. Jurors are sensitive to the nuances of the particular case, and make far finer discriminations than the critics are willing to give them credit for. The proof can be seen in the far more commonplace cases where juries convict those who have engaged in acts of private revenge. It would, in any event, be an obviously high-risk strategy for any potential defendant to assume that a jury will automatically sanction all acts of vengeance.

The Justice of the Criminal Justice System

In the Bobbitt and Owen cases it was the victim who was in effect on trial. On occasion, the evidence causes the trial to transmute from one of the accused to one of his accusers, with the conduct of those responsible for the enforcement and administration of the law becoming the focus of the jury's attention. Such a case occurred in London in 1990. Following evidence that one policeman had beaten the defendant on the way to the jail and another had fabricated a statement attributed to the defendant, the jury sent a note to the judge indicating that it was not prepared to convict (*Sunday Observer*, 11 November 1990). The court agreed to enter a verdict of not guilty despite the fact that there were five witnesses still to be heard and the prosecution had yet to make its closing argument. The verdict was more a condemnation of the police than an acquittal of the defendant.

The concern with the propriety of official conduct can extend to others involved in the administration of the criminal justice system. In 1991 Pottle and Randle (see page 38) were acquitted of helping a Soviet spy escape from Wormwood Scrubs prison. Although the facts on which the charges were based had been known as early as 1970, no formal proceedings were brought until nearly two decades later. The belated prosecution seems to have been a reaction to a book, detailing their role in the escape, that the defendants had published in 1989. The publication of the book led to demands from politicians for the prosecution of its authors. The defendants maintained at their trial that they were in the dock not so much for what they had done as for what they had written. The judge, however, instructed the jury that any alleged abuse of the legal system was irrelevant, and that the only question was whether the defendants had assisted the escape, which they did not deny. Nevertheless, the jury acquitted.

The probity of both police and prosecution was at issue in the highly publicized criminal trial of O.J. Simpson for the murder of his ex-wife, Nicole, and her companion, Ronald Goldman. This case differed from those of Bobbitt, Owen, and Pottle and Randle in that Simpson denied committing the murders. The jury therefore had a factual question to resolve – did Simpson kill the two victims? As part of Simpson's defence, his lawyers insinuated that the police investigation may have been corrupted by racism. A key prosecution witness was captured on tape repeatedly uttering racial epithets. As is the case with all general verdicts, the not guilty verdict in the case masked the reasons behind the result. It is not clear whether the jury was unconvinced by the evidence linking Simpson to the murders, or believed that law enforcement personnel had behaved so badly that justice, all things considered, warranted an acquittal. There was, of course, a link between the official charges against Simpson and the unofficial charges of police racism. If the jurors believed that the prosecution was racially motivated, they might have decided that the evidence against Simpson had been fabricated. And if they decided that the evidence had been fabricated, they might have concluded that there existed a reasonable doubt of Simpson's guilt. Post-trial comments by some of the jurors suggested that distrust of the police investigation was an important factor in their decision.

The Simpson case presented the jury with a dilemma. On the one hand, the jurors presumably had no desire to let a murderer go free. On the other, they did not wish to be seen to be condoning questionable racist practices. The question of whether or not there was a reasonable doubt as to Simpson's guilt may have been resolved in a way that allowed the jury to express its disapproval of police racism. But does it make sense to punish the police by letting a guilty defendant go free? Would it not be preferable to convict the guilty defendant and then discipline the police for any misconduct? The problem is that neither politicians nor prosecutors are inclined to discipline the police, upon whom they are dependent in their war against crime, and self-regulation, while a laudatory goal, is often difficult to achieve in practice. The failure of those in a position of authority to curb police misconduct leads to community frustration which can find expression in questionable acquittals. These verdicts often will prompt needed reforms, just as refusals of juries in England to convict petty thieves of capital offences hastened the abolition of the death penalty. Following the Simpson verdict the LA police department began to take racism more seriously.

Heightening the Jury's Sensitivity to the Demands of Justice

Some would suggest that the jury's role in achieving justice is overrated (for example, Frank, 1963; Williams, 1963; Darbyshire, 1991), and that for every case where the jury may have properly exercised its power to do justice can be found another where it has failed to avoid an injustice. Just as there have been jurors that have stood up for freedom of speech and religion, so too have there been juries which have convicted defendants thought to be witches or anarchists. It was a jury of ordinary Athenians, it might be recalled, that convicted Socrates of corrupting the youth of Greece. For every New England jury praised for its refusal to convict those charged with harbouring runaway slaves there existed a jury which acquitted a Ku Klux Klansman solely because the victim was black. Those who favour the jury system take pride when justice is seen to triumph, but are rightly embarrassed by the jury's failures. The obvious challenge is to eliminate, or at least minimize, the incidence of the latter as much as possible. The starting point is to discover the reasons why a jury might fail to prevent an injustice.

As noted at the beginning of this chapter, in many trials the law in question is not unjust and the jury is not presented with a claim that its application would work an injustice in the circumstances of the case. The jury has no reason to do anything other than to return the verdict required by the law. However, even in cases where issues of justice arise, juries can be seen mechanically applying the law. It may be because the jurors do not appreciate that they have any other choice. The typical trial judge instructs the jury that its function is to apply the law, whether or not the jurors agree with it (Devitt, Blackmar and Wolff, 1987). Further, the judge will tell the jurors that they should not be swayed by sympathy and may intimate, if not expressly state, that the jurors would be violating their oath if they were to allow such considerations to enter their deliberations.

This is not to say that judicial directions do not pay lip service to the relevance of justice. The token references, however, may serve only to confuse the jurors. Consider, for example, the following California jury instruction:

> Ladies and Gentlemen of the Jury:
>
> ...
>
> You are to be governed by the evidence introduced in this trial and the law as stated to you by me. The law forbids you to be governed by mere sentiment, conjecture, sympathy, passion, public opinion or public feeling. Both the People and the defendant have a right to demand, and they do demand and expect, that you will conscientiously and dispassionately consider and weigh the evidence and apply the law of the case, and that you will reach a just verdict, regardless of what the consequences may be ... . (Van Dyke, 1977, p. 266)

In one breath the court tells the jury that it must follow the law. In the next it says that the parties have a right not only to expect, but to demand a just verdict. Yet, the court implies that such human qualities as sentiment, sympathy and sensitivity to community opinion have no relevance whatsoever to what constitutes a just verdict. According to the instruction, justice can seemingly be achieved only through a strict application of the law. That the demands of law and justice might conflict is apparently not a possibility that the jury is allowed to entertain.

If the judges are to be faulted, it is for their failure to be more candid with jurors and to inform them that they are permitted to return a verdict contrary to the law when justice so demands. Why are judges not more forthcoming? One reason may be that some do not approve of the exercise of what they see as an extra-legal authority. In *King* v. *Shipley*[30] Ashurst J drew a distinction between a jury's rights and powers:

> I admit the jury have the *power* of finding a verdict against the law, and so they have of finding a verdict against the evidence, but I deny they have the *right* to do so. (emphasis added)[31]

Presumably a jury has to be informed of its rights but need not be told of its powers. But does the distinction make sense? When Ashurst speaks of a verdict against the evidence, whom does he envisage making the determination that the verdict is in fact against the evidence – the judge? As will be discussed in Chapter 3, there is little reason to believe that a judge's determination of the facts is any more accurate than that of a jury – and there are sound reasons for believing the opposite. On the other hand, the judge is undeniably qualified to declare that a verdict is against the law, at least where the case presents a pure question of law. An example would be where a statute required medical evidence to sustain an insanity defence, but no medical witnesses testified at the trial. If a jury were to return a verdict of not guilty by reason of insanity, it might correctly be said to be contrary to the law. But so what? The court would still be bound to accept the verdict. If judges are under a duty to accept a verdict that is contrary to the law, is it not because the jury has the right to return such a verdict?

Ashurst's focus may, in any event, have been misdirected. His concern in the above-quoted paragraph was with the rights of the *jurors*. But what of the rights of the defendant? Arguably a defendant has a right to be protected against unjust laws, sanctions and prosecutions. This is the jury's responsibility. To say that the jurors have the power to provide this protection but no obligation to do so is to emasculate the defendant's right. Even if it is conceded that the jury has only a power and not a right (let alone a duty) to return a verdict contrary to the law when justice demands, the accused arguably has a right to have a jury consider the exercise of this power. Unless the jurors are informed of their power, they will not be in a position to exercise it.

Some judges fear that, if the jury is given to understand that it may return a verdict against the law, there will be juries which will unjustifiably convict. These judges misconceive the nature of the jury's authority. Juries should be told that if they decide that justice so requires, they may acquit despite the fact that a conviction might seem to be warranted by the letter of the law. They should never be told that they may convict where the defendant has not violated the law. The latter instruction would violate both settled legal rule *and* the principle of justice that it is unjust to convict someone who has not violated the law. If, for some reason, a jury did convict in the absence of proof of illegal conduct on the part of the defendant, the conviction would be subject to reversal.[32] Similarly, while a jury is allowed to be merciful, it is not allowed to be vengeful. Like the motorist who drives on a one-way street, the jury's prerogative to return a verdict contrary to the law extends in only one direction.

Another reason why some judges may refrain from informing jurors of the full extent of their authority is that they may be afraid that the jury will usurp their own responsibility for dealing with issues of law. As with the fear that jurors will return unwarranted convictions, this too is based on a misconception of the jury's role. A jury is not allowed to question a court's evidentiary rulings or its interpretation of the law. It must accept the judge's directions as embodying a correct statement of the law. At one time there was some debate, particularly in the United States, as to whether jurors were the judges of the law as well as of the facts, but it is now settled that this is the court's responsibility.[33] This allocation is correct, for the interpretation of the law requires an expertise that the jurors do not possess. It is quite a different matter, however, for a jury to conclude that the application of the law, as authoritatively interpreted by the judge, would work an injustice in the particular case and, for that reason, acquit.

Some judges may believe that considerations of justice can best be taken into account at sentencing. At this stage the court will have before it not only the jury's verdict, but also a pre-sentence report prepared by a qualified probation officer or social worker. The court will also be able to examine the defendant's prior criminal record and consider mitigating evidence that might have been inadmissible at the trial. Deferring considerations of justice to the sentencing stage is, however, problematic. One obvious point is that justice may require an acquittal. Even if a convicted defendant is not sent to prison, the defendant will incur a criminal record that may foreclose future job opportunities. Second, the judge may lack the discretion to adjust the sentence in a way that will achieve justice. Some crimes carry mandatory, or mandatory minimum, sentences. Sentencing guidelines may also restrict the judge's discretion. Finally, part of the rationale for jury trials is to imbue the verdict with the community's sense of justice. A judge's perspective of justice may not be the same as that of the community. It is not so much that the judge does not share the values of the general community (although this, too, is not that unlikely) as that the views of any one member of a group are less likely to be an accurate representation of the whole than those of a twelve member cross-section.

Perhaps the most persuasive justification for not informing jurors of their ability to return a verdict contrary to the law is forwarded by those judges who do not wish to see juries exercising this prerogative too freely and too often. Unlike their colleagues who believe that any verdict which is contrary to the law is unwarranted, these judges are not opposed to jury justice in the appropriate case. Their fear, rather, is that, by instructing the jury that it has the power to disregard the law, they may be encouraging verdicts against the law in inappropriate cases.[34] In being less than candid with the jurors, the judges seek to restrict the jury's exercise of its authority to those exceptional cases which truly cry out for justice, where the call of justice all but drowns out the judge's instruction to adhere to the law. (Kadish and Kadish, 1973) Lord Devlin points out the hypocrisy in this position:

> [The jury's] rights are never explained to it. Jurymen are not assured that they are answerable only to their own consciences nor told in a criminal case that a verdict of acquittal returned contrary to the direction of the judge must nevertheless be accepted. If he were sitting in judgment upon others a judge might say that he thought it rather unscrupulous to bring a bunch of laymen into a process dominated by professionals and not to explain to them their rights. But ... most judges would answer by saying that the working of the system requires the jury to be bridled. If the horse takes the bit between its teeth there is nothing to be done about it; it cannot be punished for it, but it should not be taught how to do it. (Devlin, 1979, p. 101)

Judicial fears regarding the dangers of candid directions may well be exaggerated. In an instructive experiment, Horowitz divided mock jurors into three groups (Horowitz 1985, 1988). One group was instructed that its task was to return the verdict required by the law, the second that the jury was the judge of both law and fact, and the third that jurors were permitted to bring to bear their own feelings about the case and acquit if they felt that the law, as applied to the facts, would produce an unjust result. The instruction given made no difference to the verdict in a hypothetical case involving a grocer killed during an attempted robbery – all three groups convicted of murder. The instruction to the third group, which might appear to be the one most likely to lead to a verdict contrary to the law, failed to produce a single acquittal in a second hypothetical case involving a pedestrian who was run over by an intoxicated university student on a foggy night. Interestingly, two of the five juries that received each of the other two sets of instructions acquitted the student. Only in a hypothetical situation, involving the mercy killing of a terminally ill cancer patient by a nurse who had the consent of both the patient and her family, did the third instruction yield a significant increase in the acquittal rate. Although all three groups were reluctant to convict the nurse, it was the third group that was most inclined to translate its reservations into a not guilty verdict.

The results of Horowitz's experiment suggest that the directions of the court will not deflect a jury from convicting when the case for guilt is strong and no countervailing considerations of justice are present. Where the instructions may make a difference is in those cases where there are genuine issues of justice to be taken into account. A cautionary note should be sounded, however. One should not read too much into any experiment involving mock jurors. The jurors are aware that the fates of real people are not at stake and their sense of the gravity of the occasion may be correspondingly reduced. Because no defendant will actually be sentenced to prison as a result of their verdict, the jurors may be less inclined to consider the equities of the case. Furthermore, knowing that they are being observed may have an inhibiting effect on the candour of the deliberations. Despite these caveats, the studies do seem to indicate that jurors are better able to distinguish between those cases which warrant a verdict contrary to the law and those where justice will be achieved by its strict application, than judges are inclined to give them credit for. Jurors, it seems, are able to grasp the difference between serious and technical offences, and between offenders who deserve censure and those who deserve mercy.

The strategy of not informing the jury of its power to return a verdict against the law when justice demands, on the grounds that it will do so anyway in cases which cry out for justice, appears to assume that there are two discrete categories of case: those that do not require the exercise of the jury's power to do justice and those that do. It is expected that, despite the lack of guidance, the jury will be guided by its conscience in the latter but not the former category. In real life, however, cases present themselves in shades of grey as well as in black and white. Some cases will scream out for justice, but in others the cry is more muted, and a jury may have to make an effort to hear it. In between the two extremes there lies a broad middle ground where considerations of justice need to be balanced against the requirements of the law. These are cases which do not 'cry out' for justice but where a conviction for the crime charged might nonetheless be unduly harsh in light of the defendant's relative lack of moral culpability. Such cases require a tempering of the strict demands of the law but, without guidance, the jury may not be able to provide the needed moderation.

A second risk inherent in the strategy of refusing to discuss with juries their responsibility to do justice is that jurors may take seriously the judge's admonition to limit their inquiry to the proper application of law to fact. Among the jurors may be some who have reservations about the justice of a conviction, but who also consider themselves good citizens and as such, may be reluctant to disobey the instructions of a court. They accept the judge's statements at face value, and strive to apply law to fact, regardless of what they see to be the demands of justice. An example of this phenomenon is reported by Jessica Mitford in her book on the trial of Dr Spock for counselling draft resisters during the Vietnam War (Mitford 1969). Mitford interviewed jurors who admitted to misgivings about convicting but felt that they had no other choice in light of the judge's instructions. As a consequence they concurred in a verdict which conflicted with their consciences.

If jurors are told that their role is restricted to applying law to fact, the verdict that a particular jury returns will turn more on the jurors' independence of spirit and knowledge of their prerogatives than on the merits of the case. But if judges do not tell them of these prerogatives and the scope of their authority, from where are they to acquire such knowledge? In *United States* v. *Dougherty*[35] Judge Leventhal offered the following answer:

> The jury knows well enough that its prerogative is not limited to the choices articulated in the formal instructions of the court. The jury gets its understanding as to the arrangements in the legal system from more than one voice. There is a formal communication from the judge. There is the informal communication from the total culture – literature (novel, drama, film, and television); current comment (newspapers, magazines and television); conversation; and, of course, history and tradition. The totality of input generally convey adequately enough the idea of prerogative, of freedom in an occasional case to depart from what the judge says. Even indicators that would on their face seem too weak to notice – like the fact that the judge tells the jury it must acquit (in case of reasonable doubt) but never tells the jury in so many words that it must convict – are a meaningful part of the jury's total input. Law is a system, and it is also a language, with secondary meanings that may be unrecorded yet are part of its life.[36]

If Judge Leventhal is correct, it would seem that a trial judge's instruction to apply the law to the facts may serve only to induce an unhealthy sense of schizophrenia. Either the jurors will have to follow their consciences in disregard of the directions of the court or they will have to follow the court's directions in disregard of their consciences. Alternatively, the jurors will have to guess at what the court *really* means.

Even assuming that a jury, in Judge Leventhal's words 'knows well enough that its prerogative is not limited to the choices articulated in the formal instructions of the court', from where are the jurors supposed to summon the inner fortitude to defy the court's formal instructions? Some juries, aware of their prerogatives and with the strength of character to assert them, will return the just verdict. Others will not, either because they perceive their duty as that of returning the legally correct verdict or because they are reluctant to disobey the judge's instructions. Yet both juries may have arrived at exactly the same point in their analysis of the case. The difference will reflect only their belief as to how their conclusions are to be translated into a verdict. Judge Leventhal's approach appears to be a recipe designed to produce, at best, the haphazard achievement of justice. Like cases will not be treated alike, and preventable injustices may be inevitable.

If juries are to be successful in their task, they need to understand what that task entails. They should be told that they have the duty to prevent injustice and the right to return the verdict that they believe to be just, all things considered. A bill proposed in New York sought to revise the jury handbook as follows:

> [T]he handbook shall inform the jurors that in all cases they have the historical, constitutional, and natural right to judge not only the liability, guilt, or innocence of the defendant(s) under the law as charged, but to exercise their conscience in doing so and that, if they determine according to their conscience that the law as charged by the judge is unjust or wrongly applied to the defendant(s), it is their obligation, right, and duty to judge according to their conscience. (Scheflin and Van Dyke, 1991)

This message would need to be reinforced by the trial judge. A far-reaching juridical instruction to this effect was proposed as an amendment to the Oregon Constitution:

> Before the jury hears a case, and again before jury deliberation begins, the court shall inform the jurors of their rights in these words: 'As jurors, your first responsibility is to decide whether the prosecution has proven beyond a reasonable doubt every element of the criminal charge. If you decide that the prosecution has proven beyond reasonable doubt every element of the criminal charge but that you cannot in good conscience support a guilty verdict, you are not required to do so. To reach a verdict which you believe is just, each of you has the right to consider to what extent the defendant's actions have actually caused harm or otherwise violated your sense of right and wrong. If you believe justice requires it, you may also judge both the merits of the law under which the defendant has been charged and the wisdom of applying that law to the defendant. Accordingly, for each charge against the defendant, even if review of the

> evidence strictly in terms of the law would indicate a guilty verdict, you have the right to find the defendant not guilty. (Scheflin and Van Dyke, 1991)

Once a jury has been made aware of the full extent of its remit the court can proceed to explore with it the types of factor which might properly be considered in the search for justice. The requirements of the law are obviously important, and the jurors should be so informed. But they should not be left with the impression that this is the only relevant consideration. Jurors also need to be told that they must not be insensitive to the demands of conscience. The judge might further discuss with the jurors those aspects of justice which might have particular relevance to the case. Judges, of course, should not impose on the jury their view of the just verdict in the particular case, any more than judges should impose their understanding of the facts or their analysis of how the law should be applied to the facts. Nor can the range of factors which a jury might wish to take into account be restricted by a trial judge's instructions, and the judge should make that point clear as well.

Discussing standards of justice with the jury might well help to obviate the unjust acquittal. Commonly cited examples include the sectarian juries in Northern Ireland that refused to convict Protestants of crimes committed against Catholics and the all-white juries which acquitted Ku Klux Klansmen of crimes against blacks. Unlike unjust convictions, unjust acquittals are not susceptible to judicial reversal. Subsequent chapters will explore how a representative and heterogeneous jury can help to combat unjust acquittals. To the extent that such acquittals are produced by overt or covert threats to jurors, the jurors can be protected by preserving their anonymity (see Chapter 3). The judge's instructions can also play a role by forcing the jurors to recognize the potential injustice that might occur if they were to succumb to community prejudice. Although it is perhaps naive to expect a judge's discussion of justice to override parochial bias, there may be some jurors who see a genuine conflict between the responsibility to represent their community and their responsibility to do justice, for whom judicial guidance would be welcome. At present, judicial decisions tend to conflate these two responsibilities (see Chapter 5).

Lawyers, too, should be able to explore the demands of justice with the jury. No doubt many already attempt to do so in their closing speeches.[37] Some judges tolerate such tactics, but other's do not. The effect, again, may be that like cases are not treated alike. Allowing counsel to advance justice-based arguments may bring to the jurors' attention dimensions of the case that they might not have fully appreciated if left to their own devices.

Even if lawyers were to be allowed to appeal to the jury's sense of justice in their closing speeches, the foundation for such an appeal to justice would often have to be laid long before the lawyer's closing speech. Evidentiary rules, however, can frustrate the attempt to lay this foundation. Many of these rules were, in fact, born of a distrust of the jury (Thayer, 1898). The exclusion of hearsay evidence, for example, rests not so much on its lack of probative value, nor even the fact that it cannot be subjected to effective cross-examination, but rather on the fear that jurors will accord it more weight than it deserves. Rules of relevancy are based on the premise that the jury's function is to apply law to fact. Once it is acknowledged, however, that the jury's remit encompasses the search for justice, other types of evidence, currently inadmissable, become relevant. The jury would benefit, for example, from having information about a defendant's motives. Motive – the reason why a defendant did what he did – is no defence in law, yet it undoubtedly bears on an accused's moral culpability. A crime committed from an honourable motive will still be a crime, but considerations of justice may argue in favour of an acquittal. Take the case, referred to previously, of the Liverpool women charged with causing millions of pounds' worth of damage to fighter jets destined for Indonesia. Their defence was that the planes might be employed in an unjust war against the peoples of East Timor. If such evidence were to have been excluded (it was not), the jury would have been poorly placed to evaluate the defendants' claim that their acts were justified. Indeed, their acts of destruction might have appeared wanton and totally irrational. Similarly, cases of civil disobedience often raise the question of whether an individual is justified in disobeying a morally neutral law, such as one that forbids criminal trespass, in order to protest an unjust government policy. To focus exclusively on the law that has been violated without permitting evidence of the alleged injustice of the policy being protested yields a distorted picture. As Judge Jack Weinstein points out (1993), a liberal approach to evidentiary rules is often required if the jury is to do its job properly. Better still would be the reconsideration and reformation of evidentiary rules that impede the jury's search for a just verdict.

Juries would also benefit from a knowledge of the range of sanctions for the offence charged and the sentence most likely to be imposed if the accused were to be found guilty. This information is typically withheld from the jurors. Yet it may be critical both to avoid the inappropriate acquittal that results when the jury is under an erroneous impression that a severe sentence will be imposed, and the unwarranted conviction where the jury erroneously assumes that a lenient sentence will be imposed. In Michigan the 'suicide doctor', Jack Kevorkian, was found not guilty of aiding and abetting a suicide, despite admitting his 'crime'.[38] It is of course speculative, but perhaps the jurors might have been more willing to return a guilty verdict had they been assured that Kevorkian would not have been sent to prison. Conversely, it is likely that the jurors' resistance to a conviction would have been even greater had they been informed that a mandatory life sentence would have to be imposed. A jury's concern is often less with guilt or innocence than with an outcome that captures the defendant's moral blameworthiness.

What is sought, in effect, is a voice in sentencing. This need not be as extreme as authorizing jury sentencing (as occurs in the *Cours d'assises* in France where judges sit with the jury), but simply permitting juries to make recommendations regarding the appropriate sentence.[39] Russia might seem an unusual place to look for an appropriate model but juries there are given the power to recommend a verdict of 'lenience', which limits the court to a sentence that can be no higher than the average of the maximum and mandatory minimum terms of imprisonment for the crime charged (Thaman, 1995). A British jury is allowed to recommend mercy, but as is the case with so many of its other powers, the trial judge is under no obligation to inform it of this prerogative, and usually does not.[40] One might well wonder how a jury is to become aware of its power. In any event, a jury's recommendation of mercy is merely advisory and might well be ignored by a 'law and order' judge. The force of a jury's recommendation would be increased sharply if there were a requirement that the sentencing judge had to reconvene the original jury to submit to it any proposed sentence which varied significantly from its recommendation. Nor should it be assumed that the jurors would automatically disagree with the judge's proposed alteration after it was explained to them. The judge's sentence, for example, might take into account the defendant's previous criminal record, which might not have been revealed to the jury at the trial.[41]

Conclusion

This and the preceding chapter have attempted to explore the jury's role in preventing injustice and achieving justice. It is submitted that the conception of the jury's role that has been presented offers both a more accurate, as well as a richer, account of what the jury does and should be doing than the one traditionally espoused. It does not pretend that jurors have a judge's expertise in applying law to fact or a philosopher's ability to engage in abstruse, theoretical analysis. It sees the strength of the jury system in the practical wisdom and sensitivity to the demands of conscience that jurors bring to their task. The moderating influence of collective responsibility prevents the verdict from reflecting the idiosyncrasies of any single individual, as might be the case if a judge alone were entrusted with the verdict. As will be discussed in Chapter 3, the processes of the jury room – the synergism of the deliberations and the dialectics of debate – help to ensure that the theory of the case on which the verdict is based is that which best fits the facts, the law and the demands of justice.

The criminal justice system's attitude towards the jury is currently marked by antinomies and ambivalence. On the one hand, it entrusts jurors with the ultimate authority to decide guilt or innocence. On the other, it refuses to inform them of the ramifications of their verdict, although no rational human being would ever contemplate an important life choice without seeking to take account of its consequences. In matters of evidence, it treats the jurors as children, withholding from them information that reasonable persons would take into account in planning their own affairs. When jurors are confused, they are not encouraged to speak up or ask questions, as any sensible person would. Jurors are also not encouraged to take notes, although the judges openly question their ability to remember testimony in a lengthy trial. Finally, and most worryingly, while acknowledging that jurors possess the power to return a verdict against the law and the evidence, judges decline to tell them of this power on the remarkable rationale that they might be tempted to exercise it. This obduracy on the part of judges compels juries to operate in a surreptitious and furtive manner that is not in keeping with the noble purpose of their enterprise.

Any explanation as to why the jury's power to infuse their verdicts with justice lies too often dormant would place much of the blame on trial judges who fail to inform jurors of the full scope of their remit. Even if the largely semantic point that a jury has only the power and not the right to acquit contrary to the law when justice demands were conceded, a defendant arguably has the right to have the jury consider the exercise of this power. Unless jurors are informed of it, it will be exercised at best haphazardly, at worst not at all.

The judicial failure to be more forthcoming with jurors has other deleterious side-effects. It means that the jury will be deprived of the guidance that a judge might be able to provide as to the demands of justice. It means that lawyers who wish to appeal to the jury's sense of justice can do so only if they have a quiescent opponent and a tolerant judge. It means that an individual juror may hesitate to admit to the others the real concerns behind his or her reservations regarding a particular verdict, and end up advancing judicially sanitized arguments that are not as persuasive. Finally, it means that jurors, when they do decide to return the verdict that they believe that justice, and not the law, requires, will have to summon the inner courage to defy the Court's directions.

If the jury system is to thrive, rather than to become a museum piece, revered more for its history than its functionality, jurors must be given the tools to do their job properly, and should be told what that job involves.

Judges should loosen the reins by which they currently hold juries in check – not only because it is unrealistic to expect jurors to ignore their conscience, but because it stifles the very qualities that make the jury a valuable institution. To confine the jury to the application of law to fact is to restrict it to a pseudo-judicial role for which it is not particularly qualified (at least compared to the judge), while preventing it from performing the 'community conscience' role for which it is eminently suited. When a jury attempts to 'play judge', it does a disservice to the defendant, who looks to the jury to temper law with justice. Of course, a jury's decision to return a verdict contrary to the law cannot be based on whim or pure personal preference; it must be grounded in principle. The instructions of the court help to guard against unprincipled verdicts and thus serve a constructive function. Nevertheless it does not follow that this purpose is further advanced by keeping the jurors ignorant of their responsibility to prevent injustice and to seek justice, all things considered.

Notes

1 Jury trials in civil cases are virtually non-existent in Britain except for a small category of cases, mostly dealing with injury to reputation. Because any discussion of damages would therefore have relevance primarily only for the United States, and because I would like to maintain the Anglo-American focus of the book, the topic, although intriguing, will not be pursued further.

2 Cf. *Yick Wo* v. *Hopkins*, 118 US 356 (1886).

3 Typically, these laws apply only to the male partner, which, at least in the case of mature minors, raises questions of sexual discrimination.

4 This issue led to a extended debate between Lon Fuller and H.L.A. Hart (1958) in the pages of the *Harvard Law Review*.

5 See, for example, *State* v. *Western Union Telegraph Co.* (1953) 97 A.2d 480; *People* v. *McCalla* [1923] 63 Cal. App. 783.

6 US Constitution, amend. 8.

7 *Trop* v. *Dulles*, 356 US 86, 101 (1958).

8 See comments of Lord Roskill in *R.* v. *Seymour* (1983) 2 All ER 1058, 1061.

9 For a discussion of a comparable American experience, see Robertson, Rich and Ross (1973).

10 If the jurors were specifically to ask the judge, they would most likely be told that it is not a matter for their concern.

11 When dealing with a doctrine of common law, the courts have more flexibility than they do in regard to a statute. See, for example, *R.* v. *R.* [1991] AC 599 (no matrimonial exception in rape).

12 See *Duncan* v. *Louisiana*, 391 US 145, 155 (1968).

13 124 Eng. Rep. 1006 (CP 1670).

14 *Bushell's Case* 124 Eng. Rep. 1006 (CP 1670).

15 At common law a verdict alleged to be false could be challenged by a writ of attaint. The challenge would be heard by a second jury, double the size of the original. By its

verdict this second jury could reverse the decision of the first jury. Such a verdict by the so-called jury of attaint constituted a conviction of the original jurors for perjury. This logically followed, for the original jurors were chosen because of their knowledge of the facts. If they reached an incorrect verdict, then they must have sworn falsely to the facts. Penalties were harsh. The offending jurors could be arrested and imprisoned, and their lands and property forfeited to the king. Presumably those who sat on a jury of attaint were aware of these consequences and must have hesitated before subjecting fellow citizens to them.

16 This remained the legal position in England until the passage of Fox's Libel Act 1792.

17 A similar analysis was recently advanced by the United States Supreme Court in *United States* v. *Gaudin*, 115 S. Ct. 2310 (1995). The issue was whether false statements made by an accused were 'material' for purposes of the applicable statute on false reporting. The Court stated that whether or not the statements were material depended on the inferences to be drawn from the facts and thus was an issue for the jury to decide.

18 For an account of this case see McCormick (1986).

19 *The Times*, 31 July 1996.

20 Some would suggest that the office of the prosecution may, and perhaps should, exercise its discretion and not bring charges in cases of political crimes. Arguably however, if there is a plausible case to be answered, then it is the prosecutor's duty to present it to a jury. Discretion is a double-edged sword, and those who would urge the prosecutor not to proceed in cases of political crimes might be quick to condemn a decision not to prosecute in the case of a corporate crime.

21 391 US 145 (1968).

22 Dworkin draws a similar distinction between matters of policy, most appropriately decided in a legislative setting, and matters of principle, most appropriately decided in a judicial setting. See Dworkin (1978).

23 See *Daily Telegraph*, 15 January 1994. Interestingly, however, Mr Bobbitt had previously been acquitted of sexual assault of his wife.

24 See *New York Times*, 22 January 1994.

25 *Daily Telegraph*, 23 May 1992.

26 See, for example, Homicide Act 1957 s. 3.

27 See *R.* v. *Ahluwalia*, [1992] 4 All ER 889; *R.* v. *Ibrams* (1981) 74 Crim. App. R. 154.

28 See also *R.* v. *Camplin* [1978] AC 705; *R* v. *Cascoe* [1970] 2 All ER 833.

29 This is not to say that the tactic does not raise troublesome questions. The victims of a criminal assault, for example, are not parties to the criminal prosecution and not able to defend their character. In cases of murder or manslaughter, the victim is dead.

30 (1784) 99 Eng. Rep. 774. This view was countered by that of Willes, J. who said: 'Where a civil power of this sort has been exercised without control, it presumes, nay, by continual usage it *gives* the right' (ibid. at pp. 824–5).

31 Ibid. at 828.

32 See Fed. R. Crim. Pro. 29(c); Criminal Appeal Act 1968 s. 2.

33 See *Sparf and Hansen* v. *United States*, 156 US 1 (1895). A few American state constitutions, however, provide that the jury is the judge of both law and fact in state trials. See Georgia Constitution, Article I, s.1, para. 11; Indiana Constitution, Article I, s. 19; Maryland Constitution, Declaration of Rights, Article 23. However, these provisions do not seem to be taken seriously in practice. See, for example, *Sparks* v. *State*, 91 Md. App. 35, 603 A.2d 1258, 1277 (1992) ('case law has made it clear that this curious constitutional relic has ... been shrivelled up to almost nothing').

34 The point was made thus in *United States* v. *Dougherty*, 473F.2d 1113, 1114, 1134, 1136–37 (DC Cir. 1972):

> ... jury system has worked out reasonably well overall, providing 'play in the joints' that imparts flexibility and avoid [sic] undue rigidity. An equilibrium has evolved – an often marvellous balance. There is reason to believe that the simultaneous achievement of modest jury equity and avoidance of intolerable caprice depends on formal instructions that do not expressly delineate a jury charter to carve out its own rules of law. ... It is pragmatically useful to structure instructions in such wise that the jury must feel strongly about the values involved in the case, so strongly that it must itself identify the case as establishing a call of high conscience, and must independently initiate and undertake an act in contravention of the established instructions. This requirement of independent jury conception confines the happening of the lawless jury to the occasional instance that does not violate and viewed as an exception may even enhance, the over-all normative effect of the rule of law. An explicit instruction to a jury conveys an implied approval that runs the risk of degrading the legal structure requisite for true freedom, for an ordered liberty that protects against anarchy as well as tyranny.

35 473 F. 2d 1113 (DC Cir 1972).

36 Ibid. at p. 1135.

37 For a powerful example of such a closing speech, see Van Dyke (1977) at p. 239 *et seq.*

38 See *New York Times*, 3 May 1994.

39 There is, however, the danger that this may encourage compromise verdicts where jurors opposed to a conviction are persuaded to agree to a guilty verdict accompanied by a recommendation for leniency.

40 *R.* v. *Langham* [1996] Criminal Law Review 430.

41 Although it would be quite controversial, an argument could be made that juries would reach more accurate verdicts if they were informed of a defendant's criminal record. The accused, of course, would be allowed to introduce evidence of reformation and more recent good character.

3 Judge versus Jury

Whatever other functions it may serve, the jury provides a mode of decision-making. The question is whether it is a better or worse mode than the alternatives available, the most commonly suggested of which is decision-making by a judge.[1] It is not unreasonable to ask why the responsibility for deciding issues of fact, law and justice should be entrusted to 12 randomly selected individuals, 'unaccustomed to severe intellectual exercise or to protracted thought'[2] and with no particularly relevant expertise. Would it not make more sense to draw on the training and experience of professionally qualified judges to resolve these matters? The jury system is the product of historical evolution, given that the lives of the defendant and others will be profoundly affected by its verdict, but history and tradition are poor justifications for its continued use.

There are many reasons for preserving jury trial, which relate to the jury's ability to prevent injustice and achieve justice (see Chapters 1 and 2) and the critical role that the jury plays in a democracy (see Chapters 4 and 5), but this chapter will examine the jury's merits as a decision-maker. In his Hamlyn lecture (1956) Lord Devlin asserted that the reason that the jury has evolved as it has done is because that was the way in which it was found to work. But what makes it work, and does it work better than a court in terms of its capacity to reach fair, just and correct decisions? In attempting to answer this question, this chapter will compare judge and jury decision-making along a number of parameters – overall general competency; susceptibility to prejudice and corruption; the ability to determine facts accurately; and the likelihood of reaching the right result in the individual case.

The Jury and its Critics

Many view the jury as an anachronism in the modern world. Juror competency is maligned and juror bias is alleged. The correctness of jury verdicts is questioned, and juries are claimed to be responsible for miscarriages of justice that bring the legal system into disrepute. Critics of the jury seem divided only as to whether to attribute its failings to incompetence or malevolence. These are serious charges that cannot be ignored by those who champion continued resort to jury trial.

All criticisms of the jury need to be approached with caution. It is not that the jury is above criticism. On the contrary, the problem is that the jury is an all too easy target for the critic. The reasons why are not hard to discern. The jury meets in secret. No third parties are present to validate its deliberations and no minutes are kept of the deliberations. Because so little is known about how the verdict is reached, it is relatively simple for the critic to attribute all manner of shortcomings to the process without fear of contradiction. Nor does the verdict allay concerns. It is a delphic pronouncement that supplies neither reasons nor explanations. The jurors themselves are not allowed to call into question their verdict and may not even be allowed to shed light on their thinking. In Britain a juror who attempted to do so could be held in contempt of court.[3]

Not only is finding fault with the jury as easy game to play, it is a game with no clear losers. Ever since *Bushell's Case*[4] it has been the law that jurors may not be punished for their verdict. Nor are they likely to suffer stigma or pecuniary disadvantage. In most instances the jurors' identity will not even be revealed. Within days of a trial the jurors will have faded back into the obscurity from which they came. Reporters, lawyers and litigants who seek to interrogate them can be held in contempt of court.[5] Thus jurors are protected from harassment and retaliation. The jury as an institution is able to absorb attacks on it without repercussions to any of its members. As a consequence, however, the jury has become a convenient scapegoat which allows more permanent participants in the criminal justice system – police, lawyers and judges – to deflect criticism from themselves. The jury not only relieves the judge of the burden of having to make the difficult decision, but also provides the judge with a convenient skirt behind which to hide when a verdict which may have been virtually dictated by the judge's directions fails to meet with public approval.

Several strains of jury criticism can be distinguished. There are attacks on jury verdicts for perversity and on the jurors who returned those verdicts for incompetence. There is the charge that jurors indulge their biases and return discriminatory verdicts. There are also claims that juries are responsible for miscarriages of justice. Running through all of these criticisms is the unstated, but implicit, thesis that a judge would have done a better job. But is this so? Are judges less prejudiced than jurors? Are they better at ascertaining the facts, at seeing through the lying witness, at separating truth from fiction? Are they more likely to be able to achieve justice in the individual case? These are the questions that will be explored in this chapter. There is, of course, no fail-safe mode of decision-making. Human beings are fallible, and any system that relies on human beings – be they judges or jurors – will occasionally err. The only question is whether a judge-based system or a jury-based system is likely to err more often and in more serious ways.

Perversity

When used in reference to a jury verdict, the term 'perverse' seems to be employed in three different senses. The first, and least legitimate, is as a rhetorical flourish to indicate disapproval of a particular verdict. The term seems to be invoked to give legitimacy to the speaker's disagreement with the verdict or to signify the strength of his or her feeling. It is comparable to raising one's voice, or pounding one's fist on a podium, to emphasize a point. When the charge of perversity is made by the police or prosecutor following an acquittal, it might be dismissed as reflecting a natural frustration with the outcome. The claim may be even more difficult to credit when it comes from the convicted defendant because of its obvious self-serving nature. However, changes of perversity have also been made by individuals who profess to have a more detached and objective vantage point (usually politicians), although it still seems to signify little more than discontent with the outcome. Such discontent and its attempted legitimation through the characterization of the verdict as perverse conceals as unwarranted arrogance. How does the critic know that he or she is right and that the jury is wrong? The critic's position is often grounded in a subjective assessment of the evidence gleaned from secondary sources such as newspaper or television reports. Unlike the jurors, their critics may not have seen the witnesses or heard the testimony. They will not have had the benefit of the dialectical processes at work in the jury room (which will be discussed later in this chapter). Lord Devlin cuts to the heart of the matter:

> Perverse … is an inappropriate, even an impertinent, word to use about an equal when all you are saying is that you disagree with the conclusions which it is his job to reach and not yours. (Devlin, 1979, p. 141)

The second sense in which 'perverse' is used is to describe a verdict which is against the weight of the evidence. Here the underlying objection seems to be to the burden of proof which allows – indeed requires – the acquittal of one who is *probably* guilty as long as there remains a reasonable doubt as to guilt. To sit in judgement on another human being is a heavy burden, and it is not surprising that, before returning a verdict that will deprive a defendant of his liberty, the jurors will give the defendant the benefit of any lingering doubt. This human tendency to err on the side of caution is reinforced by the law's requirement of proof beyond a reasonable doubt. The prosecution need not eliminate *all* doubt, for truth in any absolute sense is impossible to attain, but it must eliminate reasonable doubt. This means that there will be trials in which the jury thinks that the defendant is probably guilty yet harbours some reasonable doubt. It is not sufficient for the prosecution to convince the jury that it is more likely than not that the defendant is guilty. If any reasonable doubt as to guilt exists, the jury is obliged to acquit. Far from being perverse, an acquittal, although perhaps against the weight of the evidence, is the legally mandated result. The quarrel of those who maintain that too many factually guilty defendants are escaping their just deserts is not so much with the jury as with the stringency of this legal burden of proof.

The third sense in which 'perverse' is employed is to describe a verdict contrary to that which a strict application of law to fact would seem to demand. Empirical studies that have sought to assess how well juries perform typically compare their verdict with that which would have been reached by the trial judge (see, for example, Kalven and Zeisel, 1966; Baldwin and McConville, 1979). Those who would abolish the jury system assume that judge–jury disagreements signify cases where the jury went astray. Rarely do they pause to consider the alternative that it is the jury which got it right and the judge who was wrong. It is conceivable that the higher acquittal rate on the part of juries signals not a greater willingness of juries to free the guilty but an unhealthy inclination on the part of judges to convict the innocent (see James Committee, 1975). But there is a third possibility which may be the most accurate of all – that judges and juries are deciding different questions, and rightly so. The critics who take the jury to task for failing to return the verdict that the judge would have returned seem to regard the jury as an *ersatz* judge. To their way of thinking the jury's objective is to replicate the result that would have been reached by the judge. Taking the analysis one step further, the critics tend to see the judge as a legal technician whose task is to apply law to fact. If the application of the law to the facts works an injustice, it is the executive's responsibility to grant clemency or a pardon. Jurors, however, are justifiably not willing to speculate on the likelihood of such a future occurrence. They see themselves as being responsible for reaching the right decision in the first instance. Jury perversity directed to this end should not be resented, nor even grudgingly tolerated, but welcomed.

Miscarriages of Justice

The past decade in Britain has been marked by several highly publicized miscarriages of justice for which the jury has been blamed. The cases of Judith Ward, the Maguires, the Guildford Four and the Birmingham Six attracted the most attention, but there were others as well (see Runciman Committee, 1993). Miscarriages of justice are obviously not confined to Great Britain (although they seem to attract more media attention there than they do elsewhere), and there are numerous documented examples in the United States (see Borchard, 1970; Frank and Frank, 1957). It should be emphasized that these cases constitute a minute proportion of all jury trials, although whether they form the tip of an iceberg is impossible to know. Even if it is the exception, any miscarriage of justice is cause for concern. Society is psychologically loath to accept the possibility that even a small number of wrongful convictions are inevitable – understandably so, for it exposes everybody's potential vulnerability. We prefer to search for rational explanations for irrational results and delude ourselves into thinking that, with the appropriate corrective, the problem would disappear.

Despite the plethora of candidates to hold responsible – eyewitnesses who were mistaken in their identifications, police who extracted unreliable confessions by inappropriate means, forensic experts who falsified test results, prosecutors who were overzealous in their efforts to secure a conviction, trial judges who admitted questionable evidence, and appellate courts which were disinclined to look beyond the formalities of a fair trial to the substantive merits of the verdict – many commentators choose to focus on the jury. It is undeniable that the jury had the last clear chance at the trial level to avoid an unjust conviction. Given the reluctance of appellate courts to second-guess the jury on issues of fact and the credibility of witnesses, this may have been, for all realistic purposes, the *last* opportunity to avoid the miscarriage of justice. But would judges have been better able to see through the dissembling witness? Would they have been less likely to have been taken in by unreliable or fabricated evidence? The Royal Commission on Criminal Justice (Runciman Committee, 1993), appointed in part to seek out and identify the causes of the miscarriages of justice, thought not. It held the jury blameless, and, contrary to the critics' expectations, concluded that there was no reason to believe 'that an alternative method of arriving at a verdict in criminal cases would have made the risk of a mistake significantly less' (ibid., p. 2).

Thirty years prior to the Royal Commission's inquiry, the Chicago Jury Project had found that judges disagreed with jury verdicts in approximately 22 per cent of the criminal trials which had been examined (Kalven and Zeisel, 1966). Of these, the jury was nearly eight times more likely to have acquitted where a judge would have convicted than the other way round. In only 3 per cent of all cases would the judge have acquitted where the jury convicted. Thus, even assuming that the latter disagreements involved genuine miscarriages of justice, trying the case before a judge alone would only rarely have reversed the wrongful conviction. There is, moreover, no strong reason to believe that the cases in which the judges would have acquitted and juries convicted constituted miscarriages of justice in the sense that defendants were convicted of crimes which they did not commit. In many instances the judge would have acquitted not because the defendant was blameless, but because the judge was prepared to interpret the relevant law in a narrow and formalistic manner which, in the given case, worked to the defendant's advantage (ibid., ch. 31).

Miscarriages of justice are a matter of legitimate concern, but the problem will not be solved simply be abandoning jury trials. On the contrary, given the judicial tendency to apply the law in a more rigid fashion than juries (the reasons why are explored later), with less consideration to the equities of the case, there is reason for believing that the transference of decision-making authority from juries to judges might result in a greater incidence of morally blameless individuals being sent to prison. Such cases, too, are miscarriages of justice.

A Question of Competency

The term 'perverse', although usually invoked to signal disapproval of a jury's verdict, implies a criticism of the jurors responsible for that verdict. Many of the jury's critics appear to believe that the ordinary man or woman is intellectually incapable of piecing together evidence, following legal arguments, and understanding the judge's directions, particularly in complex cases (Frank, 1963; Williams, 1963). The basis of these attacks on juror competency is not altogether clear. As has already been noted, third parties are not permitted in the jury room, lawyers are not allowed to question jurors and jurors may be proscribed by law from discussing their verdicts. Given the shroud of secrecy which envelops the deliberations, it is surprising that anybody could assert with any degree of confidence that a jury's comprehension of the case is flawed.[6] Indeed, empirical evidence suggests that the complexity of a case is not related to a judge's disagreement with the jury verdict: the Chicago Jury Project found that judges and juries were as likely to disagree in seemingly straightforward cases as they were in complicated cases (Kalven and Zeisel, 1966, p. 157). Moreover, when asked to give reasons why the jury might have reached conclusions different from their own, the judges rarely cited the jury's inability to understand the evidence (ibid., p. 158).

The lack of empirical support of juror incompetence has not silenced the critics. Theirs is an *a priori* appeal that has sometimes received a sympathetic audience. A few American states have made statutory provision for elite or blue ribbon juries, the constitutionality of which was upheld by the

US Supreme Court in *Fay* v. *New York*.[7] In Britain the Roskill Committee recommended replacing conventional juries with a judge sitting with two expert assessors in cases involving complex fraud (Roskill Committee, 1986). This proposal was strongly opposed by the bar, and it turned out to be the one significant feature of a generally well received reform package that was not enacted into law.

Glanville Williams' suspicions regarding juror competence are based on the evidence of incompetence that he sees in the daily lives of ordinary people (Williams, 1963, p. 272). From this, he infers that such individuals will be no more responsible when serving on a jury. There are, however, sound reasons for believing that jurors will rise to the occasion. Entrusting any individual with the liberty (and in some instances life) of another human being is a weighty responsibility – one of which few jurors will want to be seen as undeserving. The ceremony and rituals of the courtroom reinforce the solemnity of the occasion, robes and wigs being but the external manifestations of the seriousness of the enterprise. Being relieved of job-related responsibilities frees jurors to give their undivided attention to the evidence. The trial judge will set out, in measured tones, the jury's task which the jurors will then be left to fulfil in the solitude of the jury room. The natural synergism and dialectics of the jury debate (to be discussed later) lift the quality of the deliberations. Peer pressure keeps the attention of the jurors focused, and jurors challenge each other to stretch their minds in the pursuit of their common goal of reaching the correct verdict. All aspects of the jury experience combine to raise the quality of decision-making of people whose competency, seen in a different context, might seem questionable.

Arguably more of a danger to the integrity of the jury system than the case that outstrips the jury's competence is the case where the above described seriousness of purpose, which the criminal justice system has worked so hard to create and preserve, is undermined by external forces. The O.J. Simpson murder trial provides an example. According to most accounts the trial degenerated into a media circus. Thrust into the limelight and aware that lucrative book contracts awaited their verdict, the jurors were converted from anonymous entities into instant celebrities. The conception of the jury as a body of ordinary citizens, drafted from the community to perform a civic duty and then allowed to melt back into the community, was fundamentally altered. The precise effect of this transmogrification on the machinery of justice is difficult to calculate, but it is hard to imagine that it had no effect at all. By restricting press coverage of cases *sub judice*, the British courts do a better job of preserving the integrity of the jury system than their American counterparts. Of course, British judges are not restricted by written constitutional provisions which protect free speech and freedom of the press. It is ironic, however, that these rights, historically secured by the jury verdict in Zenger's case (see pp. 36–7), can prove so deleterious to the effective functioning of the modern American jury.

Some of those who profess concern about juror competency are troubled by the lack of educational qualifications of the typical juror. These are likely to vary considerably, from the juror who has not completed secondary school to the juror who holds multiple doctorates. However, the lack of formal education is not the handicap that the critics imply. Jurors receive an on-the-spot education to the extent needed to enable them to decide the particular case. Through the testimony of witnesses they learn the facts of the case. Through the directions of the court they learn the law that they are to apply to the facts. In the jury room the jurors share any extra-legal knowledge that might assist them in deciding the case.

In any event, few criminal trials are that complicated. When the Chicago Jury Project asked judges to rate the complexity of the cases heard by the juries whose verdicts were being studied, 86 per cent of the cases were described as easy to understand, another 12 per cent as somewhat difficult, and only 2 per cent as very difficult (Kalven and Zeisel, 1966, p. 154). Even difficult cases often reduce themselves to basic questions. For example, although jurors may not able to follow all of the financial machinations in a complex fraud case (the most cited example of the type of case thought to be beyond the jury's competence), they may nonetheless have an accurate overall impression of whether the defendant has behaved dishonestly (Cornish, 1968, pp. 165–7). A senior police officer offered this assessment:

> [A]ll my experience has been that juries are sufficiently mentally aware to see where there has been a 'rip-off'. I have no complaints about the way juries have dealt with any of my cases. I used to think you'd need a jury of stockbrokers, bank managers and accountants to get a conviction but now I realize ... [that all] you need are sensible people who can tell when there's been a 'rip-off'. (Baldwin and McConville, 1979, p. 62, n. 12)

In a truly complex case of fraud, it is not only the jurors who can become confused. Lord Justice Lawton tells of such a case in which he represented the defendant. A bank manager who had sat through the trial commented that only three people in the courtroom truly understood the case – and that they did not include the prosecuting counsel, the judge or Lord Justice Lawton (Harman and Griffith, 1979, p. 19) This anecdotal report suggests that the problems raised by complex fraud litigation would not disappear with a change in the decision-maker. Indeed, any such change could have its own negative repercussions. If the trial of complex fraud cases were to be entrusted to expert assessors sitting with a judge, as recommended by the Roskill Committee, a conviction might be seen by the defendants as a cynical attempt to eliminate a business rival or an exercise in scapegoating. An acquittal, on the other hand, might be seen by the public as yet another example of a capitalist clique protecting its own. Indeed, the latter perception might not be inaccurate. It would be no surprise if a panel of businessmen were to give the benefit of the doubt to a defendant who had engaged in practices not far removed from their own, even if those of the defendant fell on the wrong side of a murky line while their own were on the right side. If the verdict of an expert panel were to be perceived in this light (accurately or otherwise), it would lose its credibility in society at large. If that perception were then to be generalized, the legitimating function of jury verdicts would be lost. As Judge Gibbons observed in *In re Japanese Electronic Products Antitrust Litigation*: 'Any erosion of citizen participation in the sanctioning system is in the long run likely... to result in a reduction in the moral authority that supports the process'.[8]

Politicians who assert that the law has become too complex for jurors to understand are often reflecting on seeds that they themselves have planted. Statutes tend to be written by lawyers for lawyers in convoluted language which is familiar to those with legal training but alien to most others. Statutes are weighed down with qualifications and riddled with exceptions. Having created this linguistic monster, the politicians then assert that its application is too complicated a task to be entrusted to anybody other than a specialist. There is a paradoxical dimension to this position. On the one hand, the politicians expect the people to understand and obey the law. On the other hand, they claim that the law is too complex for ordinary persons, in the form of the jury, to comprehend and enforce. Theoretical inconsistencies aside, the real issues of right and wrong, which are at the centre of most criminal trials, are not beyond the capability of the ordinary juror.

As for the jury's ability to understand the evidence, simple trials are often made unduly complicated by lawyers – sometimes as a deliberate tactic to confuse the jurors. Often lawyers seem unable or unwilling to present their evidence in an organized, coherent and comprehensible fashion. In its inquiry into fraud trials, the Roskill Committee noted:

> The evidence before the jury may run to hundreds, or even thousands, of documents. Sometimes these are presented in huge, ill ordered bundles. Little attempt may have been made to summarise or simplify the evidence. ... Sometimes the tactics of the lawyers will seem designed to obscure rather than to evince the truth. (Roskill Committee, 1986, para. 8. 28)

Goldstein, in the aptly entitled article 'Nothing is too Complex' (1985), cut to the bone when he observed that it is the lawyer's job to make the jury understand and, if the jury does not understand, it is the lawyer who has failed, not the jury.

Similarly, juries need to have the law explained to them in clear and comprehensible language. To the jurors, the judge's instructions too often seem to be designed to obfuscate rather than to clarify the relevant legal principles. Some jury instructions require the jurors to engage in convoluted mental gymnastics: an example is the instruction that an eyewitness's previous statement that her view of the crime scene was obstructed can be considered on the question of whether the witness was telling the truth when she testified in court that her view was unobstructed but not on the question of whether her view was in fact obstructed (Uviller, 1990). Other directions are given in language that only someone trained in law could possibly understand. The juror who understands what a 'chose in action' or 'incorporeal hereditament' is does far better than the average law student. It sometimes seems as if trial judges, in their directions, address not the jurors, but judges on a higher court. Perhaps they are. No trial judge wishes the embarrassment of having a case reversed because of faulty directions. This indignity can be avoided by sticking to formulations that have been approved at an appellate level rather than experimenting with easier to understand, but perhaps less precise, instructions designed to ease the juror's task.[9] And, although, a jury is permitted to seek clarification of a judge's directions, the 'clarification' may be no more enlightening than the original.

These problems are not irremediable. Lawyers should pay closer attention to the ways in which evidence is presented. The tradition of oral testimony may not be the most effective method of presenting complex material. Technological breakthroughs, particularly in computer graphics, as well as more conventional visual aids (such as flowcharts), can be of considerable assistance. Where jurors are experiencing difficulty in understanding a witness's testimony, they should be encouraged to ask questions of the witness (see Berkowitz, 1991; Wolff, 1990; Friedland, 1990). The questions would be channelled through the trial judge, who would screen them for relevancy. Surprisingly, few jurisdictions forbid jurors from asking questions of witnesses (Heuer and Penrod, 1990), but most judges conceal the existence of this prerogative from the jury. This is unwise, for juror questions cannot only clear up areas of confusion, but also alert counsel to aspects of the case which require further elucidation. Jurors should also be allowed to propose the recall of witnesses whose testimony has been called into question by subsequent witnesses as well as suggest additional witnesses from whom they would wish to hear and whom the court might call on its own initiative. The goal in encouraging a more proactive jury is not to convert jurors into advocates or to compromise their neutrality.[10] Rather, it is to allow the jurors to have as clear and complete a picture of the facts as possible before they retire. There is little sense in a jury retiring while its members are still in a state of confusion which could be alleviated through further testimony. It is also better to allow the jurors to ask questions of witnesses than to speculate in the jury room as to what answers they would have received had they been allowed to ask questions (Frankel, 1990).

As a memory aid, particularly in lengthy trials, jurors should be encouraged to take notes. Although note-taking may not be prohibited, few judges point out its advantages. Yet educational research indicates that the taking of notes both increases attention and facilitates the encoding of ideas into long-term memory (Kiewra, 1987). This would imply that jurors who sit passively absorbing testimony are going to be less effective than jurors who take notes and regularly review them. The Royal Commission on Criminal Justice recommended that judges advise jurors to take notes and that paper and writing implements be provided for this purpose (Runciman Committee, 1993). There is also much to be said for providing jurors with pre-trial instruction as to how to take notes effectively (see Chapter 6).

Other aids to ease the jurors' task might also be considered. In lengthy trials the presiding judge might provide a running summary (perhaps at weekly intervals) of the evidence. This would also provide an opportune point at which the jurors might ask the judge questions or propose the recall of witnesses for further questioning. During their deliberations the jurors should be allowed to see transcripts of requested testimony in order to refresh their memories as to the precise statements of a witness. In the UK trial of the Guinness defendants, which lasted for over 15 weeks, the jury's request to see the transcript of part of the testimony was refused by the trial judge who stated, 'It would actually be dangerous to give you this mountain of material. I am afraid that it might swamp you'. The judge failed to appreciate that the jury needed the transcripts to fight their way out of the swamp into which they perceived themselves as having already fallen.

Summaries, notes and transcripts may help jurors to assimilate the testimony, but they will do nothing to shorten the trial. To this end pre-trial hearings (at which only opposing counsel and the trial judge would be present) should be held to prepare the case for trial.[11] Rulings on matters of law would be given at this stage so that evidentiary objections need not disrupt the trial. Witnesses whose testimony might be presented summarily should be identified and the parties directed to prepare an agreed summary of the witness's testimony which could then be read into the record. At the pre-trial hearing the judge could also elicit from each side a realistic estimate of how long it will take to present its case. With this in mind, the judge could then set fairly strict time limits for each side's presentation, with independent sanctions being imposed on lawyers who wilfully failed to adhere to these limits.

During the trial the judge should be prepared to curtail questioning of witnesses when it becomes prolonged and repetitive. The failure to do so in the O.J. Simpson trial may have contributed to a loss of concentration among the jurors. Rulings on points of law that could have been anticipated would presumptively go against the side that failed to raise the issue at the pre-trial hearing. Efficiency is not sought for its own sake, and fairness to the parties must not, of course, be sacrificed, but no party has a right to waste the court's or the jury's time.

Judges must also strive to make their instructions more comprehensible. Legal rules need to be explained in language that ordinary people can understand. Common law terms, such as malice aforethought, and Latin phrases, such as *actus reus* and *mens rea*, can be misleading if not thoroughly explained. Better still would be to redraft such arcane terminology into plain English. Instructions should be presented in a manner designed to capture the jurors attention and not, as so often appears to be the case, in a bored monotonal drone. Model directions can, and are, being developed (see Elwork, Sales and Alfini, 1982). These, of course, will have to be tailored by the trial judge to fit the particular case. Also worth considering is the possibility of giving legal directions at both the beginning and the close of the trial, as research demonstrates that an early statement of the relevant law can enhance the jurors' ability to remember and interpolate subsequently presented evidence (Sand and Reiss, 1985).

If, after these types of remedial measures have been tried, jurors are still unable to understand the issues because of their irreducible complexity, there will be time to consider more drastic remedies. Even then, rather than abolishing the right of jury trial in complex cases, more care might be put into the selection of a jury capable of understanding the evidence. In Britain, where barristers are not permitted to identify the less competent jurors through *voir dire* questioning of the jury, it was perhaps inevitable that the requirement of a unanimous verdict would have to be relaxed in order to compensate for the occasional incompetent or irrational juror. It is the shortcomings in the selection process, and not the jury system, however, that are in need of review. Moreover, *with appropriate training*, most people are capable of being effective jurors. The court should take responsibility for providing this training. This issue of the selection and training of jurors merits closer examination, which will be provided in Chapter 6.

The Problem of Bias

In most cases where there has been a miscarriage of justice, the jury did not set out to convict an innocent defendant. It may have been deceived by witnesses who misled it or by evidence that had been tampered with, but the jury itself acted in good faith. It is a case of human error, and there is little reason to believe that the substitution of one human decision-maker for another – judge for jury – would have changed the result. This was in fact the conclusion of the Royal Commission on Criminal Justice (Runciman Committee, 1993).

A far more serious cause for concern is the allegation that, in some cases, the jury has convicted an innocent defendant out of bias or it has acquitted a defendant who would have been found guilty were it not for a bias against the victim. In the first instance the jury has convicted because of who the defendant is rather than what the defendant has done; in the second it has acquitted in spite of what the defendant has done. In Northern Ireland, for example, the conviction of Protestant paramilitaries charged with crimes of violence against Catholics has long proved problematic. Parliament's response was to replace juries in terrorist cases with all-judge, or so-called Diplock, courts.[12] Where the problem in Northern Ireland was *religious* prejudice, in the United States it was *racial* prejudice. At one time, all-white juries in southern states seemed extremely reluctant to convict white defendants of crimes committed against blacks, even when the charge was as serious as murder. Some thought that such injustices were confined to the deep south and were largely a thing of the past. In a 1992 California case, however, four white Los Angeles policemen were found not guilty of the beating of Rodney King, a black motorist. What made the verdict so shocking was that the incident had been captured on videotape by a neutral observer and the videotape had been introduced into evidence. Few of those who had seen the videotape (which was also shown on national television) had expected the not guilty verdict which the jurors returned and many were quick to attribute the verdict to racial prejudice on the part of the all-white jury.[13]

A bias might be broadly defined as any irrational belief that persists despite the absence of supporting evidence and in the face of contradictory evidence. Typically courts are concerned with biases against groups, based on a characteristic such as race, religion or gender. Many biases, however, are highly individualistic (Frank, 1930). It is a not uncommon experience to have a visceral positive or negative reaction to a person to whom we are introduced. Intensive psychotherapy would probably reveal that this individual shared some characteristic, of which we were not consciously aware, with a former acquaintance who was either admired or disliked. We have then transferred our feelings about the latter to the person we have just met although they may only have the one trait in common. Rightly or wrongly (usually wrongly) we have assumed that two individuals who share a common feature are alike in other respects.

In most situations this phenomenon is harmless, since initial impressions are corrected as we come to know the new acquaintance better. But when the individual in question is a witness in a trial, the decision-maker will have no opportunity to become better acquainted with him or her. What then happens if, because of some mannerism, the decision-maker subconsciously associates the witness with a former associate who was a chronic liar? If the decision-maker unconsciously transfers this trait of untruthfulness to the witness, the witness's testimony will not be believed. Or what if the look in the witness's eyes reminds the decision-maker of a school bully? What is the likelihood of the witness's testimony being objectively assessed? This psychological blurring can, of course, be experienced by both judge and juror alike, but, as we shall see, it is more of a problem in a trial before a judge sitting without a jury.

Having conceded the obvious – that no person is free of all prejudices – we can tackle the more pertinent question of whether a judge or a jury is better able to resist prejudice. The tendency of biased individuals is to ignore or dismiss evidence that contradicts their bias. If an individual is to resist this tendency, he or she must first be aware of the prejudice. There is little basis for assuming that the typical judge possesses a greater degree of self-awareness than the typical juror. Judges are not required to submit to psychological screening as a condition of service, nor do they receive training that sensitizes them to the type of personal prejudice of which we have been speaking (although more commonly than in the past they may be required to take a course designed to heighten their sensitivity to the dangers of racial and gender prejudices).

In addition to being aware of their prejudices, decision-makers must possess the inner strength not to yield to them. Possibly, because of the careful screening that precedes judicial appointments, judges may be more likely to possess such inner fortitude than jurors. But there is obviously no guarantee. Even if judges were better able to resist their prejudices, the danger lies in respect to the specific case. Jurors can be screened on a case-by-case basis and those who are suspected of harbouring a bias that might affect their impartiality in that case can be excused. The potential thus exists for structuring a jury to prevent biased individuals from serving. In contrast, parties are not usually able to question their judge. Although procedures for challenging a judge exist, they tend not to be invoked, and the judge assigned to the case will virtually always hear it unless he or she voluntarily agrees to step down.

The ability of a jury to resist prejudice is far greater than that of an individual judge for another reason. A not atypical jury consists of twelve members of different origins, backgrounds and gender. The perspectives and values of these twelve individuals will also vary widely. A prejudice on the part of one juror will be challenged by those who do not share the prejudice or who may be biased in a different direction. A juror who asserts a prejudiced point of view will be called upon by the others to provide a rational justification for his or her opinion. If the justification fails to rise above the level of unsupported dogma, it is unlikely to persuade anybody. Another important consideration is that, on a jury, misconceptions about a particular group's beliefs, attitudes and practices can be corrected by jurors who belong to the group in question. Thus prejudice on a jury is combated by process.

Personal and idiosyncratic biases are particularly likely to be exposed by the process of group dynamics. Whatever its roots, the persistence of bias is often attributable to self-deception, and those who do not share the bias will not be deceived. Take our previous example of the decision-maker who experiences a visceral reaction to a witness who is subconsciously associated with a disfavoured person from the decision-maker's past. On a jury there will be eleven others who will be able to view the witness objectively, and who will be able to restore balance to the witness's testimony. In contrast, there is nobody to expose or challenge the warped impression of a witness that a judge might have.[14]

There is one particular strain of bias which is much more likely to infect judges than jurors – a bias which results from becoming 'case-hardened'. It is the product of overexposure to the routine of defendants who turn out to be guilty despite their initial protestations of innocence. Many defendants at trial deny that they had anything to do with the crime charged. Following their conviction these same defendants, in the hope of a lenient sentence, express remorse for having committed the crime. A judge can quickly become jaded by such reversals in position, so that when the truly innocent defendant denies involvement in a crime, the judge may be inclined to disbelieve the denial. The converse phenomenon can occur with regard to police testimony. The judge's estimation of an officer's credibility may be forged in the many cases in which the officer has testified truthfully[15] with the result that it can then become difficult to recognize the exceptional case where the officer is lying.[16] Unlike judges, jurors are not exposed to sufficient trials to become case-hardened. They approach each case (often they will hear only one) unencumbered by the psychological baggage of previous cases. They will weigh the testimony, including that of the defendant and the police, without the distorting effects of preconceptions born of prior courtroom experiences.

A related danger occurs in trials where the prosecution seeks to introduce a defendant's confession into the evidence. In a jury trial the judge will rule on the admissibility of the confession outside the presence of the jury. Consequently, the jurors will not be exposed to the contents of a confession that is held to be inadmissible and their verdict cannot be contaminated by it. In a trial before a judge, on the other hand, the judge who rules on the question of admissibility may also be responsible for the verdict. It is problematic whether, psychologically, a judge can ignore the substance of a confession which the judge has previously ruled inadmissible because of the methods by which it was obtained (see Fischoff, 1975). This is one of the concerns that has been expressed about the all-judge 'Diplock courts' in Northern Ireland (Greer and White, 1988). Similarly, a judge is often aware of extraneous information, such as a defendant's record, which might subconsciously affect the judge's ability to be impartial. As such information is withheld from the jurors, it cannot enter into their deliberations.

On the whole, the freshness of purpose which jurors bring to their role is beneficial. They will not wish to squander the limited opportunity available to them and will give the few cases that they are called upon to decide their undivided attention. For the judge there is always another case. An apparently routine case may lull the judge into a decision by rote. For jurors there is no such thing as a routine case. Furthermore, judges always have a next case and may not be able to afford the luxury of lingering on a particularly difficult case without creating a backlog. The jury has no next case pressing for its attention. It can take whatever time (within the self-defined limits of its own tolerance) is required to assure itself that it has taken into account all relevant considerations and considered all possibilities.

This section began by distinguishing between two types of discriminatory verdicts: those where the jury improperly convicts because of bias against the defendant; and those where the jury improperly acquits because of bias against the victim. There are several internal constraints within the criminal justice system that reduce the risk of a wrongful conviction. First, the trial judge can dismiss charges where there is insufficient evidence to warrant sending the case to the jury. (The specific form of this relief may vary, but both British and American trial judges have similar power.)[17] Once past the trial stage, a wrongful conviction becomes more difficult, but not impossible, to correct. In Britain the Court of Appeal may rule that the conviction is unsafe or unsatisfactory.[18] The Court has been reluctant to exercise this power, however, and Baldwin and McConville rightly lament the 5 per cent of questionable jury convictions in which there is no effective remedy on appeal (Baldwin and McConville, 1979, p. 86). Although these authors apparently tend to blame the jury, the appellate courts are also to be faulted for their reluctance to scrutinize alleged discriminatory convictions more closely. The Criminal Appeal Act 1968 established their authority to quash a conviction which is unsafe or unsatisfactory – and a verdict which is the possible product of discrimination can hardly be called satisfactory. Finally, failing judicial relief, the executive still has the residual power to grant clemency or issue a pardon. While none of these safeguards may be foolproof, they stand as potential checks against the discriminatory conviction.

The acquittal of a defendant because of prejudice against the victim is more problematic. Because of the principle of double jeopardy or *autrefois acquit*, such a verdict is final; a defendant cannot be retried for a crime of which he or she has previously been found not guilty. The preservation of this principle, however, makes little sense in cases where prejudice against the victim has led to an unjustified acquittal. In the United States the double jeopardy restriction has been circumvented by bringing the second trial in a federal rather than a state court, and by charging a violation of the victim's civil rights rather than the substantive offence that was the subject of the first trial.[19] Nevertheless, repeated prosecutions are costly, time-consuming, and, when brought in a federal court, potentially disruptive to state–federal relations. It would clearly be preferable to prevent prejudice infecting the verdict in the first place. There are several means of diminishing the risk. As noted already, the impanelling of a heterogeneous jury will provide a natural combatant to prejudice within the jury room. It would also be wise to provide jurors with instruction on how to recognize and resist their prejudices (see Chapter 6). Finally, greater guidance from the trial court regarding the demands of justice, as was advocated in Chapter 2, would alert the jurors to the dangers.

Corruptibility

Some critics of the jury believe that jurors are more susceptible to corruption than judges. For a start, there are 12 potential targets rather than one. The critics, however, also appear to assume that the moral backbone of the average juror is less firm than that of a judge. There is little empirical evidence to support this theory, and that which exists may be misleading, for the very existence of the jury may protect judges from improper overtures. After all, there is little point in bribing a judge when the ultimate responsibility for the verdict rests with a jury.

Several factors lessen the jury's vulnerability to corruption. The identity of the jurors who will hear a given case is not known until the moment of selection. From this point onwards the jurors can, if thought necessary, be sequestered or given police protection. Jurors in highly publicized trials, at least in the United States, are also likely to find their movements subject to media scrutiny so that any attempt to approach a juror could easily be captured in a news reporter's photograph. Another protection against corruption lies in the fact that, in both Britain and the United States, less than unanimous verdicts are now permissible in criminal cases.[20] The relaxation of the unanimity requirement does have a downside in that it allows those in the majority to ignore the arguments of those who disagree with them.[21] On the other hand, it has the advantage of combating the effect of the corrupt juror since, in order for a verdict to be corrupted, there would have to be at least three jurors whose votes had been compromised. At the same time as the relaxation of the unanimity requirement reduces the risk of corruption, it also increases the risks to the would-be corrupter: the more jurors who must be approached, the more likely it is that one of them will report the incident to the court or police. There is thus a natural protection in numbers – a protection that is not present when the decision-maker is a single judge.

These are other factors which increase the judge's vulnerability. Unlike the case with jurors, the judge's identity is known before trial, and the judge is not usually sequestered during the trial. Also, the incentive to corrupt the judge is greater. In a jury trial, even if half the jurors were improperly induced to vote not guilty, the only effect would be to create a hung jury. A mistrial would then be declared which, although undoubtedly a short-term victory for the defendant, would serve only as a temporary reprieve if the prosecution were prepared to retry the case. The corruption of the judge, on the other hand, would guarantee an acquittal from which a retrial would not be possible because of considerations of double jeopardy. From the long-term perspective of the criminal justice system, a corrupted judge is also a more dangerous commodity than a corrupted jury. A judge who has been once corrupted becomes a potential blackmail target in future trials. A corrupted juror, on the other hand, may never again be called for jury duty, and at worst influences only the one case that he or she hears.

Sometimes jurors or their families are expressly threatened. More commonly, however, the threat is implicit. Jurors realize that, after completion of their service, they will have to return to their community. They also appreciate that if they do so having acquitted a defendant condemned by the community, or, conversely, having convicted a local hero, they may find themselves ostracized by friends and neighbours.[22] It may well have been subtle pressures of this sort, rather than outright threats, that led to the acquittal of sectarian terrorists in Northern Ireland and white racists in the American south. Of course, the jurors in these cases may have shared the community biases. The goal should be to exhort the jury to rise above such parochialism, but judicial rhetoric to the effect that jurors are the representatives of the community may inadvertently have the opposite effect. As noted previously, judges would be better advised to stress the jury's obligation to return the just verdict.

It goes without saying that jurors and their families should be protected against all forms of intimidation.[23] In some instances this can be achieved by transferring the trial to a district where jurors will not be subject to threats. In other cases the court might order an adjournment of the trial until such time as it can be held in a less emotionally charged atmosphere. Where necessary, police protection can be provided. Those who engage in jury tampering should themselves be vigorously prosecuted. Finally, in cases where jury intimidation has been shown to have occurred, a verdict of acquittal should be exempt from the normal rules of double jeopardy (Runciman Committee, 1993).

None of the above measures, however, may be sufficient. Police protection cannot last indefinitely and those bent on retaliation may be prepared to bide their time.[24] This is particularly true of a terrorist organization that may want to make an example of the jurors for the 'education' of future juries. Postponements may allow emotions to die down, but they may flare up again when the new trial date approaches. Changes of venue may have little effect on groups with a national membership. The prospect of being prosecuted for the crime of jury tampering may not be much of a deterrent to a defendant on trial for, say, murder, and a retrial where an acquittal has been overturned because of jury intimidation may simply result in further juror intimidation at the second trial.

Given these considerations, the most effective means of protecting jurors may lie in preserving their anonymity. If the identity of the jurors is not known, neither they nor their families can be the target of threats. A number of US federal courts have recently endorsed this approach.[25] Separate access routes to and from the courthouse should be constructed so that jurors may avoid anyone who might wish to harass or intimidate them. Such measures, however, may be to little avail if jurors can be seen and identified by those in the public gallery. In some cases it has been alleged that friends or relatives of a defendant have sat in the gallery and glared menacingly at the jurors. This problem could be resolved by designing courtrooms so that those in the gallery are unable to see the jury. Indeed, improvements in the quality and sophistication of video transmissions may result in future juries watching the proceedings in a location far removed from the courtroom and the defendant. It is not at all clear that a defendant has a constitutional, natural or other right to observe or make eye contact with members of the jury.[26]

The Judge's Dilemma

Justice is an overriding concept that makes demands of all who are involved in the legal system. Police must not act arbitrarily in making arrests or take unfair advantage of those whom they arrest. Prosecutors must make charging decisions on non-discriminatory bases, and must not favour the powerful over the weak or the rich over the poor. Neither they nor the police may exercise their discretion for personal gain. For their part, judges have an obligation to be impartial to all who appear in their court and to ensure that the trial is conducted in accord with fair procedures and established rules. The jury alone, however, is responsible for returning a verdict of guilt or innocence. Unlike the decisions of police, prosecutor and judge, which at least in theory are subject to reversal, jury verdicts of acquittal are final.

In Chapter 2 it was asserted that juries judge the fairness and justice of the law. In a sense, everyone has the power to decide whether a law is unjust. Those who think that it is can refuse to obey the law in question. Indeed, anyone who wished to challenge the law may have little choice but to violate it since a court will not usually consider the validity of a statute in the absence of a genuine case or controversy. Civil disobedience is not without its difficulties, however. Considerations of self-interest can cloud a would-be civil disobedient's judgement. Anarchy would be threatened if civil disobedience were to become too widespread. Nonetheless, offences committed out of conscience are perceived quite differently by society than other offences. The very term 'civil disobedience' is less pejorative and less condemnatory than 'crime'. The terminology alone serves to distinguish these violations from those committed from a less honourable motive.

Semantics aside, whether those who engage in civil disobedience should be allowed to escape the penalty for their criminal acts is an altogether different matter. No sanction will be forthcoming if either the police decide not to arrest or the prosecutor decides not to bring formal charges. A court might also hold the law in question to be invalid or unconstitutional. Failing these interventions, the legal system will process the case in the same way as it does others in which the reason for violating the law is less noble. There is no defence of 'civil disobedience' as such. If there is allowance to be made, it is for the jury. Cases of civil disobedience are thus inextricably intertwined with the role of the jury in the criminal justice system. Those who engage in civil disobedience look to the jury's exercise of its power to acquit despite proof of factual guilt to vindicate their own decision to disobey the law.

The 'official' pre-trial screening mechanisms within the legal system consist of the police and the prosecutor. The police may decide to give an offender a caution or warning in lieu of a formal arrest. The prosecutor may decide not to press charges. Resolving cases through the exercise of police and prosecutor discretion, however, is not without its difficulties. There is a potential for arbitrariness and discrimination, and uncovering improprieties, should they occur, is problematic because of the virtual invisibility of the process. Rarely will either the courts or the general public be made aware of the exercise of discretion. Even if this were not so, without knowing how similar cases were disposed of, one could not judge whether discretion in a particular case had been exercised on a fair and even-handed basis. In the absence of records detailing all the reasons behind the exercise of discretion in all cases, baseless charges of discrimination cannot be rebutted and legitimate complaints cannot be vindicated. A more open forum may be necessary if justice is to be seen to be done.

Although both police and prosecutor have a duty to act in a just manner, the stage at which they consider a case may be premature. It is difficult to tell where justice lies until all the evidence is in. Police and prosecutors see only a part of the picture. Complainants are not always truthful, but decisions may have to be based on the assumption that they are. Witnesses for the accused may have yet to be heard. It is only at the trial that the complete picture will emerge. At this point the question becomes whether responsibility for determining guilt or innocence should be entrusted to a jury or the judge.

A judge has a duty to be impartial, and must not favour one side over the other. Although a judge owes no allegiance to a client that might compromise this impartiality, the judge may be caught by a different type of conflict of interest. The judge has a responsibility to uphold the law. To the extent that it is ambiguous or unclear the judge may need to interpret the law, but it is not for the judge to reject the law because of the result that it yields. This limitation on judicial power can lead to a dilemma. The merits of a case may appeal to a judge's sense of fairness, but the outcome that the judge deems to be fair may not be consistent with the wording of the controlling law.

A judge must look in several directions at once. The desire to reach an appropriate result in the case at hand requires that one eye be kept on its merits. At the same time the judge has to look backwards to prior decisions in construing the law which controls the case. A judge is not free to disregard precedent or interpret a legal rule in a way that conflicts with settled understandings. The doctrine of *stare decisis* requires the judge to rule consistently with holdings of previous cases involving similar facts. The judge must also be sensitive to the future effects of any decision on the development of the law. Judges are well aware of the disruptive effect of decisions that cannot be easily reconciled with precedent. Thus, although the merits of the case before the court are clearly not unimportant, they are reduced to one factor among several to be taken into account. 'There is all the difference in the world', wrote US Supreme Court Justice Felix Frankfurter, 'between disposing of a case as though it were a discreet instance and recognizing it as part of the process of judgment, taking its place in relation to what went before and further cutting the channel for what is to come.'[27]

It would be naive not to acknowledge that there may be techniques available to the judge who wishes to avoid the force of precedent (see generally Llewellyn, 1960), particularly where the earlier decision arises from the court's common law authority.[28] Often a previous case can be distinguished on its facts. However, a judge must tread this path with caution. The technique of drawing factual distinctions is in constant danger of reducing itself to the position that all cases are unique. At this point the doctrine of *stare decisis* becomes meaningless. Accordingly, a self-imposed rule of restraint requires a court to demonstrate that any distinctions which are alleged to be sufficient to warrant a departure from precedent be material. In any event, past precedent is rarely as certain as writers of treatises might make it appear. A House of Lords decision, for example, may consist of five separate opinions. In theory each of the opinions may be entitled to equal weight, but which opinion a subsequent court chooses to stress may have repercussions for the proposition of law for which the prior case is held to stand. Even where there is only one opinion, its author may have expressed the rationale for the result in different ways at various points. A subsequent judge re-examining the decision may be able to choose from a selection of formulae all carrying slightly differing connotations. The subsequent judge may also be able to dismiss as *dicta* (not essential to the previous decision) some aspect of the opinion which stands in the way of the result that the judge desires to reach. Although all of these techniques have a long and honoured lineage, they inevitably cast doubt on the certainty of past precedent.

The type of confusion that can be sown when a court attempts to stretch past precedent in order to achieve the right result in the case before it can be seen by examining two cases decided by the Court of Appeal. In *R.* v. *Williams* (*Gladstone*)[29] the defendant had come to the aid of a youth whom he believed was being attacked by another man, but who in fact had been attempting to arrest the youth for robbery. Williams was subsequently charged with assault for striking the would-be law enforcer in the face. The Court of Appeal, per Lord Lane CJ, held that Williams was entitled to raise the claim that his acts were not unlawful because, in his mind, they were done in defence of another and to prevent a crime. That the defendant was incorrect in his belief was immaterial. The reasonableness of the defendant's mistake was relevant only insofar as it shed light on the sincerity of his belief.

In *Williams* Lord Lane established what appeared to be a general principle that, in cases of public and private defence, a defendant had to be judged in accord with the facts as he believed them to be and not in accord with the facts as they actually were. Four years later in *R.* v. *O'Grady*[30] a similar issue arose. The accused had killed a man whom he thought was attacking him. The case was analogous to *Williams* except for the seemingly immaterial fact that the claim raised was self-defence. A second and ultimately more critical distinction was that the defendant in *O'Grady* was intoxicated at the time. However, the House of Lords had held previously that intoxication could serve as a defence to crimes of specific intent.[31] The offence with which O'Grady was charged – murder – was a specific intent crime. Thus *O'Grady* seemed to be a case where there was a subjective belief in the need to engage in self-defence and therefore controlled by *Williams*. Nevertheless, the Court of Appeal, again per Lord Lane, held that

> ... where the jury are satisfied that the defendant was mistaken in his belief that any force or the force which he in fact used was necessary to defend himself and are further satisfied that the mistake was caused by voluntarily induced intoxication, the defence must fail.[32]

Further confusing the issue, Lord Lane stated that, in such cases, no distinction should be drawn 'between offences involving what is called specific intent, such as murder, and offences of so called basic intent, such as manslaughter'.[33] While the internal logic in the two decisions may be impeccable, when read together *Williams* and *O'Grady* introduce an unhealthy degree of confusion into the law. In the future are a defendant's mistakes to be measured by a subjective or objective test?

Why did Lord Lane in *O'Grady* abandon the analysis that he had embraced in *Williams*? Why did he reject the specific intent-basic intent distinction which had been established by the House of Lords? It is always hazardous to analyse the unspoken reasons that lie behind a court's opinion. Perhaps Lord Lane was no longer enamoured with the subjective standard which he had articulated in *Williams*. A more powerful explanation, however, may be discovered by asking where justice lay in the two cases. The defendant in *Williams*, in coming to the rescue of a person whom he perceived to be in distress, had acted honourably. It would have been adding insult to injury had he been convicted of a crime. Lord Lane may therefore have been prepared to strain legal doctrine to achieve a just result. No comparable sympathy was enjoyed by the defendant in *O'Grady*. He had not only engaged in the socially disapproved (albeit not illegal) act of becoming drunk, but also had killed another human being. Justice in *O'Grady* was on the side of the victim, a feature of the case specifically noted by Lord Lane in his opinion.[34]

Injustice can also occur when a court tries to adhere rigidly to precedent. In *Elliot* v. *C (a minor)*[35] a fourteen year-old schoolgirl was charged with criminal damage after having set fire to a shed. Evidence of mental deficiency and doubts regarding whether the defendant truly appreciated the effect of her actions led a magistrates' court to acquit. On appeal, the Queen's Bench Divisional Court held that the defendant had to be judged in accord with what was to be expected of a reasonable person without the defendant's handicaps. The court felt constrained by the decision of the House of Lords in *R.* v.

Caldwell,[36] which had established that, in respect to crimes of recklessness (as was criminal damage, the charge involved in *Elliot*), an accused would be liable if the risk created would have been obvious to a reasonable person. That a 'reasonable person' test might not be appropriate in the case of someone who lacked the intellectual abilities of the reasonable person troubled Goff, LJ. Torn between a commitment to precedent and his desire to achieve a just result, he searched for a way around *Caldwell*:

> Where ... it appears at first sight that authority compels a judge to reach a conclusion which he senses to be unjust or inappropriate, he is, I consider, under a positive duty to examine the relevant authorities with scrupulous care to ascertain whether he can, within the limits imposed by the doctrine of precedent (always sensibly interpreted), legitimately interpret or qualify the principle expressed in the authorities to achieve the result which he perceives to be just or appropriate in the particular case.[37]

Lord Goff's search was in vain, and he reluctantly concluded that there was no basis for avoiding what he obviously regarded as an unjust result:

> I feel ... that I would be lacking in candour if I were to conceal my unhappiness about the conclusion which I feel compelled to reach.[38]

The problem is not confined to cases involving prior judicial decisions. Sometimes the words of a statute stand in the way of a court's doing justice in the case before it. In these cases it is tempting to 'interpret' the statute in a way that will permit the desired result. Such an interpretation may stretch the language of the statute in ways not intended by the legislature and may also leave the court poorly placed in future cases.

This, then, is the judge's dilemma. If the judge adheres too rigidly to precedent or the words of a statute, injustice may be done in the case before the court. If the judge stretches these to achieve a just result in the particular case, damage may be done to the 'rule of law'. Judges find themselves constrained by rules which they are powerless to reject but which they cannot advantageously apply (Pound, 1966). It is for this reason that a panel of judges, which might redress some of the other deficiencies attributed to trial by a lone judge, would not be an effective substitute for a jury. The panel would still be unable to escape from the judge's dilemma.

A legal aphorism holds that 'hard cases make bad law'. In the hard case a court must choose between a strict approach to the law, yielding a possibly unjust result in the case before it, and a more flexible approach, yielding a just result but leaving the law in a less certain and perhaps less just state overall. The aphorism implies, probably correctly, that when judges try to achieve particularized justice they risk doing irretrievable damage to the fabric of the law. The jury, because its verdict has no precedential effect, is not so restricted. Lord Devlin characterized the jury's power as follows:

> The law may be made as flexible as possible, but justice of the case cannot go beyond the furthest point to which the law can be stretched. Trial by jury enables justice to go beyond that point. (Devlin, 1956, p. 154)

The courts in Britain have shown an awareness of the judge's dilemma, and of how they believe it should be resolved. Lord Goff's quiet despair in *Elliot* v. *C (a minor)* has already been noted. Perhaps more typical, however, are the observations of Slade, LJ, in *Adams and OCS* v. *Cape Industries and Anor.*,[39] a case involving a questionable parent–subsidiary alignment:

> If a company chooses to arrange the affairs of its group in such a way that the business carried on in a particular foreign country is the business of the subsidiary and not its own, it is in our judgment, entitled to do so. Neither in this class of case nor in any other class of case is it open to this court to disregard the principle of [Slade, LJ, here cites the controlling precedent] *merely because it considers it just so to do.* (emphasis added)[40]

This vision of law reflects the positivist philosophy of English jurisprudence – a jurisprudence which traces its roots to John Austin (1895)[41] and Jeremy Bentham.[42] Austin defined law as the command of the sovereign. The sovereign was a determinate political superior to whom the citizenry gave obedience. The sovereign did not have to be an individual; it could be an entity such as a parliament.[43] The commands of the sovereign, in the form of laws, gave rise to a duty, and the failure to obey that duty could lead to sanctions. In the Austinian scheme judges were mere ministers whose role was to enforce the law of the sovereign. Where the validity of a law was called into question, the judge's task was to trace the law to its source to see if the source was authorized to issue the law. If the law emanated from a valid source, it was a valid law. Whether the law was just or unjust was irrelevant and it was not for the judge to engage in a moral discourse regarding its merits.

The 'American legal realists'[44] of the late nineteenth and twentieth centuries, many of whom were themselves judges, were not so enamoured with this positivist philosophy which seemed to exalt form over substance.[45] They looked at law more in instrumental terms. Roscoe Pound described law as a tool for social engineering (Pound, 1908) while Jerome Frank maintained that the goal of the law should be to promote justice (Frank, 1930). Where the positivists defined the judge's role in terms of implementing the laws of parliament, the realists perceived in the law and the judge's interpretation of it as a means of bettering society. Thus they were prepared to give the judge more leeway to take into account moral and social values, as well as the demands of justice, in deciding a case.[46] The strict enforcement of the law was not an end in itself, as it seemed to be for the positivists, but rather a means to an end. Although, for the realists, the judge's dilemma was less of a problem, they too were sensitive to the severe disruptive effect that the invalidation of a statute could have. Realist judges were in fact more restrained in their judicial capacity than in their academic writings, as the century-long struggle to end racial segregation in American schools demonstrated.[47]

For the judge who takes realist philosophy seriously, law can easily play second fiddle to justice. For the true positivist judge, justice is the secondary consideration, something that would be nice to achieve but not at the expense of the law. Yet both law and justice are important. The challenge is to achieve justice in the individual case while maintaining a commitment to the rule of law. Neither the positivist nor the realist judge can readily accomplish this goal. The jury is needed to close the circle.

The Mathematical Advantage of the Jury

I do not mean to suggest that the jury's role in the legal system is solely the product of default, brought on by the judge's dilemma. There is a strong positive case to be made in favour of jury decision-making. One might start with a mathematical analysis. What has become known as the 'jury problem', although it is more broadly concerned with the relative merits of group versus individual decision-making, was thoroughly analysed by the French mathematician Condorcet (1785) with the objective of demonstrating the superiority of majority voting in elections. His thesis was that, according to probability theory, the vote of the majority was more likely to be right than the vote of any particular individual. I wish to assert the more modest proposition that the vote of the majority is less likely to be wrong. This may also be the more pertinent question in respect to a criminal trial. The reason, as noted in Chapter 1, is that, in the Anglo-American criminal justice systems, avoiding a wrongful conviction of the innocent takes precedence over convicting the guilty – a priority encapsulated in the aphorism that it is better that ten guilty defendants go free than that one innocent defendant goes to jail.

Assume that X is the probability of any single individual reaching an *incorrect* decision. The probability of 12 individuals independently reaching that same incorrect decision would be $(X)^{12}$. Transposing this to the jury and substituting actual (albeit hypothetical) numbers into the equation, if the likelihood of a single juror reaching an incorrect verdict is 0.3, then the probability of a 12-person jury returning a unanimous incorrect verdict would be $(0.3)^{12}$ or 0.0000005. Although the probability of a judge making a comparable error might be, say, 0.003, or 100 times less likely than that of a single juror, this probability still pales in comparison to the accuracy of the jury as a collective body. A group decision, particularly if the decision has to be unanimous,[48] is simply more likely to avoid error than the decision of a single individual, even if that individual is a judge.

The analysis is complicated by a large number of variables, however. If one were to assume an infallible judge, then the jury's verdict could never exceed that accuracy. Of course, judges are not infallible, but the difficulty of plugging numbers into our formula, of determining how much more competent is the typical judge than the typical juror, has to be conceded. Much will depend on the capabilities of the individuals involved. The analysis also assumes that each juror is an independent entity. In reality, jurors are influenced by each other, and rightly so. The fundamental error of any formula that treats each juror as an independent entity is that it is destined to ignore the most important feature of jury decision-making – the synergistic and dialectic forces which drive the jury's deliberations. These forces, which will be examined later in this chapter, will produce a more sophisticated analysis, but may also increase the risk of 'group error'. This is why the miniscule chance of a wrongful jury conviction quoted above may not conform to the incidence of documented miscarriages of justice.

Mathematical analysis suggests that a jury is less likely to be wrong, in terms of convicting an innocent individual, than a judge. Thus, a jury is a powerful tool for the prevention of injustice. But is a jury's verdict more likely to achieve justice, all things considered? In the following sections I will attempt to flesh out the processes which underlie a jury's deliberations. In so doing, I wish to contrast the interactive dynamics of jury deliberations with the more static and individualistic process whereby a judge, sitting alone, might reach a verdict. My objective, like Condorcet's, will be able to demonstrate that a group's decision is more likely to be right than that of an individual, but in the specifically legal context.

Fact-finding

The first task of anyone who is to adjudicate a legal dispute is to determine the facts. Whether the goal thereafter is defined in terms of accurately applying the law or seeking the just result, the adjudicator is unlikely to succeed if the analysis is predicated on an inaccurate picture of the facts. Thus, in comparing the merits of judge and jury, it is important to ask which is better able to make this critical factual determination. Even conceding an intellectual and experiential advantage to the judge, a compelling case can be made that the jury is the superior fact-finder. The reason why is that whereas a judge functions as an individual, a jury functions as a collective body. Simply put, when it comes to fact-finding, twelve heads are better than one.

Why should this be so? First, it must be recognized that neither judge nor jury is in a position, nor is allowed, to conduct an independent investigation of the facts. Each must determine the facts from the evidence introduced at trial. Witness testimony is not always consistent, however, and often the challenge is to determine the true facts from the conflicting accounts of the witnesses. It is not so much that witnesses deliberately lie as that individuals who see the same incident may have different recollections of it. Few people have received training in the observation and recording of events. In the panic of such an out-of-the-ordinary incident as a crime, the critical judgement of even those who might have received such training can be impaired. In any event, accurate observation of an occurrence does not guarantee accurate testimony. Memories fade with the passage of time, details change as a story is retold. The testimony of a witness at trial may accord more with the account of events told to police in response to their questioning than with the actual events.

How does one know whether a witness is telling the truth and is this a task that a judge is better able to perform than a jury? The evaluation of credibility is not a skill that is taught in the typical course of academic legal study. It entails a determination of whether what a witness has to say is believable. The events to which the witness testifies will take place in a context, and will be measured against what is likely or not to have occurred in that context. For the decision-maker to have been in the same or similar situation, or to have knowledge of the experiences of others who were, allows for a comparison to be drawn between what occurred on those previous occasions with what the witness claims to have occurred on the occasion in question. The collective experiences of twelve disparate jurors, when pooled together, are invariably going to be more diverse than those of a single judge. Indeed, the range of the ordinary judge's experiences will often be rather narrow. Most judges will be from an upper- or middle-class background, and will enjoy the lifestyle that their professional status and salary affords. This background and lifestyle is unlikely to have brought them into contact with the police except in a professional setting. As a result, they may find it difficult to credit the testimony of a witness who claims to have been abused by the police, as their own dealings with law enforcement personnel will have always been marked by courtesy. Similarly, a judge may find it difficult to evaluate the testimony of a witness who is of a different generation (most judges are middle-aged), or from a different racial background (few judges are of ethnic minorities).[49] A jury is more likely to succeed in evaluating the testimony of such witnesses because it is able to draw on the collective backgrounds and experiences of its members, some of whom are likely to be of the same age and race as the witness. Most judges are also male (although this is slowly changing), and may experience difficulty in relating to the testimony of a female witness. On the modern jury are likely to be at least several women who can help to put the female witness's testimony into perspective for the benefit of their male colleagues.

When twelve persons share responsibility for the recollection of the evidence, critical points are less likely to be overlooked. An apocryphal story is told of the defence counsel in a murder case where the body of the victim had not been discovered. Addressing the jury in closing argument, the lawyer gestured dramatically towards the door of the courtroom.

'I have just received news of momentous proportions,' he announced. 'The victim has been found; she is alive and well, and in ten seconds she will walk through that door.'

All eyes riveted towards the door as the countdown began. Ten ... nine ... eight ... seven ... six ... five ... four ... three ... two ... one. No victim. The lawyer turned sheepishly to the jury: 'It is true' he conceded 'that the victim has, unfortunately, not yet been located, but the fact that you all looked to the door proves that you have a reasonable doubt as to whether she is actually dead.'

Pleased with himself, the lawyer then took his seat. After receiving the judge's directions, the jurors retired. Within a matter of minutes they returned and delivered a verdict of guilty. The judge and the prosecutor were astonished, for they too had been persuaded by the logic of defence counsel's argument.

Subsequently, defence counsel encountered the foreman of the jury and asked how the jurors could have reached such a verdict, and so quickly (such enquiries being permissible in the jurisdiction). 'All the jurors looked to the courtroom door,' the lawyer argued, 'Did they not understand the point I was making?'

'What you say is not quite true,' said the foreman. 'Virtually everyone in the courtroom did look at the door, but not everyone. One of our members happened to be looking at the defendant, and he didn't look at the door.'

Whether or not the above story is true, it illustrates the numerical advantage of the jury. No one individual can be looking in all directions at once. At times it may be important to be observing the witness, but at other times the reaction of the defendant to the witness's testimony may be worth noting. Human attention spans are also limited, and the occasional lapse may be inevitable. The fact that one or two of the jurors has not paid sufficiently close attention to pick up on every nuance of a witness's testimony is not fatal, as other jurors will be able to fill in the gaps. Twelve sets of eyes will also be less likely to overlook non-verbal cues that are not readily apparent. An oversight or lapse by a judge, even if less likely, can have a more devastating effect because there are no third parties to fill in the missing pieces or compensate for the judge's inattention. A judge's application of law to fact may be faultless, but if the judge applies the 'right' law to the 'wrong' facts, all of the judge's legal acumen will not prevent an erroneous verdict. Worse still, because it is an error which is the product of an assessment of the facts, it cannot be corrected by an appellate court.

Social science research confirms the superiority of the jury in this regard. Hastie *et al.* (1983) tested jurors' recollections of the evidence, and discovered that the jury's collective memory was significantly more accurate than that of any individual juror. This is only to be expected. Equally unsurprising was their conclusion that '[t]he group memory advantage over the typical or even the exceptional individual is one of the major determinants of the superiority of the jury as a legal decision mechanism' (ibid., p. 236).

The Dialectics of Deliberation

One of the most remarkable features of the jury system is that twelve strangers, from different walks of life and with widely varying backgrounds and perspectives, are able to reach unanimous agreement in approximately 95 per cent of all cases (Kalven and Zeisel, 1966, p. 453). How does this come about? We have seen that, in determining the facts, the jurors pool their recollections of the evidence. A different process, however, is at work when the jurors turn their attention to the merits of the case. It is a process involving dialogue and debate, wherein jurors challenge each other's ideas about the case and where poorly reasoned analyses are exposed and weeded out. It is a process whereby the fittest theories – those that best fit the facts, the law and the demands of justice – emerge to be the basis of the verdict.

The German philosopher Hegel attempted to explain the history of civilization in dialectic terms (Hegel, 1988). He rejected the notion of first principles from which all other principles could be derived, and instead outlined a process whereby ideas are put forward, objections to them are advanced and debated, and the original ideas either refined or replaced by superior conceptions. In Hegel's world contradictory theories – thesis and antithesis – vie with each other. Theories that are in some respect deficient will yield to those which provide a fuller, more complete and better reasoned account of whatever it is they are designed to explain. At times this struggle of ideas will produce a synthesis; at other times, a completely new way of looking at a problem will emerge. But one can be certain that whatever takes the place of the old will itself sooner or later be challenged.

The process is continual. A final end point may never be reached, but it is the process rather than the product which counts.

A similar dialectic can be seen at work in the deliberations of a jury. Hegel tended to think in terms of opposites – thesis and antithesis. The opposing positions in a criminal trial are guilt and innocence. But how is resolution to be achieved? The point of departure is the facts determined by the jury in the first phase of its deliberations. One juror will then typically offer his or her interpretation of these facts. Eleven others will reflect on, and may challenge, all or any part of the juror's analysis. Challenges demand intellectually defensible supporting reasons. If such reasons are not forthcoming then the speaker's views will be discredited, to be replaced by those of another juror, which attempt to overcome the insufficiencies of the previous account. This new alternative will in turn be subjected to the same process of challenge. Analyses rooted in prejudice will be rooted out, and constructions which lack plausibility or internal consistency will be exposed. A promising analysis that is in some way incomplete or inconsistent may be modified to effect a more complete whole. Nor need a theory of a case which is well reasoned fear being tested by challenge. Whereas weak analyses are exposed through challenge, well reasoned analyses are strengthened. Indeed, it is as a result of an analysis having survived the gauntlet of challenge that the jury can be confident of its merits. Sometimes a number of differing theories, all of which have some merit but are also in some way imperfect, may be combined to produce a superior analysis. Thesis, antithesis, synthesis – Hegel's dialectic guides the deliberations of jurors who may have never heard of Hegel.

The discourse among the jurors continues until a resolution satisfactory to all emerges. It is in both society's and the defendant's interest that the jury decide a criminal case, one way or the other. The defendant should not have to leave the courtroom under the cloud of a hung jury, with its implication that there are at least some jurors who believe him guilty. An agreement to disagree is not a desirable outcome, and it is only with the greatest reluctance that a judge will permit a jury to deadlock. When jurors report to the judge that they are experiencing difficulty reaching a consensus, the judge will typically tell them to go back and try harder, although probably not in these words. The judge is in effect attempting to ratchet the dialectic process to a higher, more sophisticated level. Usually the judge is successful. Kalven and Zeisel (1966) found that only in about 5 per cent of all cases were the jurors unable to reach unanimous agreement, and Uviller (1990) reports that what most impressed the former jurors he interviewed was the fact that '[n]ever had they been in a situation where so many different sorts of people tried so hard for so long to reconcile such various views of reality – and did so with such success'.

Philosophical theory and anecdotal reports find support in psychological research. Nemeth demonstrated the powerful role that minority opinions play in group decision-making (Nemeth, 1992). It is not so much that those in the minority are ultimately able to persuade the majority to adopt their position, although this can happen. More importantly, dissenters point out the weak points in the majority's analysis and force the majority to recheck its arguments and conclusions, thereby preventing a rush to judgement (Shaw, 1932). But dissent also has a more subtle effect. Nemeth found that one of its principal values lay as a stimulant. Lack of agreement forces a group to think in new directions. Often the result is the discovery of alternatives and insights that would have otherwise escaped notice. These alternatives and insights do not necessarily flow from positions espoused by the dissenters, however. It is rather that the fact of dissent stimulates the collective thought processes of the group. It is in this way that minority factions, regardless of the specifics – or indeed the merits – of their arguments, raise the sophistication of the group's analysis and elevate the overall quality of the decision-making process.

The Synergism of the Deliberations

There is also a synergistic aspect to a jury's deliberations. The advantage of being able to see issues from all possible perspectives, what might be called divergent thinking, was stated (perhaps even overstated) by John Stuart Mill:

> [T]he only way in which a human being can make some approach to knowing the whole of a subject is by hearing what can be said about it by persons of every variety of opinion, and studying all modes in which it can be looked at by every character of mind. No wise man ever acquired his wisdom in any mode but this; nor is it in the nature of human intellect to become wise in any other manner. (Mill, 1859)

Jurors who want to understand a criminal case need to be able to look at the case from every possible point of view, and the jurors' differing perspectives will produce a multiplicity of views. However, this is only the first step. The jurors must also be prepared to evaluate critically these perspectives; in other words, they must engage not only in divergent but critical thinking. Synergism generates the multiplicity of perspectives, and the dialectic process spurs critical thinking. On a jury the whole is greater than the sum of its parts: the breadth and depth of the group's analysis exceeds whatever would be produced if each juror were to be asked independently to record his or her analysis of the case and these were to be added together.

In the initial stages the jurors' discussions might seem disjointed and disorganized, sometimes going in a number of different directions at once, and constantly shifting direction (Kalven and Zeisel, 1966, p. 486). This scatter-gun effect is in fact an important part of the synergistic dynamic for it ensures that no theory of the case, no matter how ill-founded or far-fetched, is overlooked. A jury may journey along many wrong pathways before it discovers the true one. Working through why a pathway is wrong, however, is itself valuable for it adds to the jury's understanding of the case. Moreover, as each wrong path is eliminated, the jury is able to concentrate on those theories which hold more merit. These will then be subjected to even more intensive scrutiny, as the search for *the* theory which is free of deficiencies and will pave the way to a fair and just verdict narrows. That theory, as pointed out previously, will be the one which best fits the facts, the law and the demands of justice.

Judge and Jury Decision-making Compared

It is the dialogue and debate of the jury room, the synergism and dialectics of jury deliberations, that are missing when a single judge decides a case. A jury's analysis is more sophisticated than that of a judge not because the jurors are more learned or intelligent but because the processes of deliberation promote the sophistication of the analysis. Jurors challenge not only each other's theories of the case but also each other to find whatever experiences and insights can be brought to bear in solving their common task. The fact that the jury consists of twelve distinct individuals provides a natural protection against the deliberations being subverted by the idiosyncratic views of a single juror. No comparable safeguard protects the judge. The jury's comprehension of a case is in aggregate. No single juror may understand all of its nuances, but by piecing together their various individual understandings they are able to understand the whole. A judge, in contrast, must understand the whole of the case if he or she is to reach the correct verdict. There may be nobody to point out errors in the judge's analysis, or offer an alternative theory of the case. Even if a judge were to persuade a colleague to discuss the case or play the role of devil's advocate, that person may not have been present during the trial (and, even if present, they may not have paid close attention to the evidence) and would have to assume that the judge's depiction of the facts was correct. If the judge failed to note critical testimony or to observe witnesses' non-verbal cues, any good-faith effort to assist the judge will also fail. Again, this underlines the importance of accurate fact determination – a task which a twelve-member jury is better able to perform than a lone judge.

Trial judges may be uncomfortable with the responsibility for tempering law with justice because they may not trust their instincts about where justice lies. A judge is unable to submit his or her intuitions about the right result in the case to the dialectic processes which occur naturally in the jury room. Consequently, the judge takes refuge in the mechanical matching of facts to law,[50] searching for the most analogous precedent rather than the most meritorious result. Each draws on its strength: judges on their ability to identify and apply the law with precision; the jury on its collective common sense, and the benefits of dialogue and debate. Where a judge may employ pure logic, a jury will invoke more of a practical reason, born of experience and moderated by intuition. Where a judge may consult learned texts, jurors consult with their consciences. A jury is more likely to take account of human factors which the judge might dismiss as legally irrelevant, while a judge may wrestle with reconciliations of precedent which will not trouble a jury. The noted legal historian, Sir William Holdsworth, clearly saw the advantages of the jury's approach:

> If a clever man is left to decide by himself disputed questions of fact he is usually not content simply to decide each case as it arises. He constructs theories for the decision of analogous cases. These theories are discussed, doubted, or developed by other clever men when such cases come before them. The interest is apt to centre, not in the dry task of deciding the case before the court, but rather in the construction of new theories, the reconciliation of conflicting cases, the demolition of criticism of older views. The result is a series of carefully constructed, and periodically considered rules, which merely retard the attainment of a conclusion without assisting in its formation. ... Rules of law must struggle for existence in the strong air of practical life. Rules which are so refined that they bear but a small relation to the world of sense will sooner or later be swept away. Sooner, if, like the criminal law or the commercial law, they touch nearly men's habits and conduct; later, if, like the law of real property, they affect a smaller class, and affect them less nearly. The jury system has for some hundreds of years been constantly bringing the rules of law to the touchstone of contemporary common sense. (Holdsworth, 1966)

Conclusion

Superior decision-making processes lead to superior decisions. This, however, begs the question of what counts as a superior decision. I have argued that the jury's responsibility includes an obligation to prevent injustice and that its aspiration is to seek the just verdict, all things considered. If, on the other hand, one were to define a superior decision in terms of its proximity to the outcome mandated by a strict application of law to fact, a strong case could be made for handing over responsibility for the verdict to the judge. What I have referred to as the judge's dilemma would cease to be an obstacle. Still, the point would remain that the breadth of experience on a heterogeneous jury, the neutralization of individual bias through group dynamics, the synergistic forces that generate a multiplicity of perspectives, and dialectic process which tests various theories of the case and eliminates those which are poorly conceived, all support the allocation of responsibility for the verdict to a jury rather than to a judge. It is the integrity of the process which gives legitimacy to the jury's verdict.

The jury resolves the judge's dilemma of having to keep faith with the rule of law while at the same time achieving justice in the particular case, and relieves the judge of the temptation to sacrifice fidelity to the law to the exigencies of the case. The jury is able to prevent injustice in the case before it without having to worry about the effect of its verdict on future cases. While a court must be ever mindful of the future consequences of its rulings, a jury need not be bothered by either past or future. Its focus is firmly fixed in the present. Furthermore, unlike the judge, a jury is not required to provide reasons for its decisions; indeed, it is usually barred from doing so. As a result, no rule can emerge from the jury's verdict that can affect the freedom of future juries to pursue the just verdict in the cases which they hear. It is part of the genius of the jury system that it allows justice to be done in the individual case without damaging the overall fabric of the law (Wigmore, 1929; Devlin, 1956).

The jury, like the headache remedy in the TV commercial, is also able to provide immediate relief. A trial judge, by virtue of office, is obliged to give effect to the controlling law. It is not the judge's prerogative to invalidate a law, even one that appears to be unjust. This responsibility rests with an appellate court.[51] The latter might ultimately construe the law in such a way as to avoid the injustice in the case, but the very process of appeal is time-consuming and, for the defendant, psychologically debilitating. The latter may have to remain in jail pending the outcome. The jury's verdict of acquittal, in contrast, will result in the defendant's immediate release.

The justice of the jury is immediate in a second sense. The moral sentiments of society with which the criminal law is imbued are constantly evolving. It is impossible for the legislature to keep pace with every such shift, and, in general, it is not prudent for it to try. A legislature should proceed cautiously. To react to the social and political winds of the day can lead to ill-considered amendments to the law which in turn have to be amended if those winds again change direction. The jury permits the state the stability provided by a fixed legal order and the flexibility to avoid injustice when the law is no longer in tune with the times. It gives defendants the benefit of changing social mores while not penalizing those who adhere to the law in the statute books.

Notes

1 Another possibility is a panel of, say, three judges. (Williams, 1963, p. 298 *et seq.*) This would address some of the objections to a single judge (such as the danger that he or she might miss a critical piece of testimony or be biased in an idiosyncratic way) but not others (such as the effects of 'case-hardening', and, more critically, the judicial mentality which leads judges to apply rules in a strict and formal manner, to be discussed later). An economic objection to the cost of a multi-judge panel could also be expected. Another alternative, employed in some European countries such as France, is a mixed tribunal consisting of a judge sitting with jurors. The objection to this composite body is that it is too likely to be dominated by the judge.

2 The quotation is attributed to the Common Law Commissioners of 1853 and appears in Devlin (1956, p. 4).

3 Contempt of Court Act 1981 s. 8. In many American states, however, jurors are allowed to speak about their jury experiences on a voluntary basis.

4 124 Eng. Rep. 1006 (CP 1670) discussed in Chapter 2.

5 See, for example, Contempt of Court Act 1981.

6 Anecdotal evidence exists and simulated studies have been conducted, but both have their limitations. Anecdotal evidence is invariably incomplete, often indicating only what has happened in the exceptional rather than the routine case; and simulated studies, among other defects, lack the immediacy of a trial where a defendant's liberty hangs in the balance. Systematic study of actual juror deliberations is needed, but legislative prohibitions effectively preclude such research. Researchers are not exempt from the restrictions of s. 8 of the Contempt of Court Act 1981.

7 332 US 261 (1947).

8 631 F. 2d 1069, 1093 (3rd Cir. 1980) (Gibbons, J. dissenting).

9 See *Cage* v. *Louisiana*, 498 US 39 (1990).

10 See *United States* v. *Thompson*, 76 F3d 442 (2nd Cir. 1996) pointing out the danger of compromising juror neutrality by encouraging jurors to express their opinions prematurely in the form of non-fact clarifying questions.

11 See, for example, the UK Criminal Justice Act 1987.

12 The Diplock courts were established by the Northern Ireland (Emergency Provisions) Act 1973. Although introduced as an emergency measure and reviewable each year, these all-judge courts have continued for over 20 years.

13 This case will be discussed further in Chapter 5.

14 The problem might be eliminated through the adoption of multi-judge courts, but these are obviously expensive.

15 Of course, in some instances previous exposure to a witness may allow a judge to tell when the witness is lying.

16 This psychological tendency is reinforced by the common-sense logic that says that defendants have a strong motive to lie (to avoid jail) while the police have little to gain and much to lose (their jobs if their deceit is discovered) by lying.

17 See, for example, Fed. R. Crim. Pro. 29 (c).

18 Criminal Appeal Act 1968 s. 2(1). The proviso to this section, interestingly, allows a

dismissal of the appeal where the court finds 'no miscarriage of justice has actually occurred'.

19 This is what occurred in the Rodney King case, discussed earlier and in Chapter 5. See *United States* v. *Koon*, 34 F3d 1416 (9th Cir. 1994).

20 See Criminal Justice Act 1967, s. 17. In the United States, see *Apodaca* v. *Oregon*, 406 US 404 (1972); *Johnson* v. *Louisiana*, 406 US 356 (1972). These cases only affect a state's right to permit non-unanimous verdicts. In a federal court a unanimous verdict is required by statute.

21 There is a case for maintaining the rule requiring unanimity to convict, while permitting an acquittal by majority vote (see Byrne 1988). The existence of a significant number of jurors unwilling to vote for a guilty verdict suggests that a reasonable doubt regarding guilt persists.

22 Of course, a judge is also subject to such social pressures, but judges may be better placed to resist them.

23 It may well be that the intimidation of jurors is far less of a problem than the intimidation of witnesses. See Enright and Morton (1990, ch. 8 and citations therein).

24 This point was made by the court in *R.* v. *Hudson and Taylor* [1971] 2 All ER 244.

25 See, for example, *United States* v. *Barnes*, 604 F2d. 121 (2d Cir. 1979) *cert denied* 446 US 907 (1980); *United States* v. *Eufrasio* 935 F2d 553 (3rd Cir. 1991); *United States* v. *Crockett* 979 F2d. 1204 (7th Cir. 1992). See generally King (1986). Of course, in some instances anonymity may be to no avail. In a small community – as are many in, for example, Northern Ireland – the absence of individuals from their workplace during a lengthy trial will not go unnoticed. The inference may be then drawn that the missing persons are serving on the jury. Whether or not they or their families actually are under threat, jurors may perceive a threat. In these cases the only way forward may lie in a change of venue.

26 Such sheltering of the jury might itself give jurors the idea that they had something to fear, and a judge needs to provide a plausible reason for preserving their anonymity, such as a desire to shield them from harassment by the press.

27 *Irvine* v. *California*, 347 US 128, 147 (1954).

28 Where there is a statute on point; the wording of the statute forms an outer boundary which constricts the court's discretion.

29 78 Crim. App. R. 276 (1983), [1987] 3 All ER 411.

30 [1987] 3 All ER 420.

31 See *DPP* v. *Majewski* [1997] AC 443.

32 [1987] 3 All ER at 423.

33 Ibid.

34 Ibid.

35 (1983) 77 Crim. App. R. 103.

36 [1982] AC 341.

37 (1983) 77 Crim. App R. at 116–17.

38 Ibid. at p. 116.

39 [1990] BCC 786.

40 Ibid. at p. 820.

41 Austin's lectures were first published in 1832.

42 Bentham was Austin's friend, neighbour and mentor, and it is now thought that Austin's published lectures were based on Bentham's ideas. Much of Bentham's writings, however, remained inaccessible until well into the twentieth century when they were edited by Burns and Hart (1970). As all that was available in the nineteenth century

was Austin's published lectures, it was upon these that the English positivist traditions were built.

43 It used to be commonly said that the sovereign in the United Kingdom was 'the Queen in Parliament' (Hart, 1961). Britain's entry into the European Union may require an adjustment to this traditional mode of thinking in ways that are still unclear and a matter of heated debate.

44 The term is given to a group of American legal theorists prominent at the beginning of the twentieth century whose primary concern focused on how judges decided cases. Although sometimes classified as a 'school', the Realists did not share a common agenda, although similar themes and approaches can be discerned in their individual writings.

45 See, generally, Atiyah and Summers (1987), especially ch. 9.

46 The problem with this position is that it seemed to imply (or so its critics maintained) that the law was whatever the judge said it was. This simplistic and arguably unfair characterization of the realist position in turn suggested that the outcome of a given case would turn more on the predilections of the judge who heard the case (in a trial before a judge) than on the requirements of the law. Lawyers who took this formulation seriously, however, and many did, would jockey to have their case heard by a judge who was thought to be sympathetic to their cause. But the judge seen to be sympathetic by one side would usually be seen as unsympathetic by the other. 'Forum shopping' became the unhealthy preoccupation of American lawyers.

47 Racial segregation in state schools was finally held unconstitutional in *Brown* v. *Board of Education*, 347 US 483 (1954).

48 The mathematical analysis would have to be adjusted where a unanimous verdict is not required since the likelihood of an incorrect verdict being reached by a jury would increase. This may be an argument for restoring the requirement of unanimity. However, as this is not a text on mathematics and, as will be seen, there are many complicating variables already, a detailed mathematical analysis of the non-unanimous verdict variant will not be attempted.

49 A judge may be familiar with such individuals from previous exposure to their testimony in court, but if the judge's impressions on those occasions were misconceived to begin with, then repeated exposure may mean that the same misevaluation will not only be repeated, but be reinforced by the judge's previous experiences.

50 There are some jurisprudential theorists, however, who maintain that judges intuit rather than reason their way to the correct decision. See, for example, Frank (1930) especially ch. 12; Hutcheson (1929).

51 The legal system prefers that decisions relating to the proper interpretation of statutes and the potential overruling of precedent be made by appellate courts rather than by trial judges. The problem with shifting this responsibility to the appellate level is that the judges on the appellate court will not have been present at the trial and will not have heard the witnesses. Often the statements of fact presented by opposing counsel on appeal will diverge at critical points. A transcript may not bridge the gap, and may also fail to capture the intangibles of the case. Appellate court judges thus have less of a 'feel' for where justice lies. Such detachment might be desirable if all that were at stake were pure questions of law. However, a just outcome may be less likely to be achieved the further removed is the decision-maker from the facts and the witnesses.

4 Democracy and the Jury

On trial in every criminal case heard by a jury is not only the defendant but also the democratic premise that ordinary citizens, randomly selected, are capable of sitting in judgement on that defendant. The jury is a quintessential democratic institution, the lay cog in a criminal justice machine otherwise dominated by professionals – police, lawyers and judges. The verdict of the jury *is* the voice of the people and its methodology that of participatory democracy. Indeed, the jury offers a model of democratic decision-making that holds the potential for reviving democracy within society and empowering the people on a wide range of issues of public concern. The potential of 'citizens juries' will be examined in depth in the final chapter. The focus of this chapter will be on the democratic character of the legal jury and how it has developed and evolved over time. The overall trend has been towards strengthening the link between democracy and the jury, but in recent years there have been worrying developments, both legislative and judicial, in both the United Kingdom and the United States, that threaten this democratic link.

The Nature of Democracy

In *The Politics* (1943), Aristotle identified three primary modes of government. What distinguishes the three is not substantive policy (the same policy might be arrived at regardless of the type of government) but the process by which decisions are made. In a monarchy all power is concentrated in a single individual. It is literally the rule of one – usually a king or dictator. In an oligarchy, the responsibility for decision-making is more widely dispersed, but still limited. Often there will be a ruling subgroup or clique. Democracy, in contrast to these other two forms of government, envisages rule by all of the people. Unlike in a monarchy or digarchy, where a ruling elite makes decisions for the people, in a democracy the people decide for themselves what is in their own best interest. It is not that the people are less likely to err, but rather that they ought to be allowed a direct input into the formulation of policies that will affect their lives.

While democracy is often equated with majority rule, this stems from a confusion of theory and practice. In theory there is complete political equality in a democracy. However, where courses of action are determined by vote, those in the majority will always be in a position to outvote those in the minority. What distinguishes a democracy from other forms of government is that the minority is entitled to participate in the political process; it has the right to be heard. Even more crucially, it is entitled to have its legal and political rights respected.

Both the United Kingdom and the United States lay claim to being democracies, but in each country only an extremely small percentage of the population is directly involved in the operation of the government. The citizenry at large is not often consulted or afforded the opportunity to express their opinion on specific issues. Rather, the people are given the opportunity, at periodic intervals, to vote for legislators who in turn are supposed to represent their interests in the national assembly.[1] This, however, is a diluted form democracy – a compromise between the robust participatory democracy which envisages involvement of all the people and the need for efficiency in government. Elections conform to democratic theory to the extent that all adult citizens (except those who are disqualified for sound reasons) are eligible to vote, and each person's vote has an equal weight. Political equality, however, vanishes when the votes in an election are counted. In the first-past-the-post system which prevails in both the United States and the United Kingdom, a candidate can achieve office despite receiving only a minority of the votes cast. This may produce a strong and coherent government but not a democratic government because those who have supported losing candidates can find themselves with no spokesperson in the legislature. Although it is arguable that a legislator has a duty to represent the views of *all* the persons within his or her constituency, including those who did not vote for the candidate, in practice legislators are more inclined to be directed by their party. This is especially so in Britain, where the three-line whip remains a vibrant fact of political life; MPs who fail to support official party positions risk party censure, political ostracism and, ultimately, deselection.

Proportional representation, where each party is allocated seats in the legislature in proportion to the votes its candidates receive, might be thought to offer a solution. Voters would no longer be dependent on the willingness of legislators of other parties to represent their interests, and legislators would no longer be torn between political ideology and their obligations to an otherwise disenfranchised minority of their constituency. Each legislator's constituency would consist not of the inhabitants of a geographical district but of those voters on a nationwide basis who shared the values and positions of the party. This severing of the link between legislator and geographical constituency is not a panacea, however, since it reduces the likelihood of issues of local concern receiving consideration in the national assembly. History has also demonstrated that governments which are the product of proportional representation are often unstable. There is an increased likelihood of a divided legislature in which no single party is able to gain a majority of the seats. A coalition government will have to be formed, and minority parties may be able to demand concessions for their support far in excess of the voting bloc which they represent.[2] Mainstream voters may then find that parties representing minority interests wield disproportionate power within the governing coalition.

A model of decision-making closer to that envisaged by democratic theory can be found on the jury. Every jury is a democracy in miniature. Jurors are randomly selected and political affiliation is immaterial to selection. The fact that jurors are drawn from the local community is consistent with that corollary of democratic theory which maintains that decisions ought to be taken at a level as close as possible to those who will be affected by the decision. The selection of local jurors also allows community ethical and moral standards and, where appropriate, customs, to be taken into account in the decision-making process. Despite this link with the community, jurors arguably enjoy a greater degree of independence than legislators because they need not fear political or other ramifications from their decisions. Jurors cannot be punished for their verdicts, and this lack of accountability liberates them to fulfil their role as conscience of the community.

While the jury is chosen in accord with democratic procedures, the democratic character of the jury is most evident in its deliberations. Democracy envisages that the opinions of all will be weighed in the decision-making process. This is what occurs on a jury. The democracy of the jury room is direct rather than indirect, participatory rather than representative. Every juror is entitled to speak and to be heard. Practical constraints compel each juror to listen and respond to the arguments of the others, as a verdict is not possible without a substantial consensus, if not unanimous agreement. Each juror's vote counts, and each juror's vote counts equally. On the jury political equality is a reality. Because of this *Realpolitik*, no juror's views, no matter how aberrational, can be ignored by the others.

In *Powers* v. *Ohio*[3] US Supreme Court Justice Kennedy began his opinion by observing:

> Jury service is an exercise of responsible citizenship by all members of the community, including those who otherwise might not have the opportunity to contribute to our civic life.[4]

His point was well taken. Few citizens will have the opportunity to hold public office, but any citizen may become a juror.

The jury system symbolizes the state's commitment to democracy. If it were not such an accepted part of the Anglo-American heritage, it would be remarkable to contemplate entrusting decisions affecting individual liberty (and, in some instances, life) to people untrained in law and lacking in all legal or other relevant expertise. That a state does so is an affirmation of its confidence in its citizenry. Such confidence cannot help but strengthen the bond between citizen and state. At the same time that the jury provides a democratic link between citizen and state, moreover, jury duty serves as a reminder that, in a democracy, the people must take responsibility for the running of the state.

Democratic Selection

It is instructive to compare eligibility for jury service with eligibility to vote. In both Britain and the United States the list of prospective jurors is compiled from the electoral register.[5] This means that potential voters who choose not to register thereby forfeit the opportunity to serve on a jury. Many individuals, particularly ethnic minorities and the young, opt not to vote because they see none of the major parties addressing their concerns. It does not follow, however, from the fact that they have no interest in voting that they would not wish to serve on a jury.[6] Those who do not register to vote in a national election campaign because they perceive the issues at stake to be too remote from their everyday lives would find the opposite to be the case in a jury trial. Moreover, the sense of powerlessness derived from having but one vote among millions is not experienced when serving on a twelve-member jury, where each juror's vote can make a difference. Unlike in an election, each member of a jury also has the opportunity to make a direct and meaningful contribution to the debate. And, whereas citizens may decide not to vote because they feel they have insufficient information to select between the candidates, jurors are informed through the evidence presented by the parties. There are therefore many reasons why a decision not to register to vote should not be equated with a disinclination to serve on a jury. Unfortunately, those who fail to register to vote are not informed that, by so doing, they remove themselves from consideration for jury service.

There is little excuse for not casting a wider net in selecting a jury (Kairys *et al.*, 1977). The electoral register could be supplemented with names from telephone directories and driving licence applications. Social security and national insurance rolls would be another fruitful source of potential juror names. Some statutory provisions allow for these possibilities,[7] but they tend not to be invoked in practice. It is, of course, essential that the same person is not listed more than once, as no citizen should have a greater chance of being selected for jury duty than any other. The problem of duplicate listings, however, should not be beyond the capabilities of modern computer technology.

Although voting is a right of citizenship, no citizen is obliged to vote and, as noted, many choose not to do so. In contrast, a summons to jury duty cannot be declined. Jury duty is both a democratic right *and* a democratic obligation. Conversely, one cannot volunteer for jury service. Because a jury is limited in size, it would be impossible to accommodate everyone who might want to serve on a given case. A desire to serve is, in any event, irrelevant, and may in fact suggest a partisan interest that would render the would-be juror unsuitable for service on that case.

Once a jury pool is established it is necessary to determine which of its members will hear a particular case. Again, the requirement of political equality dictates that every individual in the pool should have an equal opportunity of being chosen. The mechanics may vary from jurisdiction to jurisdiction but, typically, juror names are placed in a box at the outset of the trial and the requisite number of jurors are drawn at random. Jury lore has it that, at one time, the drawing of the names was performed by a child. No doubt in the future the task will be allocated to a computer.

Democratic Deliberation

The grant of the electoral franchise, exercised in periodic elections, constitutes a pale form of democracy. The more robust form envisages a decision-making process enlightened by face-to-face debate between fully informed participants. Most elections, however, are typified by inadequate information and little opportunity for debate, the electorate generally being subjected to the conflicting claims and misleading rhetoric of politicians. Although an infinite amount of information may be available in theory, it may be difficult for the potential voter to compile or make sense of it in practice, since the information that does exist is often dispersed and would have to be brought together and reduced to digestible form. Understandably, few voters are inclined to take on the task.

In contrast, informed decision-making is no problem for jurors because the onus does not lie on them to discover the information that they need. At the trial the parties to the litigation take responsibility for finding and presenting the witnesses. Rules of evidence prevent the lawyers from placing the facts in a misleading light. Cross-examination can be employed to expose inconsistencies and possible misperceptions of witnesses. In their closing speeches the lawyers representing each side have the opportunity to present an integrated and coherent account of their position. Thus the jurors are presented with two, often different, versions of the facts and the inferences to be drawn therefrom. They may accept either or neither of these accounts. As to the law that the jury must apply to the facts, again the jurors are not required to do their own research. The trial judge informs them of the relevant law that they need to decide the case. By the time that a jury retires, therefore, information is not a problem; the jurors are in a position to make an informed decision.

Jury deliberations present a form of participatory democracy that is somewhat anachronistic in the modern nation-state. Nowadays, society has grown too large for town meetings to be an effective democratic forum except in the smallest of villages, and perhaps not even there. Finding a location which can accommodate all who might wish to attend such a meeting, and maintaining control over a large assembly, can prove problematic. Time limits on debate may have to be set, and not everybody will be able to talk for as long as they might wish. The contribution of a speaker from the audience rarely responds directly to the points made by the previous speaker. While a town meeting affords an opportunity to ventilate points of view, it is less likely to produce a constructive dialogue.

On a jury, in contrast, there is both discussion and debate. The fact that each juror has one vote, that each juror's vote counts equally, and that at least 75 per cent (if not 100 per cent) of the jurors must agree for there to be a verdict, promotes a constructive dialogue within the jury room. During the deliberations each juror will have the opportunity to speak and to be heard. The practical sanction for refusing to listen to the opinions of others is that the jurors whose arguments are ignored are unlikely to vote with those who ignore them. To avoid deadlock, a majority is forced to deal with the points made by those who hold to a contrary position. To avoid appearing merely obstinate, jurors in the minority need to present reasoned arguments in support of their position. The juror who has nothing to contribute but an uncompromising close-mindedness will encounter considerable peer pressure. The discussions will continue until all (or however many are needed for a verdict) are satisfied. Because they are relieved from other responsibilities during their term of service there is no artificial deadline to be met. Thus freed from outside distractions, jurors are able to focus their exclusive attention on the case before them. The community can be confident that whatever verdict is returned will be the product of the synergism and dialectics which are the hallmark of jury deliberations. Those who might disagree with the result can nevertheless respect the process by which it was reached.

Democratic decisions ought to reflect not just the will of the majority, but the will of *all of the people*. Yet elections are often won by candidates who receive a mere plurality of the vote. Again, the jury represents a closer approximation to the democratic ideal. Until fairly recently the verdict of the jury in a criminal case had to be unanimous. The verdict was, as the jurors were required to attest, 'the verdict of us all'. The value attached to unanimous verdicts has diminished in recent years and, in Britain, a judge may now accept a verdict of ten of the 12 jurors after the jury has deliberated for two hours without being able to reach agreement.[8] Although the federal courts in the United States and most state courts still adhere to the requirement of unanimity, the US Supreme Court has upheld state statutes permitting verdicts by ten to two and nine to three margins.[9] Despite these relaxations of the unanimity standard, the 75 per cent or greater consensus that is required for a verdict in a criminal case stands in sharp contrast to the percentage which suffices to win an election where the successful candidate may receive less than a majority of the votes cast. The voting mechanics on the jury are deliberately weighted against majority rule. If an error is to be made, it is in favour of acquitting the guilty rather than convicting the innocent – a scale of priorities that also finds expression in the requirement of proof of guilt beyond a reasonable doubt. The presence of dissenting jurors may indicate that some doubt, and perhaps a 'reasonable doubt', remains regarding guilt (although this specific argument was rejected by the US Supreme Court in *Johnson* v. *Louisiana*).[10]

As noted earlier, the decision to abandon the unanimity requirement was partly an attempt to combat the influence of the corrupt, irrational or eccentric juror. It may, however, have a hidden cost in respect to the dynamics of jury deliberations. Where unanimity is not required, jurors in the majority are able to ignore a dissenting minority that is not sufficiently large to prevent them from proceeding to verdict. Once the required number of votes is amassed, the majority have little incentive to listen to the dissenters. For their part, the dissenters may perceive little gain from pressing their arguments. An inclination on all sides to bring matters to the perceived inevitable conclusion may prevail, especially after a long and exhausting trial. In fact, empirical research confirms that less time is spent in deliberations where unanimity is not required (Hastie *et al.*, 1983).

In a general election, there is no accountability. Voting is anonymous, and citizens need not explain or justify their votes. Indeed, there is no requirement that voters disclose how they cast their ballot. Jurors, too, are not legally accountable for their verdicts, but are subject to an accountability of a different sort. Jurors are engaged in a collective enterprise in which they are dependent on each other for its success. The 'facts' on which the jurors base their deliberations are formed from their cumulative recall of the evidence. Any juror who fails to pay attention to the witnesses will be letting down his or her fellow jurors. The synergistic and dialectic engine of deliberations, which produces the verdict, will sputter if jurors do not contribute to the discussions or fail to take their responsibilities seriously. Jurors owe a moral obligation to both the state, which has placed them in a position of responsibility, and the defendant whose liberty has been entrusted to their care. Thus, while jurors may not be legally accountable, they are accountable to each other, to the defendant and to society at large.

Some would maintain that the democracy of the jury is an illusion, that juries are manipulated by judges. Even neutrally worded judicial directions can carry a distinct message conveyed by means of the judge's intonations and/or body language (Blanck *et al.*, 1985). An example is related by Ludovic Kennedy from the trial of Dr Stephen Ward:

> It was not that the judge had omitted what was favourable to Ward – the record belied that. It was simply a question of emphasis. When the judge was pointing out to the jury those things in Ward's favour, he often did so in a flat matter-of-fact voice. He appeared so uninterested in what he was saying that one could not be interested oneself; the mind automatically shut off from him. Yet when it came to matters which told against Ward, his tone changed; his voice and bearing became brighter, livelier, he held the attention where elsewhere he had lost it. (Kennedy, 1964, p. 220)

Jurors, the argument continues, do not wish to displease the judge, and will strive to return the verdict that they think that the judge desires. Mungham and Bankowski (1976) offer some limited anecdotal support for this hypothesis. They report juries which, during deliberations, seemed to be searching for clues as to the judge's preferences in order to enable them to return a verdict in accordance with those preferences. In Britain, where judges are permitted to comment on the evidence, it may be relatively easier to discern the trial judge's leanings than it is in the United States, where judges generally will refrain from commenting on the evidence. There is in fact a strong case for prohibiting judges from commenting on the evidence. The jurors have heard the same evidence as the judge and are able to make up their own minds as to its merits.

The extent to which a judge influences, let alone controls, a jury is hard to evaluate. Even if jurors wished to return the verdict that the judge desired, they may not be able to perceive the judge's preferences (Baldwin and McConville, 1979, p. 80). The fact that judges in the United Kingdom and the United States, unlike some of their European counterparts, do not sit with the jurors during their deliberations means that the judge is unable to express an opinion on points that arise for the first time during the deliberations. In the heat of jury room debate, judicial directions and comments can easily be forgotten. Some indication that judges are not able to control the jury's verdict may be inferred from the empirical research which reports that judges disagree with the jury's verdict in approximately one-fifth to one-third of all cases (Kalven and Zeisel, 1966; Baldwin and McConville, 1979). If juries were in fact manipulated by judges, a lower percentage of disagreement could be expected. Of course, the judges in the cases examined may have made no effort to influence the jury, and the incidence of judge–jury disagreements might well have been higher if the judge had not exerted an influence.

In any event, judicial efforts to influence the jury are not necessarily to be regretted. Juries are democratic institutions, but democratic institutions are sometimes in danger of slipping into anarchy. The directions and comments of the court may help strike an appropriate balance, keeping the jury on track without undermining its independence. Lord Devlin captured this complementarity when he observed that the 'interrelation between judge and jury ... secures that the verdict will not be demagogic ... [but also] that the law will not be applied in a way that affronts the conscience of the common man' (Devlin, 1979, p. 127).

The Democratic Dividend

The jury system is an assurance to the people that their views will not be ignored in a criminal trial and an assurance to defendants that they will not be condemned except by the judgement of the people. The risk that the state will run roughshod over the rights of the disfavoured is reduced by the fact that the jury stands witness to any potential unfairness. Seen in this light, the jury system represents a commitment to open government. In a democracy the government rules by virtue of the consent of the people. Open government is indispensable, for one cannot meaningfully consent to that which one does not know. Jury trials present the criminal law of the state, and the state's administration of that law, for public scrutiny (albeit to a representative sample of the public).

Juries are presented not just with the law, but with the law in a factual context. There are critical differences between laws as they lay dormant – as mere abstractions on a statute book – and laws as they are applied in practice. Facts reveal the true reach of the law while providing a focal point for analysis. Appellate courts are well aware of the importance of facts and will not usually rule on abstract questions of law or issue an opinion absent a genuine case or controversy. Like appellate courts, juries decide real-life cases, not hypothetical fact situations.

It was the educational benefit of jury service that so impressed Alexis de Tocqueville on his visit to America:

> The jury ... may be regarded as a gratuitous public school, ever open, in which every juror learns his rights ... and becomes practically acquainted with the laws, which are brought within the reach of his capacity by the efforts of the bar, the advice of the judge, and even the passions of the parties. ... I do not know whether the jury is useful to those who have lawsuits, but I am certain it is highly beneficial to those who judge them; and I look upon it as one of the most efficacious means for the education of the people which society can employ. (de Tocqueville, 1966, p. 285)

It might be thought that many of the benefits of jury service could be gained by simply attending a trial. There are, however, practical problems. Some people live at too great a distance from the courthouse and others cannot spare the time from work. The size of the gallery will impose a practical constraint on the number of spectators. The televising of trials, as occurs in the United States but not in Britain, would overcome some of these obstacles as well as providing an antidote to the fictionalized television dramas that depict courtroom proceedings in a distorted light. The O.J. Simpson case graphically demonstrated that live criminal trials can make for compelling viewing. The television audience for that trial formed a multimillion-member jury of the people who, at the end of the case, were able to make up their own minds about Simpson's guilt. Nonetheless, like most televised trials, which are chosen in part because of their sensationalist nature, the O.J. Simpson case was not typical,[11] and may have given the viewing audience a misleading impression of a criminal trial. The picture may become even more distorted if, as some fear, lawyers were to play to the camera in order to bolster their public image.[12] Witnesses, on the other hand, may be intimidated by the presence of the cameras, although knowing that they will be seen by friends, neighbours and those with knowledge of the case, may cause them to take greater care to ensure that their testimony is accurate.

For the audience, televised trials are not a substitute for the jury experience. A television audience is less likely to pay as close attention to the evidence as are the jurors. It does not matter if the TV viewer misses an 'episode' of the trial or is drawn away by a telephone call. Nor, more significantly, will the TV audience be exposed to the dialectics of the jury room. TV viewers may discuss the case with a friend or co-worker, but the intense and robust debate that characterizes jury deliberations is less likely to be replicated. Nor, obviously, does a television audience bear the same burden of responsibility for the liberty of the accused as does the jury. In short, watching a trial on television is a passive exercise, while jury service demands that the jurors become directly engaged in the decision-making process and take responsibility for the resulting decision.

Jury service not only educates jurors about the law and its administration, but also contributes to the jurors' personal development. Being an effective juror involves mastering a wide range of skills. During the presentation of the evidence jurors must maintain concentration and pay close attention to the witnesses.[13] They must strive to make sense of what a witness is saying, even though the witness may ramble or appear confused, and must at the same time be attuned to non-verbal cues that may indicate that the witness is not telling the whole truth. After retiring to deliberate, the jurors must teach themselves how to function effectively as a group. No umpire or referee is present to maintain order, and the jurors have to find a peaceful means for resolving differences. Jurors must force themselves to be tolerant, even if tolerance is not part of their general nature. They must listen to the opinions of others, just as they expect others to listen to their opinions, and try to see the case from perspectives other than their own. No matter what a juror might think of another juror, his or her arguments must be dealt with on their merits. Jurors must come to grips with an analysis with which they disagree and identify and articulate its flaws – if not for themselves, then for others who might not be as astute as themselves. Arguments cannot just be dismissed out of hand. Likewise, when their own points are not grasped, jurors must find ways of expressing them so that they will be understood. No juror can be left behind by those who see the case more clearly, and every step in an analysis must be explained to each juror's satisfaction. Jurors always have to be prepared to respond to the doubts and reservations of others, and thus are engaged in a constant re-examination and reappraisal of their own positions. The deliberation process can be long and tedious, but jurors must learn to exercise patience. They must persevere when deadlock might appear inevitable and seek to find a path to a verdict when all appear blocked. The trial judge is unlikely to have provided guidance with respect to any of these matters. Jurors learn on the job, and have to teach themselves 'best practice' while actively engaged in that practice.

Jury service also brings home the point that one's decisions have repercussions for others. Jurors cannot escape the fact that their verdict will affect the liberty of the defendant and the members of their community. The defendant looks to the jurors for a fair and just outcome. The community looks to the jurors to ensure that an innocent person is not convicted and, conversely, that a dangerous offender is not wrongfully released into their midst. Jurors are aware that they must both make the difficult decisions and take responsibility for them. To again quote de Tocqueville:

> The jury … invests each citizen with a kind of magistracy; it makes them all feel the duties which they are bound to discharge towards society and the part which they take in its government. By obliging men to turn their attention to other

affairs than their own, it rubs off that private selfishness which is the rust of society. (de Tocqueville, 1960, p. 284–5)

The acquisition of a 'jury temperament' and the mastery of the skills required to be an effective juror cannot help but lead to a gain in the jurors' self-confidence and self-esteem. It is not at all uncommon at the outset of a trial for jurors to have doubts as to whether they are worthy of the responsibility which has been thrust upon them and to question whether their abilities are adequate for the task facing them. Its successful completion, however, removes those doubts. The resulting gain in self-confidence will be carried over to other decision-making contexts. The specific skills that are acquired can be expected to lead to a more mature decision-making in the juror's private lives.

Beyond providing an efficacious means of dispute resolution, jury service benefits the state in subtle ways. Because jurors are likely to be satisfied with the process and outcome of the case on which they have served, they will have confidence in the verdicts of other juries. They will appreciate, even if they are not able to articulate, that there are forces at work in the jury room that lead to fair and just verdicts. They will assume that the same forces will guide other juries. Any previous fears that a juror might have of official oppression are likely to abate, for the juror will have come to appreciate that the people themselves, in the form of the jury, provide a safeguard against oppression. Through a process of generalizing from their own experiences, jurors allay whatever doubts they might have about the criminal justice system (Cornish, 1968, p. 278). This effect, moreover, is not confined to those who actually serve as jurors. Through the recounting of their personal experiences, jurors reinforce the confidence of their family and friends in the legal system. Thus the democratic bond between citizen and state is strengthened.

There is, however, a cloud on this horizon. As previously noted, both Britain and the United States have relaxed the hitherto sacrosanct requirement of a unanimous verdict. Some of the potentially deleterious effects of this relaxation have already been discussed. Hastie *et al.*, (1983) also discovered that where unanimous verdicts have been abandoned, a juror's sense of individual responsibility for the verdict is diminished. In addition, there appears to be less satisfaction with the jury experience (Nemeth, 1977). The verdict itself may lose some of its legitimacy within the community, which in turn may lead to a decreased confidence in the jury as an institution. Thus, in addition to whatever effect the abandonment of the unanimity requirement might have on the dynamics of the decision-making process, it may also merit reconsideration because of its negative psychological effect on both jurors and the public.

The Jury as Democratic Determiners of the Law

The value of a democratically composed jury is particularly important as in those areas where the jury has been entrusted with setting the legal standard to be applied. This statement might seem paradoxical. Whether or not juries once had the authority to decide questions of law (see Gordan, 1992; Howe, 1939), the lines of responsibility are now fairly settled: the legislature is responsible for enacting the law, the court for transmitting the law to the jury, and the jury for applying the law. Nobody would be so rash as to suggest that the jury has the power to create or even interpret law. As the US federal court explained in *United States* v. *Battiste*.[14]

> If the jury were at liberty to settle the law for themselves, the effect would be, not only that the law itself would be most uncertain, from the different views, which different juries might take of it; but in case of error, there would be no remedy or redress by the injured party; for the court would not have any right to review the law as it had been settled by the jury. ... Every person accused as a criminal has a right to be tried according to the law of the land; and not by the law as a jury may understand it, or choose, from wantonness, or ignorance, or accidental mistake, to interpret it.[15]

The force of this analysis notwithstanding, in a surprising number of areas the law is left for the jury to determine. Either the controlling legal standard is expressed in terms that give the jury the leeway to do this, or else the courts have construed the law in such a way that the jury is required to give it content. In the abstract, this may seem confusing, but a few examples will, hopefully, clarify what I mean. In both Britain and the United States obscenity is illegal.[16] But what constitutes obscene material? In Britain the term refers to material which will tend to deprave and corrupt those exposed to it.[17] However, expert testimony regarding a publication's tendency to deprave or corrupt is not admissible,[18] nor do victims who have allegedly been depraved or corrupted testify. Whether the publication will have the requisite corruptive effect is left for the jury to decide. Similarly, on the other side of the Atlantic, the US Supreme Court has defined obscene material as that which 'the average person, applying *contemporary community standards*, would find ... taken as a whole, appeals to prurient interest'.[19] The trial judge does not instruct the jury as to what constitutes this 'contemporary community standard' nor do expert witnesses testify as to whether the publication in question would appeal to prurient interests (although they may be permitted to state whether, in their opinion, it has redeeming literary merit). Rather, the jurors set the legal standard. In order to ensure that the 'contemporary community standard' accurately reflects the community as a whole, however, the jury needs to embody the full range of perspectives that exist within the community. Thus, it is vital that it be democratic in its composition.

The authority of an American jury to determine the requirements of the law can extend to issues of constitutional law. The eighth amendment to the US Constitution prohibits cruel and unusual punishment. In *Gregg* v. *Georgia*[20] the US Supreme Court held that capital punishment was not cruel and unusual *per se*. Although the determination of whether the death sentence ought to be imposed in a given case could, after this ruling, have been left to either judge or jury, most states chose to leave the issue to the jury. This allocation of responsibility is consistent with the Supreme Court's pronouncement that the eighth amendment takes its meaning from 'the evolving standards of decency which mark the progress of a maturing society'.[21] Who better to determine the society's standards of decency than the people themselves? Parenthetically, it might be noted that the theme of justice requiring individualization, discussed in preceding chapters, has also been recognized by the Supreme Court in the capital punishment context. In *Eddings* v. *Oklahoma* the Court declared that the death penalty must be imposed with reasonable consistency, and that 'a consistency produced by ignoring individual differences is a false consistency'.[22] It is for the jury to take into account individual differences.

In Britain the Theft Act 1968, among its other elements, requires the Crown to prove that the defendant has appropriated the property of another *dishonestly*. Dishonesty has proven difficult for the courts to define, and the issue has been left to the jury. In *R*. v. *Ghosh*[23] the Court of Appeal held that a defendant acts dishonestly if his conduct would be regarded as dishonest by the ordinary standards of reasonable and honest people.[24] The jury does not, however, receive guidance from either the court or witnesses as to what reasonable and honest people would regard as dishonest. No sociologists or other experts testify to the point, nor are the results of opinion polls admissible into evidence. The trial judge does not define dishonesty. Instead the courts simply trust that twelve men and women drawn at random from the community will, among themselves, be able to say whether or not the defendant acted dishonestly. For better or worse, each jury sets its own standards of dishonesty. To achieve some comparability it is desirable that juries be democratically composed.

The legal definitions of obscenity and dishonesty are not isolated examples. Some crimes, such as manslaughter, turn on the reasonableness or unreasonableness of the defendant's conduct. In *R*. v. *Adomako*[25] an anaesthetist had failed to respond to obvious signs that his patient's life was in danger. Medical witnesses had described the defendant's conduct as 'abysmal' and a 'gross dereliction of duty'. The issue before the House of Lords, however, was not the appropriate medical, but the appropriate *legal*, standard to be applied. It held that, in order to convict, the jury had to find that the defendant's conduct amounted to *gross* negligence. But how negligent must one be before one's negligence can be characterized as gross? This, said their Lordships, was a question for the jurors to determine. Lord Mackay, who wrote the opinion for the court, was untroubled by the fact that the decision provided the jury with little in the way of guidance:

> It is true that to a certain extent [gross negligence] involves an element of circularity, but in this branch of the law I do not believe that is fatal to its being correct as a test of how far conduct must depart from accepted standards to be characterised as criminal. This is necessarily a question of degree and an attempt to specify that degree more closely is I think likely to achieve only a spurious precision. The essence of the matter, *which is supremely a jury question*, is whether, having regard to the risk of death involved, the conduct of the defendant was so bad in all the circumstances as to amount in their judgment to a criminal act or omission. (emphasis added)[26]

Although the focus of this book has been on criminal cases, the jury's involvement in the setting of legal standards in tort law is even more pronounced. In Britain most tort cases are decided by a judge sitting without a jury[27] but, in the United States, jury trials are common. Jurors are typically instructed to decide whether the defendant acted as would a reasonable person of ordinary prudence under the same or similar circumstances. By their verdicts juries establish the legal duties owed by members of the community to each other, and set the standards of care to which they will be held accountable. The trial courts provide no benchmark against which the reasonableness of a defendant's conduct is to be measured. The jury establishes its own benchmark by looking at the experiences of its members to determine what is reasonable. A democratic jury provides the widest possible range of experiences against which this assessment can be made. Nor does the standard of reasonableness remain fixed; it varies with the facts and circumstances of the individual case. The determination is not a function of legal or judicial rule but rather of the collective common sense and sound judgement of the jurors who hear the particular case.

In Britain, in contrast, juries rarely sit on tort cases and judges charge themselves with determining whether the defendant has behaved as would a reasonable person. It is arguable, however, that too many judges are too far removed from the ordinary members of the community in terms of values and lifestyle to be able to answer this question as accurately as could a jury composed of a cross-section of that community. By virtue of their legal background and training, judges are not ordinary persons. The cases which they hear in court are the exceptional ones and can easily give them a distorted perception of the types of aberrational event that it is 'reasonable' to foresee. The British political theorist, Sir Henry Sidgwick, saw clearly the deficiencies of the judge in this situation:

> These are cases in which the estimate of culpability involves more than merely knowledge of the rules of law and ascertainment of particular facts; it involves the application of a standard which can never be quite definite and can only attain adequate definiteness for practical purposes through experiences of similar affairs: – as when the question is whether a man has taken 'reasonable care' to avoid causing mischief in certain circumstances. (Sidgwick, 1919, p. 492)

The Democratization of the British Jury

The concept of a jury of one's 'peers' is usually traced to the Magna Carta but, regardless of whether this provision was intended to apply to legal trials (see Darbyshire, 1991), it has never been taken literally. Originally jury service in England was restricted to householders and property owners,[28] the apparent rationale being that only these individuals had a sufficient stake in society to be trusted to take their responsibilities seriously. Such persons also were thought to be better educated, more intelligent and less susceptible to corruption. The practical effect, however, was to limit jury service to the upper and middle classes. Most defendants, on the other hand, tended not to belong to these classes. The combination of these sociological realities exposed the true nature of what it meant to be tried by a jury of one's peers. It was not a right to be tried by one's equals as much as an assurance that one would not be tried by one's inferiors.[29]

Another effect of the property requirement was to restrict jury service to males. With rare exception women at common law were not able to own property. Even after this restriction was removed by statute,[30] the traditional female role of homemaker/childraiser meant that few women worked. Those who did were poorly paid and were therefore unlikely to become property owners. Thus, although sex discrimination in respect to jury service may have been formally abolished in 1919,[31] this reform was to have little practical impact as long as the property requirement remained in force. Thirty-five years after the passage of the Sex Discrimination Removal Act, Lord Devlin, commenting on his days as a trial judge, observed that he 'had never seen more than four women on a jury and you are almost as likely to find none as three; two is the commonest number and one is quite usual' (Devlin, 1956, pp. 21–2). The jury was not only predominantly male, but the males were generally middle-aged or older, the reason being that younger men were less likely to own property.

In 1965 the Morris Committee, reflecting the growing dissatisfaction with the elitist nature of juries, proposed a conception of the jury as a cross-section of the community drawn at random. Accepting the Committee's recommendations, parliament formally abolished the property requirement for jury service in 1972.[32] By 1972, however, the requirement had already lost much of its force since it had not been adjusted upwards to keep pace with inflation. The final abolition may therefore have been more symbolic than real. Nonetheless, it did signify that the justifications which had helped to preserve the requirement for centuries had ceased to be persuasive. The claim that those with property were more likely to be educated had become increasingly untenable with the trend to universal education. The assertion that the upper classes were less susceptible to corruption was always somewhat suspect, and became more so with increased public awareness of the extent of white-collar crime; and the notion that property ownership could be equated with intelligence seemed more grounded in self-serving myth than in reality.

While the symbolic importance of the abolition of the property requirement should not be underestimated, neither should it be exaggerated. When juries were composed of 'middle-class, middle-aged and middle-minded' Englanders, the values that the jurors could be expected to apply and the verdicts that they could be expected to reach were fairly predictable. On 'the new democratic jury', where the underclasses served alongside the upper classes, where women sat next to men, and where the voices of ethnic minorities could be heard, the results were far less certain. This may have caused consternation to some within the political and legal establishments. At the same time as the property qualification for jury service was being abolished, a concomitant movement arose to reclassify crimes so that they would be tried in magistrates' courts, where juries were not available.[33] Over the past two decades, this process of reclassification has accelerated, with the result that about 98 per cent of all criminal cases are now tried in magistrates' courts (Padfield, 1995, p. 195).[34] The warnings of Sir William Blackstone, writing with prescience two centuries previously, were studiously ignored:

> [T]he liberties of England cannot but subsist so long as this palladium [Blackstone was referring to the jury] remains sacred and inviolate; not only from all open attacks, (which none will be so hardy as to make,) but also from all secret machinations, which may sap and undermine it; by introducing new and arbitrary methods of trial, by justices of the peace. ... And however *convenient* these may appear at first (as doubtless all arbitrary powers, well executed, are the most *convenient*,) yet let it be again remembered, that delays, and little inconveniences in the forms of justice, are the price that all free nations must pay for

> their liberty in more substantial matters; that these inroads upon this sacred bulwark of the nation are fundamentally opposite to the spirit of our constitution; and that, although begun in trifles, the precedent may gradually increase and spread, to the utter disuse of juries in questions of the most momentous concern. (Blackstone, 1979, Bk.4, p. 349)

So who are these magistrates to whom the liberty of the criminal accused has been now entrusted? Like jurors, magistrates possess no formal legal training.[35] Unlike jurors, however, they are not the product of random selection. Prospective candidates for the magistracy are nominated by local advisory committees, carefully screened, and appointed by the Lord Chancellor's department. Magistrates are usually older and 'respected' members of the community. Most will be from the middle and upper classes, and conventional in their lifestyles. Few would be characterized as dissident or radical. Ethnic minorities tend to be underrepresented (King and May, 1985). Ironically, given their historical exclusion from juries, women may be overrepresented, the explanation being that wives of prominent businessmen are strong candidates for appointment, not only because of their standing in the community, but also because they have the time to devote to the magistracy. As magistrates do not receive a salary, they need to have the financial security not to have to worry about remuneration, and the spouses of successful businessmen are in such a position. The businessmen themselves are usually less willing to spare the time to be magistrates.

Whether or not magistrates are better decision-makers than jurors is not the issue. The point, rather, is that the magistracy is a distinctly less democratic body than the jury. By diverting criminal cases from Crown Courts, where a jury is available, to magistrates' courts, where it is not, parliament sabotaged its own democratic reforms. The jury system may have survived the direct attacks of those who wanted to eliminate it entirely, but the rise of the magistracy may yet prove to be a more decisive indirect attack. Those who favour the jury's elimination have in fact not been overly concerned with how abolition might come about or with the internal consistency of the arguments used to achieve it. The Roskill Committee (1986) recommended removing complex fraud trials from the jury's domain because such cases were said to be too complicated for ordinary citizens to understand. The James Committee (1975) was of the view that there were offences that were too trivial to justify the juror's time – offences which today account for approximately 98 per cent of all criminal trials (Padfield, 1995, p. 195).[36] It might be recalled that the juryless Diplock courts in Northern Ireland were established because it was thought that jurors were too susceptible to threats and intimidation.

In Chapter 3, the particular danger of case-hardening that threatens the judge was noted. Its source was identified as the exposure of judges to cases that fall into a pattern where the defendants swore their innocence at trial and then their regret for having committed the crime at sentencing. The symptoms of case-hardening include a tendency to be unduly suspicious of the testimony of defendants and to be too uncritically accepting of the testimony of the police. It was then observed that jurors, unlike judges, do not hear enough cases to become case-hardened. They approach the limited number of cases that they hear without any preconceptions. Magistrates are more like judges than jurors in this regard for they too enjoy long-term appointments. Becoming case-hardened may be as much a danger for the magistrate as it is for the judge.

The creeping expansion of magistrates' court jurisdiction may ultimately result in the slow death of the jury system but, at present, jury trial remains available in Crown Court. It is in Crown Court that the most serious crimes are tried. Although statistically miniscule in comparison to the number of cases heard in magistrates' courts, these cases are more likely to raise issues of moral blameworthiness. Here too, however, there has been an attempt to undermine the democratic character of the jury. At approximately the same time as the property qualifications for jury service were being repealed, the Director of Public Prosecutions began the practice of vetting jurors in politically sensitive cases. Pre-trial checks of prospective jurors' backgrounds were carried out by police, with the aim of alerting the prosecutor to those persons who might not be suitable jurors in the particular case. These could then be asked by the Crown to stand by.[37] As a result of vetting, jurors who were not disqualified by law could nonetheless find themselves excluded from jury service because of their background, associates or political views. It could be expected that the resulting juries would be more conservative and more prone to convict, and, indeed, this was presumably the purpose behind the vetting. Although the practice was criticized by Lord Denning in *Ex Parte Brownlow*,[38] vetting was upheld by the Court of Appeal in *R.* v. *Mason*.[39]

If a juror of dubious reliability managed to slip through the vetting net, there was another mechanism in place to neutralize the juror's effect. Again, at about the same time that the jury was becoming a more democratic body by virtue of the abolition of the property requirement, the government introduced legislation to allow for non-unanimous verdicts.[40] After a jury has deliberated for two hours without being able to reach a unanimous verdict, a judge may accept a verdict of ten to two. One effect of this reform is to allow a conservative majority on the jury to ignore the voice of one or two liberal dissenters (Sealy and Cornish, 1973). It also has the effect of allowing the majority to ignore the viewpoint of an ethnic or racial minority member of the jury.

The Democratization of the US Jury

In Britain trial by magistrates has displaced trial by jury in all but the most serious of criminal cases. Similarly, there is a declining incidence of jury trials in the United States, but for a different reason. Decision-making authority in criminal cases cannot be legislatively shifted to non-jurors, as it has in Britain, for the right to a jury is guaranteed by the US Constitution.[41] The reason for the reduction in jury trials in America is that the overwhelming majority of cases are 'plea bargained', the defendant agreeing to plead guilty in exchange for a reduction in the charges, a dropping of some of a number of charges or a favourable sentence recommendation. The shadow of the jury looms large in the plea bargaining process, however. Each side's best guess of how a jury would decide the case influences its bargaining position. For this reason, the statistical incidence of jury trials gives a misleading impression of the impact of the jury on the criminal justice system.

The real difference between the jury in Britain and the United States relates not to the percentage of cases that it hears but to the respect in which the institution is held. Whereas juries seem to be the target of a constant sniping campaign in Britain, and at best grudgingly tolerated, the jury in the United States is viewed as an integral and valuable part of the criminal justice system. The US Supreme Court's description of the jury as a bulwark of liberty, and 'an inestimable safeguard against the corrupt or overzealous prosecutor and the compliant, biased or eccentric judge'[42] is one with which lawyers, politicians and the public alike would concur. This reverence is due in part to the jury's role in American history. The first colonists left England to escape political persecution. It might be recalled that William Penn, who founded Pennsylvania, was one of the original defendants in *Bushell's Case* (discussed in Chapter 2). The colonists found in the jury a mechanism for resisting the power of a British government to which they no longer felt loyalty. The acquittal of John Peter Zenger (also discussed in Chapter 2) symbolized the jury's defiance of British rule. When British rule was finally overthrown, the right to jury trial was enshrined in the US Constitution and all state constitutions.

This is not to say that the American jury has been a model of democracy. As in Britain, property ownership was initially a condition of eligibility for service (Altschuler and Deiss, 1994). This requirement fell fairly quickly, but other exclusionary practices remained. Women did not become eligible for jury duty until nearly the beginning of the twentieth century, and it was not until 1975 that true equality between the sexes in respect to jury service was constitutionally mandated.[43] More serious still was the exclusion of blacks and ethnic minorities from juries. The struggle to desegregate the jury mirrored the struggle to desegregate other aspects of American life. Unlike in Britain, however, where reform was forged in parliament, in the United States it was the judiciary (and the US Supreme Court in particular) that was primarily responsible for effecting change.[44]

In *Strauder* v. *West Virginia*[45] the Supreme Court held that a state statute that prohibited coloured persons from serving as jurors violated the equal protection clause of the US Constitution. The statute at issue in this 1880 case was discriminatory on its face, but in the following year the Court found unconstitutional a law which, although objective on its face, was discriminatorily applied so as to exclude blacks from jury service.[46] Nor is the reach of the Supreme Court's rulings limited by race. In *Hernandez* v. *Texas*,[47] where persons of Mexican descent had been excluded from serving on juries, the Court held that the systematic exclusion of *any* identifiable class of the community could violate the fourteenth amendment:

> Throughout our history differences in race and color have defined easily identifiable groups which have at times required the aid of the courts in securing equal treatment under the laws. But community prejudices are not static, and from time to time other differences from the community norm may define other groups which need the same protection. Whether such a group exists within a community is a question of fact. When the existence of a distinct class is demonstrated, and it is further shown that the laws, as written or as applied, single out that class for different treatment not based on some reasonable classification, the guarantees of the Constitution have been violated.[48]

Throughout the course of its rulings, however, the Court has been at pains to emphasize that a defendant does not have a right to have members of his or her background or race included on the jury.[49] There is no affirmative right to a jury of one's peers as such.

Much of the discrimination in jury selection has been the product of a more subtle process than overtly discriminatory legislation. Historically, many states relied on prominent citizens – so-called 'key men' – to nominate prospective jurors. These key men tended to be white middle-class males whose range of acquaintances was often restricted to individuals of a similar background as themselves. Few knew persons of other races to nominate for jury duty, even if they might wish to do so.[50] The result was that the conscious and subconscious prejudices of the selectors were reflected in the jury's composition. It was not until passage of the Federal Jury Selection and Service Act of 1968[51] that the 'key man' approach to jury selection was formally rejected in favour of a policy of random selection. This Act, however, applied only to the federal courts. As the overwhelming majority of criminal prosecutions are brought in state courts, and as many states continued to accord a role to prominent local citizens in jury selection, the 'key man' system survived. Legal challenges to the practice have not proved successful.[52]

Even before passage of the 1968 Act, it was becoming increasingly evident to the Justices on the US Supreme Court that a ban on discrimination in jury selection would not, by itself, produce racially integrated juries. A steady stream of cases in the first half of the twentieth century attested to the resilience of the all-white jury.[53] As a result, the Supreme Court began to search for a more effective approach to the problem. The first indications of a shift in the Court's thinking appeared in *Smith* v. *Texas*,[54] where the Court referred to the jury as a 'body truly representative of the community'.[55] This description seemed to envisage juries which actually mirrored the communities from which they were drawn, as opposed to juries which were simply selected pursuant to non-discriminatory criteria. In *Glasser* v. *United States*[56] the Court advised that jury selectors 'must not allow the desire for competent jurors to lead them into selections which [did] not comport with the concept of the jury as a cross-section of the community'.[57] Articulating the new vision of the jury that appeared to be emerging, Justice Frank Murphy wrote in *Thiel* v. *Southern Pacific Co.*[58] that the 'American tradition of trial by jury, considered in connection with either criminal or civil proceedings, necessarily contemplates an impartial jury drawn from a cross-section of the community'.[59]

Three decades later, in *Taylor* v. *Louisiana*,[60] the Supreme Court finally put constitutional teeth into its evolving image of the jury. Under review was a Louisiana statute which exempted from jury service women who did not file a written request to be allowed to serve. The law in question did not prohibit women from serving; on the contrary, it implicitly recognized their right to serve. It was the fact that in order to become a juror a woman had to take affirmative steps not required of a man which was challenged. The Supreme Court found a constitutional violation, but not of equal protection. Rather, the Court held that the Louisiana statute failed to satisfy the cross-section demands of the sixth amendment.[61]

> [T]he exclusion of women from jury venires deprives a criminal defendant of his *Sixth Amendment right to trial by an impartial jury drawn from a fair cross section of the community*. (emphasis added)[62]

The sixth amendment provision to which the Court referred traces its roots to the common law concept of vicinage (Connor, 1909), which contemplated jurors drawn from the local community. This made sense at a time when jurors were selected because of their personal knowledge of the circumstances of the case. Local residents were more likely to have such knowledge. After the jury was transformed from a group of fact-knowers to one of fact-finders, the requirement of vicinage persisted as an assurance to defendants that they would be judged by persons familiar with their character as well as that of their accusers. This rationale had a particular poignancy in the American colonies. One of the many issues which united the colonists was their opposition to the English government's practice of returning defendants to England to stand trial. The sixth amendment guarantee of local jurors served as a protection against such reverse 'transportation' as well as the converse danger of jurors being imported from outside the jurisdiction.

There is a critical difference, however, between the common law concept of vicinage and the Supreme Court's requirement of a jury drawn from a fair cross-section of the community. The focal point of vicinage was the physical location from which the jurors were chosen. It was a concept grounded in geography. When filtered through the sixth amendment, and interpreted by the Supreme Court in *Taylor* and subsequent cases, the focus shifted from geography to the racial, ethnic and gender composition of the jury. The Court had apparently discovered (a cynic might say invented) a previously hidden dimension of vicinage.

The shift from an analysis based on equal protection to one based on a requirement of fair cross-section representation might not, at first glance, appear especially significant. Both lines of analysis reach the same end point: that a jury from which identifiable groups in the community have been excluded does not accord with constitutional standards.[63] However, the two constitutional guarantees – equal protection and fair cross-section representation – embody distinct philosophical traditions. Equal protection traces its lineage to the principle of justice that similarly situated individuals should be treated similarly. What matters for constitutional purposes is that any differences which are alleged to justify dissimilar treatment be shown to be material to the task in relation to which the allegedly discriminatory line has been drawn. If race is irrelevant to the function of being a juror, as it would seem to be, then discriminations based on race are in violation of the equal protection clause.

In contrast, cross-section representation locates its philosophical roots in a concern for democratic values – a point explicitly recognized by Justice Hugo Black in *Smith* v. *Texas*:[64]

> For racial discrimination to result in the exclusion from jury service of otherwise qualified groups not only violates our Constitution and the laws enacted under it but is at war with our basic concepts of a democratic society. ...[65]

A jury which comprises a fair cross-section of the community is a democracy in microcosm. No one can be excluded from such a jury without good cause any more than they could be excluded from a democratic society. The verdict of a democratic jury must reflect the judgement of all the community's members and not just that of the majority. Cross-section representation, when coupled with the requirement of unanimity, fosters verdicts that reflect the democratic judgement of *all* the people.

There can be occasions when the demands of fair cross-section representation and equal protection find themselves at odds. Say that a jury is chosen by a process of random selection. The community is racially mixed but the jurors chosen are all of the same race. There is no evidence of discrimination; the jury is simply a statistical anomaly. Nonetheless, it cannot be said to be representative of a fair cross-section of the community. Some have suggested that the proper course in such a situation is for the judge to take positive steps to integrate the jury by summoning additional jurors from the minority population. This would yield a more representative jury but by means that would be in tension with equal protection principles since similarly situated individuals would not have been similarly treated. Supplemental jurors of the excluded race would have an infinitely greater chance of being selected for the reconstituted jury, as they would be the only group eligible for selection.

There may also be differences in respect to the proof required to establish the respective constitutional claims. A petitioner who alleges a violation of the equal protection clause must establish that there has been discrimination by state officials. Proving discriminatory intent is often problematic, as few will admit to having consciously acted in a discriminatory manner. On the other hand, in theory the lack of such proof should not be fatal to a fair cross-section claim, for its essence lies in the fact that the jury pool does not accurately reflect the composition of the community. How that has come about, while not irrelevant, would not appear to be critical. However, in *Duren* v. *Missouri*[66] the Supreme Court seemed to attempt a degree of assimilation:

> In order to establish a prima facie violation of the fair cross-section requirement, the defendant must show (1) that the group alleged to be excluded is a 'distinctive' group in the community; (2) that the representation of this group in venires from which juries are selected is not fair and reasonable in relation to the number of such persons in the community; and (3) that this underrepresentation is due to systematic exclusion of the group in the jury selection process.[67]

The first prong of the *Duren* test – that the group be 'distinctive' – answers the question of what groups should be considered in determining the profile of a cross-section of the community. But what makes a group distinctive? Claims of 'distinctiveness' by youths, the elderly, manual workers, the unemployed, and men with beards have all been rejected by the courts.[68] The judges seem to be fixated by race, gender and ethnic distinctiveness. Missing from the typical judicial opinion is any analysis of whether the group in question will bring to the jury room a perspective that might otherwise not be considered. However, it is arguably the distinctiveness of a group's perspective and not the distinctiveness of the group that should matter.[69] If a group has a unique perspective to offer, then the exclusion of that group will mean that this perspective is less likely to enter into the dialectics of the jury's deliberations.

The second prong of the *Duren* test is that the representation of the group in question be fair and reasonable in relation to their numbers in the community. This quasi-mathematical requirement has generated the very types of practical problem that it was designed to solve. The courts have struggled with the question of how far the percentage of a group on the jury has to deviate from its percentage within the community before a constitutional violation will be found.[70] How to calculate the variation has also proved problematic for judges whose forte is not in statistical analysis.[71] Even if the idea of fair and reasonable representation is accepted, it does not address the problem of distinctive groups whose numbers are small. Such groups are statistically unlikely to be included on the actual jury and their possibly unique perspective may be lost.

The third prong of the *Duren* standard – systematic exclusion – would seem to be the most crucial. Indeed, it might well be asked why, if systematic exclusion is present, it should make any difference whether the excluded group is distinctive. Likewise, why should the size of the group matter? Both size and distinctiveness would seem superfluous if there has been systematic exclusion. But, then again, fair cross-section representation analysis would itself seem superfluous, as proof of systematic exclusion would usually warrant a finding of a violation of equal protection. This is not invariable, however, as a court might find the systematic exclusion that would justify a finding of a sixth amendment violation but without the intent to discriminate that is necessary to sustain an equal protection claim.

The practical effect, however, is that a jury which would be unconstitutional under the sixth amendment in a criminal prosecution for, say, assault would pass constitutional muster if the victim of the assault were to sue the assailant in a civil court, where the parties would be restricted to an equal protection challenge to the jury's composition (the sixth amendment being inapplicable to civil cases). This is no mere hypothetical possibility but what actually happened in *Ricketts* v. *City of Hartford*.[71] From a political and philosophical perspective, if not from a strict legal perspective, the inconsistency is troubling.

The US Supreme Court's conception of community, as we have seen, is defined not in the geographical terms of vicinage but in the sociopolitical terms of gender, race and ethnicity. But is the Court's concern with the harm to those excluded or the harm to the defendant? This is a theoretically critical question for it bears on the issue of whether a defendant should have to be a member of the excluded group in order to have standing to raise an alleged constitutional violation. In *Taylor* v. *Louisiana*[73] it was a male who complained that women had been unconstitutionally excluded from the jury which heard his case. Likewise, in *Peters* v. *Kiff*[74] a white defendant challenged his conviction on the ground that blacks had been wrongfully excluded from his jury. In both cases the challenge was successful. Decisions such as these seem to be exceptions to the general rule that a court will consider only the rights and interests of parties before the court. In these cases it is not clear that the defendant was harmed in the sense that a differently constituted jury would have reached a different verdict. The harm was to those who had been excluded from jury service. Such exclusion marks the group in question as inferior. As the Supreme Court said in *Strauder* v. *West Virginia*.[75]

> The very fact the colored people are singled out and expressly denied by a statute all right to participate in the administration of the law, as jurors, because of their color, though they are citizens and may be in other respects fully qualified, is practically a brand upon them, affixed by the law; an assertion of their inferiority, and a stimulant to that race prejudice which is an impediment to securing to individuals of the race that equal justice which the law aims to secure to all others.[76]

In *Ballard* v. *United States*[77] Justice Douglas went further, stating that the harm extended 'to the jury system, to the law as an institution, to the community at large, and to the democratic ideal reflected in the processes of the courts'.[78]

The Supreme Court's commitment to a jury which is representative of a fair cross-section of the community is called into question, however, by its decisions on the size of the jury and the need for a unanimous verdict. In *Williams* v. *Florida*[79] the Court held that juries of six were constitutionally permissible in criminal cases. Justice Byron White, speaking for the majority, described the common law tradition of twelve as an 'historical accident ... without significance except to mystics'.[80] The correctness of this observation aside, it is mathematically less probable that a jury of six will comprise a fair cross-section of the community than a jury of twelve (Zeisel, 1971) since there are fewer places to be filled and a correspondingly reduced probability that a representative of a minority group will fill one of them. Conversely, there will be an increased likelihood of the all-white jury that the Supreme Court's decisions seemed directed at avoiding.[81] The Supreme Court's decisions permitting less than unanimous verdicts[82] may achieve the same effect by indirection. Where unanimity is not required, the majority need not listen to the dissenters once the requisite number of jurors needed to return a verdict agree. Empirical research noted earlier indicates that minority factions are less likely to participate when unanimity is not required and that overall deliberations are not as extended. (Hastie *et al.*, 1983; Nemeth, 1977). In many cases the dissenters will be members of an identifiable minority group within the community. It makes little sense in insisting that 'distinctive' groups be included in the jury pool if their voice can then be ignored. The true danger in six-person juries and the abandonment of the requirement of unanimity on twelve-person juries lies in the threat to the dynamics of jury room deliberation.

Democracy and the Peremptory Challenge

The requirements of non-discrimination in jury selection and fair cross-section representation are best viewed as complementary. Both requirements, however, are directed to the composition of the pool from which the jury is selected; neither addresses the composition of the jury which decides the actual case. The jury pool may be democratic in character, but the jury may not. To understand why, one might consider the situation of woman jurors post-*Taylor* v. *Louisiana*. In *Taylor*, it will be recalled, the Supreme Court invalidated a statute that excluded women from jury service unless they took positive steps to include themselves. The thinking behind the statute was that women, because of household and childcare responsibilities, were too valuable to be spared and in any event would probably not wish to serve. The Supreme Court's decision, however, did not preclude trial judges from excusing women who cited these 'hardships' in open court. Many did, with the result that juries after *Taylor* continued to be predominantly male.

A more sinister threat to a democratically composed jury in the United States lay in the use of peremptory challenges to exclude wholesale classes of jurors. Peremptory challenges, as will be discussed further in Chapter 6, permit a party to excuse jurors without having to give any reason. Thus a juror may be challenged whom a lawyer suspects, but is unable to prove, is biased. In most instances this will facilitate the impanelling of an impartial jury. However, some lawyers have used the peremptory challenge to remove all jurors of a particular race or ethnic background. It would seem intuitively objectionable, however, for a party to be able to achieve by indirection the all-white jury which would be unconstitutional if mandated by statute. In *Swain* v. *Alabama*[83] the Supreme Court agreed and held that it would be unconstitutional for the prosecution to use its peremptory challenges to strike minority jurors in all cases 'whatever the circumstances, whatever the crime, and whoever the defendant or the victim'.[84] The practical problem lay in satisfying this test, as a defendant would not necessarily know of challenges which had occurred in trials in which he or she had not been a participant, and public records were unlikely to identify the race of jurors who had been excused pursuant to peremptory challenge. Also, the requirement of demonstrating an across-the-board abuse of the challenge allowed a prosecutor with a discriminatory bent to escape censure by the simple expedient of not discriminating in every case. In fact, the use of peremptory challenges to exclude all members of a particular race was likely to be confined to cases where race was an issue.

In *Batson* v. *Kentucky*[85] the Supreme Court reconsidered *Swain* and held that the prosecution's use of its peremptory challenges to exclude all black prospective jurors in the case was unconstitutional. Interestingly, the constitutional provision which the Court found to have been violated was not the sixth amendment's requirement of fair cross-section representation but the equal protection clause: '[Equal protection] forbids the prosecutor to challenge potential jurors solely on account of their race or on the assumption that black jurors as a group will be unable impartially to consider the State's case against a black defendant.'[86] The Court further indicated that it was not necessary for the defence to show across-the-board discrimination in a series of cases, as had been required under *Swain*. *Batson* was followed by a series of decisions in which the Supreme Court extended the reach of its holding to civil as well as criminal cases,[87] to defence lawyers as well as prosecutors,[88] and to defendants who were not of the same race as the challenged jurors.[89] More recently the Court has held that the principle of *Batson* forbids peremptory challenges based on gender.[90]

In retrospect it can be seen that the US Supreme Court's efforts to democratize the jury have proceeded through three distinct stages. In the first the Court invoked equal protection principles to preclude intentional discrimination in the creation of a jury pool. The fair cross-section decisions introduced a second phase in which the failure to achieve a representative jury pool could itself be the subject of constitutional challenge. In the final stage the Court turned its attention away from the pool from which the jurors were selected to the actual composition of the jury in the given case. However, the focus of all the Court's decisions has been on exclusion rather than inclusion, and the Justices have consistently maintained that a defendant has no right to have members of his or her race, gender, or ethnic background included on the jury.

Conclusion

Historically, the democracy of the jury was distorted by the absence of the poor, racial and ethnic minorities, and women. These battles have now largely been won. In Britain the property requirement for jury service was abolished by statute, as was the restriction on women serving as jurors. In the United States, laws which excluded women and minorities from jury duty were held unconstitutional by the courts. Those that escaped judicial censure were quietly repealed. By the late twentieth century the jury, at least in principle, had become open to all. Today there is a threat to the democracy of the jury from a different quarter. Ironically, it arises in respect to that segment of the population which at one time was regarded as the jury's backbone – individuals of education and high socioeconomic status. The source of the threat lies in legislative exemptions and judicial excusals from jury service.

Often statutes will exempt designated categories of individuals from jury service. In Britain judges, lawyers, their clerks and others concerned with the administration of the law, as well as the clergy, are ineligible.[91] In addition, members of parliament, the European Assembly, and the armed forces have the right to be excused.[92] Others excusable as of right include those in the medical and related professions – doctors, nurses, midwives, dentists, veterinarians, and pharmaceutical chemists.[93] Those over the age of 65 can also request to be excused.[94] In the United States the specific categories vary from state to state, but the general pattern is similar. Some groups, like the police and fire-fighters, are excused because they are deemed too valuable to be spared for jury service; others, such as lawyers and judges, are excused because they are thought likely to have too great an influence on other jury members. Although most categories of exemption can be explained by one of these two rationales, the justification for some categories is more of a mystery. Van Dyke discovered a broad spectrum of state occupational exemptions from jury service which included accountants, morticians, funeral directors, farmers, commercial airline pilots, and telegraph and telephone operators (Van Dyke, 1977, p. 127) Regardless of rationale, the effect of these exemptions is to diminish the democratic composition of the jury.

Statutory exemptions apply to blanket categories. In addition, judges have the discretion to excuse prospective jurors on an individual basis. The general catch-all ground is hardship – that jury service would create an undue burden for the person in question. Those who bear the primary responsibility of caring for the sick, the elderly or children are often excused on this ground. Hardships may also be based on physical disability. Also recognized are claims of economic hardship by, most commonly, sole proprietors whose businesses would suffer in their absence. In *Thiel* v. *Southern Pacific Co*,[95] the US Supreme Court, while striking down an exclusion on daily wage-earners from jury service, stated that 'a federal judge would be justified in excusing a daily wage earner for whom jury service would entail an undue financial hardship'.[96]

The more complex a case, the longer the trial is likely to last. The longer the trial, the greater the financial hardship to the jurors. The greater the financial hardship, the stronger the incentive to avoid jury service. It is not simply the low *per diem* remuneration[97] that causes concern, although most persons of moderate income will suffer economically during their term of jury service unless their employer is legally required, or voluntarily prepared, to carry on paying their salary. There is also a more subtle factor at work. If a trial is to be of substantial duration, and trials of over six months are no longer that rare in the United States (a 1990 California sex abuse trial lasted for two years and nine months!), an employee who holds a responsible position in a company may find it jeopardized. The workload of the juror cannot be left to accumulate in the juror's absence, and a replacement may need to be employed. Following completion of jury service, the juror may experience difficulty in reclaiming his or her former job. It is also not uncommon for those who have served on a lengthy trial to discover that their contemporaries have been promoted while their position in the company hierarchy has remained static.

The effect of exemptions and excusals, like the effect of discriminatory practices of former times, is to distort the democratic composition of the jury – but in a different direction. The unemployed and retired can afford the luxury of jury duty; the self-employed and those in the professions cannot. If not statutorily exempt from service, they contrive to have themselves excused. Judges are rarely in a position to investigate the merits of hardship claims, and most will accept a claim at face value. As a consequence of exemptions and excusals, the responsibility of jury service is disproportionately borne by the young, the old, the unemployed, and those who are financially supported by a spouse, partner or parent. Ironically the modern-day jury is increasingly likely to be composed of the very persons who, at an earlier stage of jury history, would have been legally excluded from service.

In terms of democracy, this means that the jury is a less representative body. That the distortion results from exemptions and excusals rather than from discriminatory laws and practices does not alter the effect, which is likely to become exacerbated as the trend to longer and longer trials continues.

What, if anything, can or should be done? For a start, the legislature needs to re-examine the rationale for each statutory category of exemption. All blanket exemptions are suspect, for they inevitably will have a greater distortive effect on the representativeness of a jury than excusals granted on an individual basis. Only legally trained individuals who might exert an undue influence on the deliberations and those who provide essential (narrowly defined) services to society should be exempt. Beyond these limited categories, all excusals from jury service should be granted on an individual basis. The presumption should be against an excusal. Instead, courts should examine the reason for the request and attempt to accommodate the juror's concerns without excusing him or her from service altogether. Thus, for example, if a juror claimed that a physical handicap prevented attendance, the court should arrange for transportation to and from the courthouse. Within the courtroom, seating arrangements might be altered to accommodate the needs of those with hearing or visual impairments. Childcare facilities should be provided so that parents of young children will be able to serve. Better compensation would undoubtedly help to minimize the economic hardship of jury service, and mandatory legislation should require employers to continue to pay an employee's salary during the term of his or her service. The legislation should also guarantee that employees are not disadvantaged by jury service.[98] Even with these changes, the self-employed and those in positions of responsibility within a company may be reluctant to be absent from work for extended periods. In lengthy trials, a judge might consider substituting the occasional evening for afternoon session, or a Saturday for a weekday session, to allow jurors time to tend to their business affairs. Even an extended lunch hour might help to minimize the disruption to the juror's employment.

The struggle to democratize the jury has been a continual one. The nature of the specific challenge may change with time, but the goal remains the same: to ensure that the verdict of the jury remains the voice of the people – of all the people.

Notes

1 This statement is only partially true in respect to Britain. Parliament is composed of the House of Commons and the House of Lords. The House of Lords is not an elected body. Membership is acquired through heredity or appointment by the government.

2 This has proved to be the case, for example, in Israel where minority religious parties, holding a handful of seats in the Knesset, hold the balance of power between the two major parties, neither of which is able to command a majority. As a result, they are able to obtain cabinet posts in exchange for their support.

3 499 US 400 (1990).

4 Ibid. at 402.

5 See, for example, Juries Act 1974 s.3 (UK); Federal Jury Selection and Service Act, 28 USC s.1863 (b) (2) (US).

6 It could be argued that those who do not care enough to register to vote have an

insufficient interest in the country's well-being to be allowed to serve on juries. This argument, however, fails to take into account the reasons for not registering.

7 For example, the Federal Jury Selection and Service Act of 1968 provides that voter lists can be supplemented when they fail to produce a fair cross-section of the community. 28 USC 1863 (b) (2).

8 Juries Act 1974 s.17. Where the size of the jury is between eight and eleven, all but one of the jurors have to agree on the verdict. Ibid.

9 *Johnson* v. *Louisiana*, 406 US 356 (1972); *Apodaca* v. *Oregon*, 406 US 404 (1972).

10 406 US 356 (1972). The Court reasoned that a dissenting minority did not mean that the majority had not been persuaded of the defendant's guilt beyond a reasonable doubt. The Court also noted a logical fallacy in the argument. On a jury that was unable to agree (or deadlocked) there would perforce be some jurors who were not persuaded that defendant's guilt had been proved beyond a reasonable doubt. If this were taken as conclusive proof of reasonable doubt, the remedy should be dismissal of the charges and not a retrial as is accepted.

11 The case was distinguished, among other ways, by the sheer number and quality of the lawyers involved, the meticulousness with which each item of evidence was poured over and, outside the courtroom, the battle for public opinion which was being waged.

12 One could argue that knowing that they will be on television encourages lawyers to be better prepared as they will not wish to present themselves to the general public as incompetent. In the heat of the trial lawyers are likely, after perhaps an initial period of self-consciousness, to forget about the presence of the camera.

13 Even though jurors are able to compensate for each other's lapses, jurors must not count on this back-up. It would be most undesirable if all the jurors were not to pay close attention to the evidence on the assumption that the others would.

14 24 F. Cas. 1042 (No. 14,505) (CCD Mass. 1835).

15 Ibid. at p. 1043.

16 See, for example, Obscene Publications Act 1959.

17 See *DPP* v. *Whyte* [1972] AC 849.

18 See *R.* v. *Anderson* [1972] 1 QB 304.

19 *Miller* v. *California*, 413 US 15 (1973) (emphasis added).

20 428 US 153 (1976).

21 *Trop* v. *Dulles* 356 US 86, 101 (1958).

22 455 US 104, 112 (1982).

23 [1982] 2 All ER 689.

24 The jury must also find that the defendant realized that his conduct would be so regarded.

25 [1994] 3 All ER 79.

26 Ibid. at p. 87.

27 Juries are still available where a charge of fraud has been lodged against the party applying for the jury; or when a claim of libel, slander, malicious prosecution, or false imprisonment has been filed; or where the case in question raises similar issues. Supreme Court Act 1981 s.69.

28 See Juries Act 1825.

29 There was one noteworthy exception, however. An alien who was indicted for a crime was entitled to a jury *de mediatate linguae*, composed of half foreigners. See Larue (1976).

30 Married Women's Property Act 1882.

31 Sex Disqualification (Removal) Act 1919. s.1.

32 Criminal Justice Act 1972, consolidated in Juries Act 1974 s.1.

33 Freeman (1981) makes the point that the two events may not have been unrelated.
34 See, for example, Criminal Law Act 1977 s.14 *et seq.* This Act incorporated the recommendations of the James Committee (1975), which had been set up to consider the appropriate distribution of business between Crown Court, where jury trial was available, and magistrates' courts, where it was not.
35 The exception is the stipendiary magistrate, who is legally qualified, but these are relatively few in number and utilized primarily in major metropolitan areas.
36 One should not, however, be too quick to attribute an anti-democratic motive to this reclassification of offences. Some MPs may have been persuaded by the economic savings that would be realized from reducing the business of the Crown Courts, and others by penological considerations. Magistrates are limited in the term of imprisonment that they can impose following a conviction. To those who believed that prison sentences were becoming excessive in length, the reclassification of offences was seen as a salutary development.
37 This practice, discussed further in Chapter 6, allowed the Crown to identify jurors who would be excused from serving as long as a sufficient number of jurors remained.
38 [1980] 2 All ER 444, at 452–3.
39 [1980] 3 All ER 777.
40 Juries Act 1974 s.17.
41 US Constitution, amend VI. There is, however, an exception for petty offences. See *Baldwin* v. *New York*, 399 US 66 (1970).
42 See *Duncan* v. *Louisiana*, 391 US 145, 156 (1968).
43 See *Taylor* v. *Louisiana*, 419 US 522 (1975).
44 Part of the explanation lies in the power of the judiciary in the two countries. In the United States, a court may invalidate a legislative enactment that conflicts with the Constitution. British courts are precluded from invalidating a statute properly enacted by parliament.
45 100 US 303 (1880).
46 *Neal* v. *Delaware*, 103 US 370 (1881).
47 347 US 475 (1954).
48 Ibid. at p. 478.
49 See, for example, *Virginia* v. *Rives*, 100 US 313 (1879).
50 See *Rabinowitz* v. *United States*, 366 F. 2d 34, 40–41 (5th Cir. 1966).
51 28 USC ss.1861 *et. seq.*
52 See, for example, *United States* v. *Tropiano*, 418 F.2d 1069 (2d Cir. 1969) *cert. denied*, 397 US 1021 (1970); *United States* v. *Ditommaso*, 405 F.2d 385 (4th Cir. 1968) *cert. denied*, 394 US 934 (1969).
53 See for example, *Avery* v. *Georgia*, 345 US 559 (1953); *Hill* v. *Texas*, 316 US 400 (1942); *Norris* v. *Alabama*, 294 US 587 (1935); *Carter* v. *Texas*, 177 US 422 (1900). See, generally, Schmidt (1983).
54 311 US 128 (1940).
55 Ibid. at p. 130.
56 315 US 60 (1942).
57 Ibid. at p. 86.
58 328 US 217 (1946).
59 Ibid. at p. 220.
60 419 US 522 (1975).
61 US Constitution, amend. VI.
62 419 US at pp. 522, 535–6 (1975).
63 The sixth amendment, as will subsequently be discussed, applies only in criminal

cases. A civil litigant who wished to challenge the composition of the jury would be restricted to a claim under the equal protection clauses of the Constitution.

64 311 US 128 (1940).

65 Ibid. at p. 130.

66 439 US 357 (1979).

67 Ibid. at p. 364.

68 See, for example, *Ham* v. *South Carolina*, 409 US 524 (1973) (beards); *Fay* v. *New York*, 332 US 261 (1947) (manual labourers); *Barber* v. *Ponte*, 772 F.2d 982 (1st Cir. 1985) *cert. denied*, 475 US 1050 (1986) (youths); 738 (1991); *Silagy* v. *Peters*, 905 F.2d 986 (7th Cir. 1990) *cert. denied* 111 S.Ct. 1024 (1991) (the elderly).

69 See *Thiel* v. *Southern Pacific Co*, 328 US 217, 230 (1946) (Frankfurter, J, dissenting).

70 In *Swain* v. *Alabama* 380 US 202 (1965), the Supreme Court stated that a 10 per cent absolute disparity was insufficient to make out a constitutional violation, but subsequently in *Alexander* v. *Louisiana*, 405 US 625 (1972) the court found a constitutional violation when there was only a 7 per cent absolute disparity (but a 33 per cent comparative disparity). The difference between absolute and comparative disparity is examined in note 71.

71 Some courts have adopted a test of 'absolute disparity', wherein they subtract the group's percentage incidence in the jury pool from its percentage incidence in the community. Where the minority in question is small, this method of calculation will invariably lead to a finding of no constitutional violation. So, for instance, in *United States* v. *Horne*, 4 F.3d 579 (8th Cir. 1993), where the district was 2.9 per cent black, but there were no blacks in the jury pool, the court stated that the 'appellants have failed to present adequate evidence that the representation in the venire was not fair and reasonable in relation to the admittedly small number of Afro-Americans in the district ...'. The absolute disparity test has been used in some Supreme Court decisions. See, for example, *Castenada* v. *Partida*, 430 US 482 (1977); *Swain* v. *Alabama*, 380 US 202 (1965). A 'comparative disparity' test, in contrast, calculates the ratio of a group's percentage in the jury with its percentage in the population. Thus if a particular group represented 20 per cent of the community but only 10 per cent of the jury pool, an absolute disparity test would calculate the underrepresentation as 10 per cent (20 per cent minus 10 per cent) while a comparative disparity test would measure it at 50 per cent (10 per cent divided by 20 per cent). The comparative disparity test also breaks down when the numbers involved are small (for example, if a particular group represented 2 per cent of the community but only 1 per cent of the jury pool, the comparative disparity would still be 50 per cent). More sophisticated than either of these methods is one which calculates the likelihood that the discrepancy was the result of chance. See Gobert and Jordan, s.6.17 (1991).

72 74 F3d 1397 (2nd Cir. 1996).

73 419 US 522 (1975).

74 407 US 493 (1972).

75 100 US 303 (1880).

76 Ibid. at p. 308.

77 329 US 187 (1946).

78 Ibid. at p. 195.

79 399 US 78 (1970).

80 Ibid. at p. 102.

81 In *Ballew* v. *Georgia*, 435 US 223 (1978), the Supreme Court held that juries of less than six were not constitutionally permissible. The decision is also noteworthy because it constituted a high water mark in terms of the receptivity of the Court to social

science studies of the jury. Justice Blackmun carefully reviewed the post-*Williams* research which indicated that juries of less than twelve were not as effective deliberators and more likely to reach an incorrect verdict.

82 *Apodaca* v. *Oregon* 406 US 404 (1972); *Johnson* v. *Louisiana* 406 US 356 (1972). A less than unanimous verdict is not permissible when the jury consists of six members. *Burch* v. *Louisiana*, 441 US 130 (1979).

83 380 US 202 (1965).

84 Ibid. at p. 223.

85 476 US 79 (1986).

86 Ibid. at p. 85.

87 *Edmonson* v. *Leesville Concrete Co.*, 500 US 614 (1991).

88 *Georgia* v. *McCullom*, 505 US 42 (1992). This decision was particularly problematic from a strictly constitutional perspective. The Constitution applies only to state and federal entities. While a prosecutor could be deemed a state official for the purpose of satisfying the constitutional requirement of 'state action', the same could not be said of private defence counsel. The Court overcame this objection by reasoning that peremptory challenges were a matter of state creation, occurred within the structure of a state court system, and furthered the state's interest in the impanelling of an impartial jury.

89 *Powers* v. *Ohio*, 499 US 400 (1991).

90 *JEB* v. *Alabama ex rel TB*, 114 S.Ct. 1419 (1994).

91 Juries Act 1974 Part I, Sch. 1. There are also categories of individuals, primarily those who have been convicted of a serious crime or are on probation, and the mentally ill, who are disqualified from jury service. See Juries (Disqualification) Act 1984; Juries Act 1974, Sch. 1, Part II. See also Criminal Justice and Public Order Act 1994, s.40 (disqualification of those on bail).

92 Juries Act 1974, Sch. 1, Part III.

93 Ibid.

94 Ibid.

95 328 US 217 (1946).

96 Ibid. at p. 224.

97 In California, for example, jurors are paid US$5 per day. See California Civil Procedure Code s.215 (West 1982).

98 See, for example, Jury Systems Improvement Act, 28 USC 1875 (protecting jurors from intimidation, discharge, or coercion because of service on a jury).

5 Justice versus Democracy

The previous chapter discussed the democratic dividend of jury service to both jurors and the state. But of what value is a democratic jury to the defendant whose liberty is at stake, and what, if anything, does such a jury contribute to the realization of justice? The courts have not always been clear in their answers. Where once the Justices of the US Supreme Court purported to be vindicating the right of the *citizen* not to be discriminated against in jury selection, they now speak of the right of the *accused* to be tried by a jury drawn from a fair cross-section of the community. Is the implication that the verdict of a jury that is not of such a composition somehow suspect? Is it because jurors cannot be relied upon to be fair and impartial in judging persons of a different background from themselves? One could certainly argue the opposite – that jurors from a different background will be able to perceive a case more objectively and dispassionately without the danger of subconscious identification. But what, then, is one to make of the oft cited, although seldom implemented, right to a jury of one's peers? Could it be that part of the rationale for democratizing the jury is to increase the probability that among the jurors will be some whom the accused would count as peers?

In the judiciary's desire to end discrimination in jury selection and impanel a jury that can be fairly characterized as a representative microcosm of the community, little thought appears to have been given to the ability of such a jury to achieve justice. Whether two such seemingly self-evident goods as justice and democracy are compatible may depend on how jurors perceive their role. This will turn in part on the judicial messages transmitted to them – whether expressly or by implication – as to why a democratic jury matters. It is the relationship between democracy and justice, at times comfortable and at other times uneasy, which will be examined in this chapter.

Peers and Prejudice

The tension that can arise between democracy and justice is illustrated by the case of the four white Los Angeles police officers charged with the beating of a black motorist, Rodney King. The assault had been captured on videotape by a passer-by, and the videotape had been shown on national television. Following a change in venue, the trial was held in Simi Valley, a suburban community with a black population of only 1.5 per cent. Simi Valley was also home to many retired police officers. The jury which heard the case, although randomly selected, contained no blacks. The jury acquitted, despite the fact that the videotape was introduced into evidence. The rioting in Los Angeles which erupted following the verdict was telling evidence to the fact that, while the verdict may have reflected prevailing community standards in Simi Valley, it did not accord with the views of the more racially and culturally diverse Los Angeles community.

Changes of venue are ordered to avoid prejudice to an accused. In the King case, the trial had been transferred to Simi Valley to avoid the potential prejudice to the white defendants that might have infected the trial if it had been held in Los Angeles, where the assault had occurred. The case illustrates one of the pressure points between justice and democracy. The purpose of a change in venue is to increase the probability of a just verdict by removing the contaminant of local prejudice. The jury that heard the King case, however, was not democratic in its composition, at least not in the racially mixed sense that seems to be envisaged in US Supreme Court decisions. The problem was that, while the jury may have been representative of the community from which the jurors were drawn, the community was not representative of the Los Angeles area in which the crime had been committed.[1]

Further evidence that there may be differences in outlook, opinion and ultimately verdict between a non-representative jury and society at large can be garnered from the O.J. Simpson murder prosecution. Just as in the King case, most of the jurors in the O.J. Simpson trial were of the same race as the defendant and of a different race than the victims. But where in the King case the jury was overwhelmingly white, in that of Simpson it was overwhelmingly non-white. There was, however, a second 'jury' in the Simpson case, in addition to that which sat in the jury box, consisting of the national audience which watched the trial on television. The predominantly black in-court jury quickly reached a unanimous verdict of not guilty, while the more heterogeneous jury of the public seemed to be less persuaded of Simpson's innocence. Several caveats should be noted: the public's perceptions may have been distorted by inflammatory news coverage and commentary to which the real jurors, who were sequestered, were not exposed; the television audience may not have viewed the proceedings with the same degree of concentration as the real jurors; the opportunity for reflection and group deliberation afforded the real jury may not have been available to the public generally; and, of course, the television audience did not carry the burden of responsibility for Simpson's liberty. These differences notwithstanding, the dissonance between public opinion and the verdict of the actual jury in a case where both were exposed to much the same body of evidence suggests that a more diverse and heterogeneous jury might not have been so quick to acquit Simpson. Interestingly, in a subsequent civil suit, a predominantly white jury found Simpson liable for the two deaths, admittedly by the lesser civil standard of a preponderance of the evidence, and awarded the victim's families damages of $8 million.

Cases in which there is a change in venue raise questions about what it means to have a jury which is democratic in its composition. Juries are usually drawn from the district in which the crime was committed. The community in which a crime occurs is likely to have the greatest interest in its resolution. In this conception of community, geographical boundaries demarcate the democratic cross-section whose opinion is sought. When there has been a change in venue, a different community is substituted for that in which the crime took place. This substitute community may not contain the same racial and ethnic mix as the community in which the crime occurred. Thus selecting a cross-section of it will not necessarily yield – and in the Rodney King case did not yield – a similarly composed jury to that which would have been impanelled had the change in venue not been ordered. The trial judge in that case may have been right to order a change in venue, but might be faulted for not transferring the case to a district whose racial and ethnic composition was more similar to that of the Los Angeles community where the assault had occurred. But if this be the objective, why not simply mandate that the jury ultimately selected to hear a case mirror the racial, gender, religious, ethnic (and whatever other characteristics are deemed relevant) composition of the community in which the crime took place?

The Rodney King and O.J. Simpson cases also highlight another tension in the realm of jury rhetoric. It is often claimed that there is right to 'a jury of one's peers'. The concept of peers seems to trace its roots to the Magna Carta. As observed previously, among the English nobles it may have been an assurance that one would not be judged by persons of inferior rank. In the less class-conscious 'new world' of the United States, the Supreme Court defined peers as 'persons having the same legal status in society' as the accused.[2] Those today who assert the right to a jury of one's peers have yet another concept in mind. What they seek is a jury composed of persons of the same race, class or ethnic background as the accused – black jurors in the trial of a black defendant a female jury when the accused is a woman, and so on.[3] The argument advanced to support this conception of a jury of one's peers is double-edged: first, that non-peers are more likely to be prejudiced against the defendant; and second, that peers are best able to understand and put into perspective the actions of the accused. The somewhat unsettling undercurrent is that only peers are capable of being fair and impartial.

Both O.J. Simpson in his criminal prosecution and the police defendants in the Rodney King case were tried by a jury of their 'peers'. On each jury persons who were predominantly of the same race as the defendants predominated. Not only did the jury in the King case contain no black members but it was drawn from a community permeated by the views of the ex-policemen who had chosen to retire in the area. These jurors were undoubtedly able to empathize with the situation of the police. Similarly, the jury in the O.J. Simpson case could be expected to have known, either as a result of personal experience or that of friends and relatives, what it meant to be a black man who was the target of an investigation by white police. Both juries could be expected to identify with the defendants, but not so much with the victims or their families, who were of a different race. In contrast, the predominantly white jury in Simpson's civil suit may have been better able to empathize with the white victims than with the black defendant who claimed to have been the victim of police racism. None of these juries, however, could be said to be heterogeneous in its racial and ethnic balance.

By definition a jury composed exclusively of a defendant's peers will be homogeneous and unrepresentative. If the goal is a heterogenous jury, then the concept of peers may have no place. A possible compromise would be to seek a jury which contains some members whom the defendant would count as peers. This would have the advantage of giving expression to the defendant's perspective of events, but not to the exclusion of all other points of view. If unanimity were also to be required, then those who shared the defendant's perspective could not be ignored; they would have to be convinced.

Proportional Representation

Even in the case of a heterogeneous community, the randomness of random selection can generate an unrepresentative jury. If the black population of a community is 25 per cent, the most likely number of blacks on the jury will be three, but two or four will be only slightly less common. In a small percentage of cases there could be as many as six (or more) or as few as none. All this is consistent with mathematical theory. However, theory will inevitably be distorted by the politics of jury selection. Disqualifications, exemptions, excusals, challenges for cause, and, in the United States, peremptory challenges, will cause the composition of the jury to deviate, sometimes markedly, from that predicted by pure probability.

Judicial decisions which have addressed the composition of the jury have been concerned primarily with the deliberate or systematic exclusion of various groups from service. If an imbalance in the jury is caused by the luck of the draw, the courts will not intervene. But from the perspective of the black defendant who is tried by an all-white jury, it matters little that the jury is the result of random selection or the product of cynical design. The disadvantage is exactly the same. The legal effect, on the other hand, is not. The American courts will find a constitutional violation if state officials have acted improperly, but will do nothing if the segregated jury is the result of chance. The same is true in Great Britain.[4] The obsession in both countries is with process rather than product.

The nature of the problem is illustrated by *United States* v. *Nururdin*.[5] The accused, who was black, lived in an inner-city neighbourhood. He was tried by an all-white jury generated by random selection. He argued that suburban whites could have little appreciation of inner-city life or the relationship between white Chicago police and black community residents. Sociologically, his point was well taken. As a matter of law, it was irrelevant, and the court rejected it. The result was consistent with those Supreme Court pronouncements to the effect that a defendant has no right to have members of his or her race included on the jury.

Let us assume for the sake of argument that the goal is a jury which is representative of society. How might the legal system go about achieving such a jury? One possible solution might be thought to lie in some form of proportional representation. There would, however, be immense practical problems. How would one go about the task of selecting such a jury? Would there be separate pools of black jurors? Hispanic jurors? Catholic jurors? Jewish jurors? Young jurors? Old jurors? Male jurors? Female jurors? Homosexual jurors? The list would be endless. Moreover, on how many lists would a person with multiple defining characteristics – such as a young, black, unemployed, female Catholic – appear? If more than one, then the democratic requirement of political equality in jury selection will have to be set aside. Proportional representation may make sense in a legislature of several hundred members, where accommodation of each group receiving a minimum number of votes in an election is feasible because of the large number of spaces available. But there are so many distinctive groups in most societies that having all of them represented on a jury of twelve would be a physical impossibility, even granted that any given juror would probably be a member of more than one constituency. Expanding the size of the jury would help to overcome this difficulty,[6] but at a cost which would be both economic (more jurors to be paid) and functional (the larger the jury, the more unwieldy its deliberations).

An alternative approach would be for a court to intervene only when random selection has failed to produce a jury which roughly reflected the demographic make-up of the community, or which failed to include a juror who shared the defendant's most salient characteristics. Assume, for example, that a randomly selected jury contained no blacks, although the community itself was racially mixed or the defendant was black. The judge would then seek out black jurors to rectify the imbalance. This was in fact the proposal submitted to the Court of Appeal in *R.* v. *Ford*.[7] The Court, while acknowledging a trial judge's residual discretion to dismiss a juror who should not be serving, rejected the defendant's claim for a more racially balanced jury. To achieve such a jury when it was not produced by random selection would require the trial judge to replace one competent juror with another of a different race. This the trial judge had no authority to do, the judge's discretion being limited to the discharge of incompetent jurors. If the court were to go further and dismiss a qualified juror in order to make room for one of a different race or religion, it would unfairly impugn the integrity of the juror who was dismissed.

The debate was joined in 1993 by the Royal Commission on Criminal Justice (Runciman Committee, 1993). It recommended allowing both the prosecution and defence to apply for a multi-racial jury in cases which had a racial dimension to them and where it was unlikely that an all-white jury would be able to provide a fair trial. This proposal, however, has not been taken on board by either parliament or the judiciary. It is not without its conceptual difficulties. What would be the role of the minority jurors in such a scheme? In an election, where candidates run for office on a platform endorsed by a political party, it is reasonable to assume that votes for candidates of a particular party represent support for the party's platform. Thus if seats in the legislature were to be allocated based on the percentage of votes which the party receives, it would not be unreasonable to expect its delegates to vote in accord with the party's official position. The situation of jurors, however, is altogether different. One does not run for jury service nor do jurors have platforms to which they have made a public commitment. A juror will inevitably be of a particular race, religion, gender and ethnic background, but it would be inaccurate to equate these characteristics with a political or philosophical agenda. Can it be automatically assumed that a black juror will reflect a 'black viewpoint'? Indeed, is there such a thing as a 'black viewpoint'? The very idea smacks of the stereotyped thinking that underlies most prejudices. Even if, as a matter of statistical probability, a member of a particular racial or ethnic group might be more likely than other members of the population to hold to a certain set of beliefs and values, there would be innumerable exceptions. When dealing with such small numbers as the one or two minority members of a jury, statistical probabilities count for little. All that matters is the perspective of the particular jurors selected to serve. The views of these individuals may or may not accord with those of the group to which they belong.

Theoretical and practical objections combine. For proportional representation to function effectively in the jury context, jurors would have to be selected because they embodied the predominant values of the constituency to which they were deemed to be members. A battery of tests would be necessary: first, to ascertain the views of that constituency; and second, to determine whether a prospective juror subscribed to those views. Alternatively, a juror, regardless of personal belief, could be charged with representing the views of the constituency of which the juror was deemed to belong. However, a juror who did not share the opinions of that constituency might well not be an effective advocate for the constituency. All this assumes, of course, that the group in question had a firm opinion on the issues raised by the case, and that the juror was familiar with that opinion. Neither of these assumptions is necessarily true in practice. Often the critical issues which ultimately emerge in a criminal trial cannot be anticipated.

Even if a juror had insight into the position of the group of which the juror was deemed to be a member, there would remain the bothersome question of whether the juror should vote in the way that the group would prefer in circumstances where that would conflict with the juror's conscience. The juror who did not agree with the views of the group would be faced with an inherently unappetizing trilemma. The juror could support the position of the group contrary to his or her own personal beliefs and suffer the inevitable psychological ambivalence in so doing. Alternatively, the juror could vote in accord with the dictates of his or her conscience, in effect disenfranchizing the group from the slot that had been allocated to it. The third option would be for the juror to espouse the position of the group during deliberations, but vote in accord with conscience when it came to the verdict. A persuasive juror might sometimes find the other members of the jury convinced by a position that held no personal appeal. None of these alternatives is particularly attractive. The tension is created by the conflict between the demands of representative democracy and the jury's responsibility to see that justice is done in the individual case. Proportional representation, while perhaps ensuring a diverse and heterogeneous jury, would exacerbate that tension to breaking-point.

Democracy's Threat to Justice

In Chapter 1 an analogy was drawn between jurors and the members of Rawls' 'original position' (see pp. 20–21). Both groups are brought together to decide questions of justice. Both are provided an environment free of distraction in which to conduct their deliberations and are shielded from outsiders who might improperly attempt to influence them. Each is advantageously placed to reach an *informed* decision – those in the original position because its members apparently know all they need to know to reach a decision, and the jury, because it has been presented with the testimony of the witnesses, the opposing theories of counsel, and the legal directions of the court. Both benefit from the synergism and dialectics of the deliberation process.

There are, on the other hand, differences between the jurors and members of Rawls' original position, most notably the fact that real-life jurors are not insulated by a 'veil of ignorance'. They are aware of their race, sex and individual characteristics and are capable of appreciating the impact that their decisions may have upon their lives. The values, attitudes and experiences of a lifetime are not likely to be erased or even suspended when a citizen enters the jury box. The critical question is whether such influences will enhance or detract from the jury's search for justice.

The danger of prejudice cannot be ignored. A juror's life experiences can leave a deposit of irrational biases which may affect the juror's reaction to the witnesses and their testimony, and predispose the juror to reject certain types of arguments. The juror with a deeply religious upbringing, for example, may feel an instinctive revulsion towards the doctor charged with committing an illegal abortion, although the doctor may have acted in order to save the mother's life. Even if this constitutes a defence in the jurisdiction, the juror may resist it. The effect of a juror's biases may carry over to the deliberations and may lead to the rejection of opinions not because of their merits but because of their source. A juror who is racially prejudiced may discredit not only the testimony of witnesses of the disfavoured race but also the analysis of jurors who are of that race.

There are several ways of dealing with the dangers of prejudice. One would be to take greater care to remove biased jurors from the panel. For Britain, this would require a far more active screening programme along the lines of that which already takes place in American courts. An alternative approach would be to sensitize jurors so that they would be aware of their biases and be better able to resist them. Both of these options will be examined more closely in Chapter 6. For now, I wish to consider two other possibilities. One is the default position of doing nothing – of allowing jurors to give free rein to their prejudices in the jury room. The other is to channel juror biases in such a way that they will serve a constructive purpose.

It might prove useful to begin by sketching the current attitude of the British and American legal systems to the issue of juror screening (a more in-depth analysis will be presented in Chapter 6). In Britain courts do not actively seek to discover whether jurors are biased. Barristers are not allowed to investigate or question prospective jurors.[8] Nor are the judges receptive to evidence that prejudice has infected the deliberations; the general rule is that jurors are prohibited from impeaching their verdict.[9] The issue of bias thus never surfaces. Like ostriches, the judges bury their heads in the sand and pretend that a randomly selected jury is an impartial jury, at the same time closing their minds to all psychological, sociological or empirical evidence to the contrary.

In contrast, the American judiciary accepts that prospective jurors may be biased and often goes overboard in the attempt to ferret out biased jurors. Lawyers may both investigate and question prospective jurors. The process of questioning jurors – *voir dire* – can last longer than the trial itself. Even then, the courts implicitly recognize that whichever jurors are selected to hear the case will be prejudiced in some way or another. Being human means having prejudices. However, it is envisaged (rationalized?) that these prejudices will not only not interfere with the deliberations, but will advance the deliberations in a constructive way. What the courts seem to have in mind is a process where conflicting biases play off against each other and lead the jurors to a fair and impartial verdict.

Taylor v. *Louisiana*[10] was the first US Supreme Court decision to find a *constitutional* right to a jury drawn from a fair cross-section of the community. In the course of its opinion the Court alluded to the political function of the jury. Referring to the Federal Jury Selection and Service Act of 1968, Justice Byron White observed:

> In passing this legislation, the Committee Reports of both the House and the Senate recognized that the jury plays a political function in the administration of the law. ...[11]

But what is that political function? Is it – as arguably it is in the case of a legislator – to represent the views of a constituency? To be fair to Justice White, he probably had a different political function in mind. Elsewhere in his opinion, he referred to the need to preserve public confidence in the jury system. As the jury is the state's chosen decision-maker in serious criminal cases, public confidence in the jury is essential to public confidence in the criminal justice system. The perception that certain segments of the community have been excluded from jury service erodes confidence in the jury's verdict, particularly among the group which sees itself to have been excluded. There will be the inevitable suspicion that some invidious reason underlies the exclusions. Conversely, the inclusion of members of the defendant's race and ethnicity will help to allay such suspicions. The minority members of the jury are present not as mere observers, but as full participants. They are able to advance arguments, put forward perspectives and contribute to the deliberations. That they also have a vote in the final verdict ensures that their views cannot be ignored – at least where a unanimous verdict is required.

It is in this way that the ideal of a multi-cultural, multi-racial, sexually integrated jury is thought to inspire public confidence. It legitimates the jury's verdict, whether or not that legitimacy is deserved. In the past the jury used to attest that its verdict was 'the verdict of us all'. The 'all' referred to the 12 members of the jury. Nowadays the 'all' might be said to refer, symbolically, to all segments of the community. This use of the jury, however, is somewhat troubling to the extent that it appears to exalt from over substance and to place the appearance of fairness and justice above its actuality.

Decisions of the Supreme Court on the subject of the peremptory challenge (discussed in the preceding chapter) carry further the idea that diversity on the jury is prized for reasons other than what it might contribute to the achievement of justice. Peremptory challenges permit a party to excuse a limited number of prospective jurors without having to state reasons why they should not serve. As a result, an accused can remove persons who are suspected of being biased, but whose bias is not sufficiently obvious to justify a challenge for cause. Part of the purpose of allowing peremptory challenges is to promote the *accused's* good opinion of the jury (Blackstone, 1765). A defendant is more likely to accept the verdict of a jury in whose selection he was allowed to participate than that of one perceived to have been imposed on him. On the other hand, the exercise of peremptory challenges, particularly against members of an identifiable segment of the community, will detract from the representativeness of the jury and may reduce the public's confidence in its verdict.

The fate of the peremptory challenge thus became linked to the question of whether priority should be given to preserving the democratic character of the jury or to preventing potential bias from obstructing the achievement of justice. In Great Britain the response could not have been more unequivocal – parliament abolished the peremptory challenge.[12] An accused can still challenge jurors for cause, but without the opportunity to question prospective jurors which is available to American lawyers, the ability of a barrister both to detect and to establish bias are severely limited. Unless the barrister or the defendant is aware of a reason for suspecting a juror's impartiality, or the juror volunteers such information, the juror will be permitted to sit. The resulting jury may be more democratic, in that it is the undiluted product of random selection, but whether or not its members are biased is virtually impossible to determine.

Although the peremptory challenge has yet to be abolished in the United States, the judiciary's indulgent attitude towards it appears to be changing. Supreme Court decisions beginning with *Batson* v. *Kentucky*[13] signalled that the courts are prepared to interfere with its exercise if to do so would lead to a more democratically composed jury. In *Batson* and its progeny the Supreme Court indicated that neither the prosecution nor the defence may use its peremptory challenges to strike a class of jurors on the assumption that members of that class cannot be impartial in the particular case before the court. What was once an unfettered right of a party to excuse jurors was converted into a judicially controlled prerogative. The defendant's good opinion of the jury which decided his or her fate was subordinated to the public's good opinion of the non-discriminatory nature of the state's criminal justice system.

After a *prima facie* showing of discrimination in the exercise of a party's peremptory challenges has been made, the party alleged to have engaged in the discrimination has the burden of proffering a neutral explanation for the challenges.[14] This stands the theory of the peremptory challenge on its head. The original idea was to allow a defendant to excuse jurors without needing to give any reasons. It was sufficient that bias was suspected, and even this did not have to be stated in open court. Post-*Batson* peremptory challenges, in contrast, may have to be explained and justified on a public record. In theory the justification need not rise to the level required for a challenge for cause, but in practice there may be little difference. At best the peremptory challenge has been converted into a watered-down version of the challenge for cause.

There is a hidden danger here. Often it is not easy to demonstrate that a juror is biased. It is not a character trait that will be readily admitted. Intensive questioning may be required in order to elicit statements that will at best give rise to an inference of bias. However, unless questioning of jurors (as permitted in the United States but not Britain) is combined with the right of peremptory challenge, it loses much of its efficacy. Most judges, not wishing to be seen to be questioning a juror's truthfulness, are disinclined to excuse jurors for cause where the juror has asserted the ability to be impartial. In fact, however, jurors are often less than candid. Those who wish to be on a jury in order to vent their prejudices may be the last to admit to them when questioned. Others may believe that they are capable of rising above their prejudices and see no need to make a public admission of their shortcomings. Where a juror's biases are on a subconscious level, such that the jury may not even be aware of them, the lawyer may have to resort to a series of highly probing questions. Such questioning, however, risks antagonising the juror. A lawyer may be prepared to accept this risk as long as the fallback of a peremptory challenge remains available. The lawyer who judges that the questioning has alienated a juror may then excuse the juror by means of a peremptory challenge. However, if there is a possibility that the peremptory challenge will be rejected, the lawyer will have to think twice before potentially disadvantaging the client by aggressive questioning.

In *Batson* and its progeny the Supreme Court seemed to be more preoccupied with preserving the racial, ethnic and gender diversity of the jury than with the danger posed by biased jurors. Perhaps the Justices believed that any bias which might be brought to the jury room by any individual juror would be offset by the biases of the other jurors. What the Court had previously referred to as a 'diffused impartiality'[15] would insulate the fairness of the deliberations. How this is to come about will be explored subsequently but the concern here is with the inferences that might be drawn from a selection process where jurors are challenged, excluded and sometimes reinstated because of their race, gender or ethnicity. If jurors perceive that they owe their place on the jury to the group to which they belong, might not they reason that it is their duty to represent the views of that group (Van Dyke, 1977; Abramson, 1994)?

Conscience versus Constituency

There are two visions of the proper relationship between the jury and the community which seem to be competing with each other. One holds that because it would be impractical for the community as a whole to adjudicate every legal dispute, the jurors are its representatives. It follows that if the jurors fail to reflect the views of that part of the community which is their natural constituency, then the perspectives of that constituency may not receive an airing, in which case the verdict cannot be said to be that of the community as a whole. The competing vision acclaims the jury as the conscience of the community. It is through each juror's exercising an independence of judgement that the jury fulfils this community conscience role. The intriguing question is whether these two visions of the jury's role are compatible.

An analogy might be drawn to the position of the legislator. Do legislators owe an allegiance to their constituents or their conscience? The fact that a legislator is popularly elected might suggest an obligation to the voters. However, the electorate may have voted in the way that it did because they saw in the candidate a higher intellect that could be brought to bear on complex problems. In these circumstances, for the candidate, once elected, simply to parrot the views of the constituency would be to lose the benefit of the legislator's presumed superior abilities (Mill, 1861). In addition, the assertion that a legislator should reflect the views of the constituency assumes not only that the constituents are as capable as their legislator, but as informed. Few members of the public, however, enjoy the luxury of being able to investigate the merits of pending legislation. In any event, capturing the mood of the constituency, even if a legislator were to be so inclined, is problematic, particularly since on controversial issues the public is rarely of one mind. Accepting as reflective of public opinion the views of the vocal minority who make personal contact may be misleading, and opinion polls tend to measure spontaneous reactions which cannot be equated with reflective and considered judgements. Nor is strength of feeling usually captured in an opinion poll. Public opinion is also elusive because it is often in a state of flux, and an opinion poll provides only a snapshot of it at a particular moment in time.

All of the above considerations argue in favour of a legislator exercising an independence of judgement. It is, moreover, not as if the legislator is totally unrestrained. Party manifestos and election commitments cannot be ignored entirely, and there will eventually be another election at which the legislator who repeatedly fails to represent the views of his or her constituents may be voted out of office. Considerations of practical politics thus exert a moderating influence on independent judgement.

But what of the jurors? They have made no advance commitments to any constituency. They are not under the restraining influence of a political party. There is no indebtedness to voters who elected them, and no future election to hold them to account. No legal or practical constraints intrude on their independence. Their sole duty is to their office as juror. Strengthening the case for jurors exercising an independence of judgement is the fact that the public is even less likely to be knowledgeable of the facts giving rise to a criminal prosecution than it is of the background to a legislative bill. While polls purporting to measure the public's attitude towards pending legislation may proliferate, rarely is a poll taken regarding a prospective defendant's guilt or innocence (the high-profile case, such as that of O.J. Simpson, being the exception). Thus it is extremely difficult for jurors to have insight into the views of their 'constituents' before they hear the evidence, even if they had an interest in discovering these views. After the trial has begun, the judge will instruct the jurors that they are not to discuss the case with members of the public.

Although, unlike legislators, jurors may not be selected because of their superior intellectual abilities, like legislators they are well placed to exercise an informed independence of judgement. Indeed, jurors may be in a better position to do so than legislators. Although legislators may hold hearings in which they receive testimony, not all those who might be able to make a relevant contribution will be afforded the opportunity to appear. Time constraints may restrict the length of the hearing and the selection of witnesses may lie within the control of the party which has the most members on the committee. In a jury trial, by contrast, the choice of witnesses is left to the opposing parties. Neither side may exercise an arbitrary veto on who can testify for the other, and each side can be counted on to present all evidence that supports its case. There are no comparable time constraints to those facing the legislators. Even though a jury may receive a fuller picture than a legislative committee, both are in a superior position to make an informed decision than members of the public, who may have not had any exposure to the relevant evidence. For this reason jurors or legislators who vote according to the perceived views of a constituency do their constituents a disservice.

The Primacy of Justice

In the United States, the confusion as to whether the jurors owe a duty to conscience or constituency has been exacerbated by decisions of the US Supreme Court. In most criminal cases the courts are concerned with whether the accused has received a fair trial. The jury selection cases are the exception. Here the courts are also concerned with the rights of those who have been improperly excluded from service. In *Carter* v. *Jury Commission*[16] and *Turner* v. *Fouche*[17] none of the appellants had themselves even been the object of a criminal prosecution. These class action claims were filed on behalf of black citizens who had allegedly been excluded from jury service. The Supreme Court not only heard the cases but held that the appellants' constitutional rights had been violated. In decisions such as these a democratically composed jury becomes not a means to a fair trial but an end in itself.

While it will be subsequently argued that democratic juries promote the search for justice, let us assume, for the sake of argument, that this was not the case. If the courts had to choose between justice and democracy on the jury, which should take precedence? In establishing his principles of justice, Rawls espouses a serial or lexical ordering in which liberty takes precedence (Rawls, 1972, pp. 5-11). Much as one might desire to be economically well-off, it is more important to be in a position to determine one's own plan of life. Without liberty a rational life plan would be impossible. However, each person's liberty is circumscribed in that he or she may not unduly infringe on the liberty of others. Whether or not a defendant has impinged on the liberty of another in an impermissible way is what is at issue in a criminal trial. In that trial the defendant's liberty is at stake. Issues of liberty are paramount and cannot be allowed to take a back seat to issues of political ideology. Kant (1959) makes the telling point that persons should be treated as ends in themselves and not as a means to an end. A criminal defendant whose freedom is at stake in a criminal trial should not be used as a means of promoting democracy within society at large.

The hierarchical ordering that subordinates democracy to justice can also be seen in jury selection. The logic of democracy would argue in favour of seating jurors irrationally prejudiced against an accused to the extent such prejudice existed within society. Yet jurors are required to be impartial and those who are not may be challenged for cause. Even the appearance of partiality may justify a challenge. Thus, for instance, jurors who are distantly related to a party, lawyer or witness in a case may be excused even though the relationship would have had no bearing on their verdict. Some American courts are prepared to accept challenges based on what might be called generic biases. To return to an example used previously, a juror's strong religious beliefs might lead to a challenge for cause where a doctor is prosecuted for committing an illegal abortion. To strike for cause all of those who are opposed to abortion on religious grounds may exclude a significant segment of the population which would clearly be entitled to a vote if a referendum were to be held on the issue of abortion. The absence of this vein of opinion will arguably detract from the democratic character of the jury. Nevertheless, it is felt in such cases that democracy must take a back seat to the fairness to the accused.

It has already been noted that a court may order a change in venue when prejudice threatens the fairness of the trial. In these instances, the defendant's interest in a fair trial takes precedence over the democratic interest in local jurors. Justice must be seen to be done, and if there is reason to believe that a community would be biased, a change in venue may be ordered even without proof of bias. In *Rideau* v. *Louisiana*,[18] where the defendant's confession had been broadcast repeatedly on local television, the US Supreme Court held that the trial judge had erred in refusing to grant the defendant's motion for a change in venue. The Justices declined to examine a transcript of the *voir dire* in order to determine if any juror's impartiality had been compromised. According to the Court, '[d]ue process of law ... requires a trial before a jury drawn from a community of people who had not seen and heard Rideau's televised interview'.[19]

Democracy and justice clash in a different way when a defendant seeks not to escape from local prejudice but to benefit from it. Consider the trial of defendants charged with crimes of violence against blacks in a community where racial prejudice is rampant. The defendants, rather than having on interest in seeking a change in venue, count on local prejudice against the victims to lead to their acquittal. Such cases raise the question of whether the *prosecution* should be allowed to seek a change in venue. The sixth amendment to the US Constitution grants an accused, but not the government, the right to a jury of the 'district wherein the crime shall have been committed'.[20] Part of the rationale behind the constitutional mandate is to allow community values to be brought to bear on the decision-making process. But what if the community values are themselves rooted in prejudice? The problem lies in a conception of community that takes account of the interests of the defendants but not those of the victims.

Few would consider it just if a blatantly racist jury were to be allowed to decide the guilt of racist defendants. There is a strong argument in such cases for granting a change in venue, even though it would be at the expense of local decision-making. The Federal Rules of Criminal Procedure in fact allow a judge to order a change in venue 'in the interest of justice'.[21] Unlike the Constitution, the federal rule does not distinguish between defence and prosecution. This solution, however, does nothing to reconcile the tension between democratic values and the demands of justice. The clearly preferable approach would be to rid the jury of prejudice. This might be achieved through better screening of prospective jurors, as well as pre-trial training of jury members (see Chapter 6). More frank discussion by the trial court of both the dangers of prejudice and the demands of justice would also help.

These adjustments to the democratic composition of the jury highlight a crucial difference between voting in an election and serving on a jury. In an election a citizen is free to vote in any way he or she chooses. If a voter refuses to support a candidate because of the candidate's race or sex, we may condemn the voter as crass or misguided, but there would be no denying the right to make that choice. In an election people are free to vote not only according to their preferences but also their prejudices. In a criminal trial, on the other hand, the liberty of the accused hangs in the balance. The jury has an obligation to protect the defendant against an unjust conviction and there can be no place for jurors voting according to their prejudices.

A Balancing of Biases

Justice, it has been argued, must take priority over democracy. It does not follow, however, that a democratically selected and representative jury need be incompatible with justice. On the contrary, hopefully, one would promote the other. A democratically composed jury does, as we have seen, lend an aura of legitimacy to the verdict by certifying that it represents the judgement of all sectors of the community. This legitimization function is not to be lightly dismissed, but it is of secondary importance. It is more critical that the verdict is, in fact, just.

One of the previously discussed advantages of a democratic jury lies in its ability to combat prejudice. At a minimum a jury, composed of men and women, of different races and from different ethnic backgrounds, is likely to inhibit expressions of racism and sexism. Individuals who might use offensive racial and sexual language among those whom they see as kindred spirits will be more inclined to restrain themselves when members of the target group are present. Although the suppression of such speech will no doubt contribute a more civilized tone to the deliberations, the victory will be pyhrric if the underlying biases remain. A more meaningful way in which a heterogeneous jury can combat prejudice is by exposing the myth behind the stereotype. Listening to a cogent, well constructed argument by a black juror, for instance, may do more to dispel a myth of racial inferiority than any number of sociological tracts.[22]

One sometimes gets the impression that there are those who believe that there is a moral superiority to a jury composed of minorities and women who have themselves been the victims of discrimination, that such persons will be more principled and unprejudiced as a result of their own experience. The reasoning that leads to this conclusion is not usually articulated. Those who engage in 'scientific' jury selection (see Chapter 6) are inclined to presume the opposite, and probably with more cause. Human beings are not saints. It would certainly not be surprising to find that a lifetime of being discriminated against leads to a distrust of those who are of the same background as the perceived oppressors. This common sense dictate underlay the jury selection strategy in the O.J. Simpson criminal case. The defence south a predominantly black jury because it envisaged that such a jury would be a particularly receptive audience to the implicit charges of racism that were to be levelled against the investigating police officers. Many of the jurors were likely to have personally experienced discrimination at the hands of the police. This is not to say that the investigation in the Simpson case was, or was not, corrupted by prejudice, but only that the jurors may have been predisposed by their own experiences to believe that it had been. The point is that minority jurors, far from being free of prejudice, are likely to bring to the jury their own distinctive strain of the virus.

A different premise, however, may underlie the relevant judicial decisions. It is that, regardless of whether or not the legal system is able to eliminate the prejudices of individual jurors, it may be able to control the prejudice of the jury as an institutional entity by including on it individuals with a broad range of biases. The various biases of the jurors will combine to produce what the US Supreme Court has referred to as a 'diffused impartiality'.[23] The Court, unfortunately, has neither explained what it meant by this term nor been explicit about the process which it sees at work. The California Supreme Court in *People* v. *Wheeler*[24] was more forthcoming:

> [T]he only practical way to achieve an overall impartiality is to encourage the representation of a variety of ... groups on the jury so that the respective biases of their members, to the extent they are antagonistic, will tend to cancel each other out.[25]

Is there any logical or psychological basis for assuming that this cancellation effect will take place? Perhaps the California judges envisaged a process along the following lines. On a jury on which there is a wide range of prejudices, no subset of jurors will be so numerous or powerful that it will be able to impose its biases on another subset which does not share those biases. It will soon become apparent that maintaining antagonistic positions rooted in prejudice will lead only to a stalemate that is not in the jury's interest. The jurors have a job to do – to reach a verdict in the case – and squabbling over prejudices will only serve to deflect them from that goal. The jurors will therefore recognize that it is in their collective interest to lay their prejudices to one side and deal with the case on its merits. Prejudices are thus not so much cancelled as neutralized, with individual agendas being displaced by collective goals.

There are several fragile points in this analysis. First, there is the assumption that each subgroup will recognize its biases. Although most people are quick to see the prejudice in others, they find it harder to see the bias in themselves. Indeed, they may honestly believe that they are unbiased. In the minds of such jurors there is no prejudice for them to agree to set aside. At the same time, the biases of one group of jurors about another may make each suspicious of proposals from the other to lay bias to one side and get on with the task at hand. A second fragile point in the analysis is the assumption that biases can in fact be set to one side. Some jurors may be capable of this, but others may not. For a cancellation effect to occur, the conflicting biases may have to be of roughly comparable strength. When they are not, those whose biases are less strongly held may be willing to put aside their biases while those whose biases run more deep may not. Jurors who are prepared to decide the case on its merits will be sabotaged by those who cling to their prejudices. A third questionable assumption is that the jurors will prefer a consensus verdict to stalemate. Sometimes a stalemate is seen by one faction or the other as the 'best possible result' under the circumstances. A minority of jurors whose arguments for acquittal are grounded in prejudice against the victim may prefer a breakdown in deliberations to a conviction. In these circumstances, deadlock is at least a short-term victory for the defendant who is able to avoid prison, and the prosecution may decide not to pursue a retrial. Conversely, those who favour a conviction because of an irrational prejudice against the defendant may take a sadistic pleasure in seeing the defendant agonize under the Damoclean sword of a potential retrial. Thus a minority may see it as being in their interest to deadlock the jury. It might be recalled that it was largely to foil the efforts of just such a minority that the requirement of a unanimous verdict was watered down.

The Dynamics of the Democratic Jury

A democratically selected jury may or may not neutralize juror biases. To the extent that it does, it is less the product of a cancellation of biases and more the result of exposure to people from different backgrounds and with different perspectives. When people from similar backgrounds, with similar prejudices, are brought together on a jury, they reinforce each other's prejudices. Racial and ethnic stereotypes will go unchallenged because the same stereotypes will be subscribed to by all. On a heterogeneous jury, in contrast, jurors will challenge each other's biases. Irrational biases yield not because they are cancelled by equally irrational biases but because their falsity is exposed through dialogue and debate.

A heterogenous jury will also produce the synergism which leads to a case being considered from a multiplicity of perspectives. Ultimately, a jury has to construct a coherent account of events that accords with the evidence and their own common-sense understandings about how human beings behave. Reasoning on a jury often proceeds by analogy. Jurors submit other real-life factual situations of which they are aware and against which the facts of the case can be compared. These analogies may be drawn from the jurors' personal experience or their knowledge of the experience of others. Empirical research has revealed that jurors spend nearly 25 per cent of their time discussing personal experiences (James, 1959). These experiences provide the interpretative filter through which the jurors give meaning to the facts of the case.

Sometimes one member of the jury will contribute an insight that might not otherwise have been available. Such an example occurred in a California trial of a black defendant who had been arrested on York Boulevard in the early morning. A black juror reflected:

> It seemed like the only reason that the defendant [was charged] was that someone in the gas station across the street looking out into the light in the dark could identify the run-of-the-mill black man from 90 to 100 feet away. They arrested him in the area of York Boulevard ... I was raised and born in Los Angeles so it

> is nothing new to me. If you are black and you're on York Boulevard at four o'clock in the morning, they are going to pick you up. They will pick me up on York Boulevard walking at four o'clock in the morning. This was the only thing that they seemed to have against the man, so we acquitted him. (Davis, 1973, pp. 112–13)

If there had not been a juror familiar with the relationship between police and blacks in the neighbourhood, the nature of the confrontation might not have been appreciated. What might have passed as a routine arrest based on probable cause was placed in the context of an ongoing tension between the police and the black community. This is not to say that the juror was correct or incorrect in his analysis, but rather that the other jurors were exposed to an altogether different way of looking at the facts. The minority juror was not needed to cancel or counteract potential racial prejudice on the part of the other jurors as much as to provide a perspective which might not otherwise have been considered.

This case might be compared with that of *The People* v. *Young Beartracks*, reported by David Swett (1969). Witnesses testified that the black defendant had killed the victim after the latter had put him 'in the dozens'. None of the witnesses, however, was able to state with precision what they meant by this slang expression. Among the defendant's peer group it apparently referred to an extreme form of verbal harassment, so extreme that it might well have put the defendant in fear for his safety. Whether such knowledge would have made a difference to the all-white jury's willingness to accept the defendant's claim of self-defence is hard to tell. What was clear was that the absence of a minority juror created a cultural and linguistic vacuum that prevented the jury from fully understanding the nature of the confrontation between the defendant and his victim.

The same breadth of perspective is gained by having both men and women on juries. In certain types of cases, such as those involving domestic violence and child abuse, it can be expected that women will have a unique perspective to offer. Likewise, in other cases, such as those involving violence on a sports pitch or in a bar, men may better understand the contextual ground rules. In these cases the views of one group or the other may be entitled to particular weight. Even in such cases, however, the views of the other sex will lend a balance to the analysis. In *Ballard* v. *United States*[26] Supreme Court Justice William O. Douglas stated:

> It is said ... that an all male panel drawn from the various groups within a community will be as truly representative as if women were included. The thought is that the factors which tend to influence the action of women are the same as those which influence the action of men – personality, background, economic status – and not sex. Yet it is not enough to say that women where

> sitting as jurors neither act nor tend to act as a class. Men likewise do not act as a class. But if the shoe were on the other foot, who would claim that a jury was truly representative of the community if all men were intentionally and systematically excluded from the panel? The truth is that the two sexes are not fungible; a community made up exclusively of one is different from a community composed of both; the subtle interplay of influence one on the other is among the imponderables. To insulate the courtroom from either may not in a given case make an iota of difference. Yet a flavor, a distinct quality is lost if either sex is excluded.[27]

Justice Douglas was unable to pinpoint the precise differences that a sexually integrated jury would make, while nonetheless asserting his belief that it would make a difference. The 'subtle interplay' between the two genders of which he speaks may be another way of describing the dynamics of jury deliberations. Men and women may not interpret the same events in the same way. Gilligan (1982) asserts that women tend to emphasize relationships and the psychosocial dimensions of conduct, whereas men are more likely to think in terms of abstract rules and rights (see also Dooley, 1991). Women also may be more willing to trust in their feelings, while men tend to prefer a logical analysis. This is not to say that all women are illogical or incapable of being rationale, or that all men are insensitive to feelings and emotions. Without conceding the truth of these broad-brush generalizations, the point is this: it is the synthesis of the two perspectives which produces the more complete and superior analysis.

Both British and American courts have held, as was discussed in Chapter 4, that a defendant has no legal right to have a member of his race or ethnic background on the jury. The various illustrations presented here, however, indicate that there can be advantages in having on the jury a person with a similar background to that of the accused; in other words, a true 'peer' of the defendant. These advantages were recognized at an early stage of jury history, when mixed juries (juries *de medietate linguae*), half composed of countrymen of the defendant, were convened in cases where the defendant was a foreigner (Larue, 1976). The purpose was to protect the defendant against possible prejudice. The implicit assumption of prejudice, however, proved incompatible with the self-image of a maturing democracy, and eventually the jury *de medietate linguae* was discarded. However, the advantage in bringing to the deliberations perspectives that might not otherwise have been considered may not have been given its due. This benefit may have been worth preserving, even if not in the crude form of the jury *de medietate linguae*. Of course, it may not always be possible to include a member of the defendant's peer group but, when the opportunity presents itself, a trial judge should not be disposed to excuse the individual in question. That juror, more than the lawyers or the witnesses, is likely to be the person best able to put the defendant's actions into perspective.

Nor should it be assumed that a peer of the defendant will automatically support an acquittal. The juror may reveal that the defendant's conduct was unacceptable among their common peer group, and that any statements to the contrary are disingenuous. Certainly, there is the risk that a juror who identifies too strongly with an accused may be irrationally biased in his or her favour as well as the danger that a juror from the same neighbourhood as the accused and with common acquaintances may feel under pressure to vote for an acquittal in order not to incur the ire of the defendant's friends and family. These factors must not be ignored but instead balanced against the contribution that the juror can make. The answer will lie not in an unbending rejection of such jurors, but in ensuring that any and all jurors, including those who fall into this category, are impartial. Impartiality will be discussed further in Chapter 6.

Instead of one juror providing a core insight that cuts to the heart of the matter, more commonly different members of the jury will make contributions that bring different aspects of the case into clearer focus. The jurors collectively may be able to appreciate subtleties that may have escaped any given individual juror's attention. Two jurors may have each noticed a peculiar facet of the case but it may take a third, who noticed neither, to appreciate the significance of the two observations taken together. The perspectives of jurors from different backgrounds combine to expand and enrich the quality of the deliberations. A group of jurors representative of a cross-section of society will contribute the greatest number of perspectives which might shed light on the resolution of the case at hand. US Supreme Court Justice Thurgood Marshall arrived at the same point but from the opposite direction:

> When any large and identifiable segment of the community is excluded from jury service, the effect is to remove from the jury room qualities of human nature and varieties of human experience, the range of which is unknown and perhaps unknowable. It is not necessary to assume that the excluded group will consistently vote as a class in order to conclude, as we do, that their exclusion deprives the jury of a perspective on human events that may have unsuspected importance in any case that may be presented.[28]

The point might be reinforced by considering a superficially attractive alternative to a democratic jury – a jury composed of society's most able citizens, who could be counted upon to bring a high degree of competence to their task. Indeed, a select group of specially qualified experts might be seen as a suitable compromise between a panel of law-trained but case-hardened judges and a jury of ignorant amateurs. An elite jury would appear particularly valuable in cases that raised issues requiring a background or expertise in a specific field. So, for instance, a jury of psychiatrists might be impanelled to evaluate an insanity defence, and a jury of financial experts to unravel a case of complex fraud. Such specialist juries have a long pedigree, from the medieval London juries of cooks and fishmongers convened to try those charged with selling adulterated food (Cornish, 1968, p. 33) to the blue ribbon panels approved by the US Supreme Court in *Fay* v. *New York.*[29] In more recent times, however, specialist juries have fallen into disfavour. They were abolished in Britain in 1949 and are implicitly at odds with the US Supreme Court's decisions on fair cross-section representation.

The theoretical objection to a specialist jury is that those on it will be too much alike. Its members are likely to come from similar backgrounds and to have had comparable experiences. Disagreements might still arise, for experts often subscribe to different schools of thought. No expert, however, would be likely to introduce a perspective that had not already been considered by the others. Old arguments would simply be rehashed and the dialectic process would be stale. On a randomly selected jury, in contrast, there is a more dynamic process at work. The absence of experts on the jury is not fatal, for expert witnesses can be called to testify by the respective sides. Moreover, such a jury will be able to debate the experts' opinions without the baggage of commitment to a particular expert school of thought. Added to the debate will be a lay perspective or, more likely, a large number of different lay perspectives, as each juror brings to the jury room a unique perspective which is the product of his or her background and experiences. These differing perspectives fuel the synergism of the deliberations. Diversity broadens perspective and enriches the deliberations. If fair cross-section representation is desirable, it is because it brings to the jury the widest possible range of perspectives.

Unfortunately, the US Supreme Court seems to have moulded its democratic jury in terms of race, gender and ethnicity. The Justices of course may be using these characteristics as a proxy for the arguably more pertinent quality of diversity of perspective, but a reader of the Court's decisions might be forgiven for thinking that these characteristics have independent significance in the Court's thinking. In *Lockhart* v. *McCree*[30] the Court held that jurors whose philosophical and moral opposition to capital punishment might substantially impair their ability to carry out their sentencing responsibilities were properly subject to challenge for cause. It rejected the argument that chose who shared a common philosophical perspective could constitute a 'distinctive' group for fair cross-section purposes.[31] The decision ignores the value of having a multiplicity of perspectives on the jury. Opponents of capital punishment have a legitimate point of view to offer –

one that challenges supporters of the death penalty to justify its imposition in the given case. The dialectic process will suffer if either group is denied access to the debate. Not only will the perspective of the death penalty opponents be lost at the penalty stage under *Lockhart*, but also at the stage of guilt determination, for the holding allows such jurors to be removed from both phases of the trial. Yet empirical studies (rejected in *Lockhart*) indicate that supporters of the death penalty are more likely to believe police testimony and disbelieve that of the defendant. They are, not uncoincidentally, also more likely to convict.

A number of American federal courts have fashioned a functional approach to cross-section representation that recognizes both racial/gender/ethnic differences and the importance of a diversity of perspective. Their test of 'distinctiveness' (or cognizability, as it is sometimes referred to in the decisions) asks whether:

1 the group in question is defined and limited by some factor such as race or sex which gives the group an identifiable composition;
2 there is a common thread in attitude, ideas or experience that runs through the group; and
3 the community of interests among members of the group is such that it cannot be adequately represented if the group is excluded.[30]

The first factor may be included out of deference to Supreme Court precedent. The second and third, however, point out the value of diversity and what would be lost if the jury were not a democratic body in fact.

Conclusion

Both non-discrimination in jury selection and the pursuit of justice are undeniably worthy goals. Effectively used, they complement each other. The challenge is to harness the broadened perspective brought about by a democratically constituted jury without injecting into the decision-making process the less salient features of racial, gender and ethnic politics. The constituency model of the jury seems to envisage justice emerging from a jury divided into factions, where each faction represents the views of a particular constituency. The jury room, however, is not the place for jurors to vent their political or ideological preferences. On the other hand, differences of perspective can advance the jurors' common search for a fair and just verdict. They are relevant to the extent that they shed light on the interpretation of the facts and issues in the case under consideration.

The strength of the jury lies is its ability to combine a diversity of perspective with a singularity of purpose. The advantage of a democratic jury lies in the collective wisdom that emerges when a cross-section of society comes together, pools their knowledge and debates issues of common concern. It is the interaction among jurors – challenging each other's assumptions and biases, sharing experiences, and offering perspectives that might otherwise have not been considered – that makes the jury so potent a decision-making body. These processes, which make for a better informed and more thoroughly tested verdict, flourish best on a democratically composed jury. The power of such a jury lies in its capacity to combat prejudice, to foster dialogue and debate, and to activate the dialectic and synergistic processes that are most likely to carry the jury to a just verdict. Seen in this light, there is no conflict between justice and democracy.

Notes

1 When the defendants were subsequently retried before a more diverse jury for various federal civil rights violations arising from the same incident, two of the four officers were convicted. *Los Angeles Times*, 18 April 1993.
2 *Strauder* v. *West Virginia*, 100 US 303, 308 (1880).
3 See, for example, Note (1970). See, generally, Larue (1976).
4 See *R.* v. *Ford* [1989] QB 868.
5 8 F3d 1187 (7th Cir. 1993).
6 In ancient Athens any citizen could serve on a jury. This was in keeping with the general commitment to democratic decision-making. The jury was unrepresentative, however, in that women and slaves were not deemed citizens and were thus not eligible for jury service. See, generally, Dunn (1992).
7 [1989] QB 868.
8 As noted in Chapter 4, in certain sensitive cases, jurors have been vetted by the police in response to a request by the Crown.
9 See *Vaise* v. *Delaval* (1785) 99 Eng. Rep. 944 (KB).
10 419 US 522 (1975).
11 Ibid. at p. 529.
12 See Criminal Justice Act 1988 s.118.
13 476 US 79 (1986), discussed in Chapter 4.
14 Ibid. at p. 97.
15 See *Thiel* v. *Southern Pacific Co.*, 328 US 217, 227 (1946).
16 396 US 320 (1970).
17 396 US 346 (1970).
18 373 US 723 (1963).
19 Ibid. at p. 727.
20 US Constitution, amend VI.
21 Fed. R. Crim. Proc. 21(a).
22 Of course the opposite may occur. While a cogent analysis may dispel a myth of inferiority, an ill-conceived and illogical analysis may reinforce it.
23 *Thiel* v. *Southern Pacific Co.*, 328 US 217, 227 (1946).

24 22 Cal. 3d 258, 583 P.2d 748 (1978).
25 583 P.2d at 755.
26 329 US 187 (1946).
27 Ibid. at pp. 193–4.
28 *Peters* v. *Kiff*, 407 US 493, 503–4 (1972).
29 332 US 261 (1947).
30 476 US 162 (1986).
31 Ibid. at p. 174.
32 See, for example, *Willis* v. *Zant*, 720 F.2d 1212 (11th Cir. 1983), *cert denied*, 467 US 1256 (1984) (where the test was first enunciated); *United States* v. *Fletcher*, 965 F.2d 781 (9th Cir. 1992); *United States* v. *Canfield*, 879 F.2d 446 (8th Cir. 1989); *Ford* v. *Seabold*, 841 F.2d 677 (6th Cir. 1992) *cert denied*, 488 US 928 (1988); *Barber* v. *Ponte*, 772 F2d 982 (1st Cir.) *cert denied*, 475 US 1050 (1986).

6 The Selection and Training of Jurors

Unlike in some continental European countries, such as France, the trial judge does not sit with the jury during its deliberations. The Anglo-American judge instructs the jury as to its duties, but has no control over how it carries them out. The deliberations of the jury are closed to the public, and jurors are generally forbidden to disclose the substance of their discussions. One cannot assess the reasoning that went into the jury's verdict because the jury provides no reasons. Any attempt to question the jurors about what transpired in the jury room, even by (or especially by) the lawyers in the case, may be deemed in contempt of court. Although easing restrictions on disclosure in order to facilitate good-faith research on juries has often been advocated (see, for example, Runciman Committee 1993), these restrictions have proved remarkably resistant to change.

Although the quality of the jury's deliberations may not be subject to scrutiny, the criminal justice system does have in its power the ability to assure itself about the quality of its jurors. A commonplace aphorism in the computer world is 'garbage in, garbage out', meaning that the computer's output cannot be expected to rise above the level of the human input of those who program it. An exact parallel cannot be drawn to the jury but it may not be an unreasonable assumption that the quality of jury deliberations will be in direct proportion to the aptitude and skills of the jurors. At a minimum jurors must possess the ability to be fair and impartial. While fairness and impartiality may not by themselves guarantee a just verdict, they may be a necessary condition for its achievement.

A fair and impartial jury is not, as the British judges in particular have been inclined to maintain, simply the natural product of a randomly selected jury.[1] Its creation requires a concerted effort on the part of both court and counsel. Care must be taken to select jurors who have the capacity to be fair and impartial, and this potential needs to be nurtured and developed through appropriate training. Unfortunately, for entirely different reasons, neither Britain nor the United States shines when it comes to the selection of jurors, and neither makes much of an effort to teach its jurors how to be fair and impartial. Before examining these points further and seeing what can be done to improve the situation, we should first examine the nature of impartiality.

Impartiality

What do the courts mean when they describe a juror as impartial? Platitudes about the value of impartiality abound, but giving content to the concept is more difficult and challenging. The problem is that all adults have values and beliefs which make impartiality in any *tabula rasa* sense of the term impossible. The challenge is to define impartiality in a way that takes account of the moral, political and psychological baggage that prospective jurors bring with them, and at the same time provides a meaningful criterion for the purposes of jury selection.

Lord Coke equated impartiality with 'indifference' (Coke 1832, s.155(b)). This term, however, may have been ill-chosen. Jurors who are satisfied to base their verdict on a flip of the coin or a roll of the dice may be indifferent but they certainly should not be described as impartial. Jurors should not be indifferent in the sense of not caring about what verdict they reach. They cannot be indifferent to the demands of justice. More accurately, Coke was concerned with neutrality (see generally Montefiore, 1975). Prior to hearing the evidence, jurors should not be inclined to favour either side. They should have no interest in the outcome of the case other than to reach a fair and just verdict. More critical than an initial indifference, however, may be the willingness to set aside any pre-trial biases and consider the evidence, the arguments of counsel and the comments, if any, of the judge on their merits. Openmindedness, and the willingness to listen to others – including other jury members – are the cornerstones of juror impartiality.

Coke's full statement required an impartial juror to be 'indifferent as he stands unsworn'. The critical point in time, as Coke saw it, was prior to the introduction of any evidence. In a criminal trial, however, jurors are not supposed to be indifferent at this point. The presumption of innocence demands that they be biased in favour of the accused. It is the state's obligation to overcome this institutionally created bias by proof beyond a reasonable doubt. The concept of impartiality therefore needs to be read in a cultural context. In a legal order where the defendant and the state started on an equal footing or where the accused was presumed guilty, impartiality might take on an entirely different meaning than it does in the Anglo-American criminal justice system.

Thus the criminal justice system does not want its jurors to be indifferent at the outset of a case. But what if, after presentation of the evidence, the jurors are indifferent to the two side's positions? Again an institutional bias asserts itself. The prosecution bears the burden of establishing guilt by proof beyond a reasonable doubt. A jury which is equally unpersuaded by the prosecution and the defence or, in Lord Coke's terminology, is 'indifferent' to the two sides' positions, is obliged to find against the prosecution. The legal system demands that the jury convert its indifference into a verdict in favour of the defendant.

For the purposes of the jury system, impartiality cannot simply be equated with the absence of partiality. If partiality is conceived of as a negative and its absence as a neutral state, impartiality is a positive state. In the impartial juror qualities of character are as important as qualities of intellect. Impartial jurors must be able to detach themselves from any pre-trial prejudices that they might have. They must be prepared to suspend judgement until they have heard all of the evidence, while affording the accused the presumption of innocence to which he is legally entitled. They must accept the institutional bias that requires the state to establish guilt by proof beyond a reasonable doubt, even if they may not personally agree with that bias. Impartial jurors must also be amenable to persuasion. They must be willing to listen to the arguments of counsel, as well as to the opinions of the other jurors, and to weigh these on their merits.

If the above conditions were to be satisfied, it would not really matter *for purposes of impartiality* how the jurors were selected or whether they were representative of a fair cross-section of the community. Indeed, from the perspective of impartiality, it would not matter whether the selection process excluded particular segments of the community from jury service. Such factors, however, as discussed in previous chapters, matter deeply for the value of democratic decision-making. And democratic decision-making, as we have also seen, stimulates the synergistic and dialectic processes of jury deliberation. It is these processes, in the hands of impartial jurors, that can be expected to produce a fair and just verdict.

The Relationship between Knowledge and Impartiality

A high value is not usually placed on ignorance, but, curiously, the ignorant juror often appears to be prized by the legal system. Ignorance, however, is employed in a specialized sense. It is not intended as a commentary on a juror's general knowledge, but rather is used in reference to the juror's knowledge of the particular case, and the juror's acquaintance with the parties, witnesses and lawyers in the case. The concern is that such knowledge could interfere with the juror's ability to be impartial.

There is an irony in the Anglo-American preference for 'ignorant' jurors. Originally jurors were chosen because of their personal knowledge of the facts, parties and circumstances of the case to be decided. The metamorphosis to the present position was gradual. Even after it was determined that familiarity with the facts was not desirable, the common law requirement that jurors be from the vicinage and the American constitutional requirement that the case be heard in the district in which the crime occurred increased the likelihood that jurors would have such familiarity. An advantage of local jurors was that they were better able to asses the credibility of their witness-neighbours. The disadvantage, on the other hand, was that their knowledge of the parties and witnesses might lead them to decide the case on grounds other than the evidence presented in court.

Over time some of the dangers diminished. With the expansion in population and the reduced dependency of community members on each other, it became increasingly less likely that a prospective juror would be familiar with all that went on in the community. At the same time, however, as some dangers receded, others came to the fore. Developments in the field of communications have expanded the information available to the ordinary citizen. To the traditional newspapers have been added, first, radio and television, and then computerized information. These increase the likelihood that prospective jurors will have a fairly general knowledge of, although perhaps not a personal familiarity with, the details of a pending case.

The courts have struggled to delineate the appropriate relationship between knowledge and impartiality in light of these technological advances. A range of approaches could be conceived: at one extreme all prospective juror who had any knowledge of a case would automatically be excused; at the other, knowledge *per se* would be irrelevant, with the only question being the effect of the information received on the juror's ability to be impartial. In between these two poles lies room for a variety of tests based on presumptions about the relationship between knowledge and impartiality. A court might consider, for example, the likely effect that the juror's knowledge would have on a reasonable person. This would obviate the need of having to decide whether jurors were being disingenuous in asserting that they could set aside their pre-trial knowledge and decide the case on the evidence presented in court. It would also have to be determined in whose favour any presumption would run. A court might, for instance, presume impartiality, despite pre-trial knowledge, and place on the challenging party the burden of demonstrating partiality; or, conversely, the court could presume partiality once pre-trial knowledge was shown, with the side seeking to have the juror included having the burden of rebutting the presumption.

The decisions of the US Supreme Court which have addressed the relationship between knowledge and impartiality in the context of media reporting of a case reflect the complexity of the problem. In *Irvin* v. *Dowd*[2] the Court began its analysis with a frank recognition of the fact that:

> In these days of swift, widespread and diverse methods of communication, an important case can be expected to arouse the interest of the public in the vicinity, and scarcely any of those best qualified to serve as jurors will not have formed some impression or opinion as to the merits of the case. This is particularly true in criminal cases. To hold that the mere existence of a preconceived notion as to the guilt or innocence of an accused, without more, is sufficient to rebut the presumption of a prospective juror's impartiality would be to establish an impossible standard. It is sufficient if the juror can lay aside his impression or opinion and render a verdict based on the evidence presented in court.[3]

In this passage the Court appeared to presume impartiality despite the media's coverage of the case, placing the burden of rebutting that presumption on the challenging party. In applying its test, however, the Court seemed to reverse its position, finding that persistent and prejudicial news reports had so permeated the community as to make impartiality impossible. Significantly, it chose to disbelieve the declaration of jurors that they could render an impartial verdict and tendered its own psychological analysis of the processes of the mind:

> The influence that lurks in an opinion once formed is so persistent that it unconsciously fights detachment from the mental processes of the average man. ... No doubt each juror was sincere when he said that he would be fair and impartial to petitioner, but psychological impact requiring such a declaration before one's fellows is often its father.[4]

Thus the Court in effect presumed partiality rather than impartiality and adopted a theory of opinion formation that made the rebuttal of this presumption a virtual impossibility.

The Court has also demonstrated that it is prepared, under appropriate circumstances, to infer impermissible knowledge on the part of prospective jurors. In *Rideau* v. *Louisiana*,[5] a local television station had, on repeated occasions, broadcast the defendant's confession to the crimes with which he had been charged. The Court held that the refusal of the defendant's request for a change of venue denied him due process. This relatively unremarkable holding was supplemented by reflections on the more general question of the desirability of 'knowledgeable' jurors. Justice Stewart, speaking for the majority, observed that '[f]or anyone who has ever watched television the conclusion cannot be avoided that this spectacle, to the tens of thousands of people who saw and heard it, in a very real sense *was* Rideau's trial and any subsequent court proceedings would be but a "hollow formality"'.[6]

The Court in *Rideau* did not find it necessary to inquire into whether any individual juror's impartiality had been compromised and declined the invitation to examine a particularized transcript of the *voir dire* examination in the case. It reasoned that, whatever such an examination might reveal, due process of law required that the trial be held before a jury drawn from a community of people who had not seen or heard Rideau's televised 'interview'. Justice must not only be done, it must also be seen to have been done. While the decision in *Rideau* may have turned on the extreme facts of the case, the Court's analysis, besides suggesting the extraordinary proposition that the trial judge should have granted a change in venue even if none of the jurors had seen, or were aware of, the television broadcast, appeared to indicate that impartiality presumes lack of knowledge about the facts of a case.

The Court seemed to change tack in *Murphy* v. *Florida*,[7] where it held that mere exposure of some jurors to adverse publicity about the defendant did not presumptively deny him due process. A noteworthy feature of the decision is that the Court did what it had declined to do in *Rideau*: it examined the transcript of the *voir dire* to determine whether any of the jurors were in fact biased against the defendant. Cases such as *Irvin* and *Rideau* were distinguished as involving widespread community bias.[8] However, the Court provided no psychological basis for its supposition that widespread community bias rendered individual jurors' assertions of impartiality less reliable.

To return to basics, there are clearly some types of knowledge that it is desirable for a juror to hold. Jurors should have a knowledge of the function and purposes of the trial, and the roles of the various participants, including themselves, within it. They should be familiar with such institutional premises of the criminal justice system as the presumption of innocence and the requirement of proof beyond a reasonable doubt. A rudimentary knowledge of English and a certain amount of general knowledge may also be necessary so that the juror is able to understand and assess the testimony of witnesses, the arguments of counsel and the directions of the court.

The more perplexing question is when it can be said that a juror has too much knowledge. To excuse all jurors who have learned about a case through the media would seem to penalize well informed citizens. The more knowledgeable the juror on current events, the less likely that he or she would be able to satisfy a concept of impartiality which holds advance knowledge undesirable. This would mean that individuals considered to be model citizens in other respects would be deemed unfit for jury service. Such an approach would seem inexorably to lead to juries composed of those who were representative of the 'average stupidity', as Herbert Spencer once put it (Spencer, 1868, p. 182), or worse. Regardless of whether such stupidity is prevalent in the community, it is doubtful that this is what the US Supreme Court had in mind when it called for a jury drawn from a fair cross-section of the community. To the contrary, it could be argued that eliminating the better-read sector of the population from jury service is at odds with the concept of cross-section representation. An elite panel composed of the best and brightest members of society may not be the objective, but neither is a jury of ignoramuses. In any event, in an era in which 24-hour news coverage is available and information pours from newspapers, radio, television and now computers, finding jurors who know nothing about a highly publicized case may not be that easy.

So where are we left? Arguably, it is only when a juror's ability to decide a case fairly has been undermined by pre-trial knowledge of some sort that the juror should be excused. This is not a concession to the pervasiveness of the modern media. Similar principles were articulated in the 1807 prosecution of Aaron Burr for treason – a case that was as heatedly discussed and debated as any twentieth-century trial. Chief Justice Marshall's remarks at that time on the relationship between knowledge and impartiality have a contemporary ring:

> Were it possible to obtain a jury without any prepossessions whatever respecting the guilt or innocence of the accused, it would be extremely desirable to obtain such a jury, but this is perhaps impossible; and therefore will not be required. The opinion which has been avowed by the court is, that light impressions which may fairly be supposed to yield to the testimony that may be offered, which may leave the mind open to a fair consideration of that testimony, constitute no sufficient objection to a juror; but that those strong and deep impressions which will close the mind against the testimony that may be offered in opposition to them, which will combat that testimony, and resist its force, do constitute a sufficient objection to him.[9]

The Myth of the Impartial Juror

Does the impartial juror exist? The original conception of impartiality reflected society's relatively naive understanding of the human mind. Since then, Freud and his followers have sensitized us to the effect of subconscious motivations and early childhood experiences, as well as the fact that even apparently long-forgotten incidents can unwittingly affect our decision-making processes (Freud, 1949). Political and moral judgements, shaped in part by who we are and what we have experienced, can affect the way we look at things. Everyone has certain defining characteristics. Some, such as race and gender, are determined by birth; others, such as membership in social organizations, are the product of choice. It would be unrealistic to expect a prospective juror not to be influenced by the values, as well as the prejudices, of these primary group affiliations. A juror whose primary group sees society as racist will approach jury service with a quite different attitude than that of a juror whose primary group believes that the state is even-handed in its dealings with its citizens. Even before the first piece of evidence is introduced, a juror may form a subconscious bond with a defendant or lawyer who is perceived to be a member of the juror's primary group. For the same reason, a juror may identify with a key witness for one of the sides.

Psychological research has shown that, when negative acts are committed by members of one's primary group, there is a tendency to attribute the cause to external factors; when the same acts are committed by someone who is not a member of that primary group there is a greater willingness to attribute the cause to an evil disposition (Hewstone, 1990). This implies that, in a criminal justice setting, jurors will be more likely to decide that the criminal acts of a fellow primary group member – an 'insider' – were the product of forces beyond the defendant's control, while those of an 'outsider' were directly attributable to the defendant's *mens rea*. This may lead to the outsider being convicted for a minor crime of which the insider would have been acquitted. This process of identification would help to explain the statistics which indicate that white juries in the United States have tended to impose the death penalty primarily in cases of black defendants charged with crimes against white victims (Cowan *et al.*, 1984); and why predominantly Protestant juries in Northern Ireland were willing to acquit Protestant paramilitaries of crimes committed against Catholic victims (Greer and White, 1988). This is not to say that the 'identification' hypothesis provides a complete explanation of any given verdict. The more moderate, and probably more accurate, thesis is that the sense of identification which a juror might have with a party or witness may affect the juror's interpretation of ambiguous evidence or tip the balance in a marginal case. Credibility assessments are also likely to be affected by the extent to which jurors 'identity' with a witness. On a homogeneous jury these effects can be expected to be more pronounced because all of the jurors are likely to form the same identifications because of their common background.

Psychological studies have confirmed a correlation between, on the one hand, such variables as occupation (Broeder, 1965; Hermann, 1970), gender (Stephan, 1974; Strodtbeck and Mann, 1956), race (Broeder, 1965) and socioeconomic status (Simon, 1956; Adler, 1973) and, on the other, juror attitudes. When evidence is susceptible to more than one interpretation, that which a juror will give to it will often turn on the juror's value system: evidence which conflicts with the juror's fundamental values may be accorded less weight or disbelieved entirely. Researchers have also identified so-called 'authoritarian personalities' (Adorno *et al.*, 1950; Bray and Noble, 1987) whose characteristics include a tendency to rigidity and conservatism. Authoritarians both believe in the value of punishment and are uncommonly predisposed to impose it on others. Not surprisingly, authoritarian jurors are inclined to favour the prosecution. In the eyes of such a juror, neutral evidence may be given an interpretation that supports the juror's desire to return a guilty verdict. Conversely, Boehm (1968) identified anti-authoritarian personalities who have the opposite tendencies. Boehm concluded that both authoritarians and anti-authoritarians were not as desirable jurors as those whom he labelled 'equalitarians' who had no strong predispositions in either direction.

What are the implications of this social science research for the legal system and its search for the impartial jury? One needs to begin by accepting the reality that everyone is influenced by their affiliations and experiences in ways that render true impartiality an illusion. But this is not to say that it is an illusion that is not worth preserving. Public confidence in the jury system and the willingness of the defendant, as well as the community, to accept the legitimacy of a verdict is built upon the perception that the verdict has been returned by persons who can be characterized as impartial.

In part, the task of the trial judge is to dampen the influences that undermine impartiality by emphasizing that which unites the jurors – their common search for a fair and just verdict. The judge should impress upon the jurors the responsibility with which they have been entrusted. The defendant, the court and the state all look to the jury to achieve justice. A juror's values and primary group perspectives are not to be ignored (even if this were somehow possible) but, as seen in the preceding chapter, need to be constructively channelled so that they promote the search for a fair and just verdict.

To assert that true impartiality is a myth, moreover, is not to deny that there are some individuals who are more impartial than others. Like justice, impartiality should be viewed as an aspirational ideal. Commitment to this ideal challenges jurors to rise above their prejudices in the effort to achieve justice. A juror should, perhaps, have to reach a threshold level of impartiality in order to be permitted to serve and those who do not should be dismissed for cause. Once past this threshold, the search is for the jury which comes closest to the aspirational ideal of the impartial jury. However, it may be that the time and effort expanded in such a search could be more profitably put to use in training jurors to be impartial. With appropriate training most individuals are capable of being competent jurors. Indeed, if the state expects its jury system to function effectively, it must be prepared to provide such training. Of what this training might consist will be explored in a subsequent section.

The Search for Impartial Jurors

To recapitulate, the challenge facing the legal system is, first, to identify prospective jurors who have the qualities of character, temperament and mind that will enable them to be impartial, and, second, to provide the training that will bring out these traits to best advantage. The key to finding jurors with the capability of being impartial often lies in identifying subconscious biases. Eliminating blatantly prejudiced jurors would not seem to be a problem. It is, however, in Britain, where judges are reluctant to deviate from the jury produced by random selection and barristers are not allowed to question or investigate prospective jurors. In the United States the tools for detecting biased jurors are available but have been exploited by lawyers to pack the jury with individuals who have a subconscious prejudice in favour of their client's position. There are lessons to be learned from examining each of the respective approaches.

Jury Selection in the United Kingdom

In the past, when jurors were chosen because of their knowledge of the facts of a case, a certain amount of bias was inevitable. Jurors could hardly be expected not to take into account the past history of their dealings with the parties and witnesses and, indeed, it was thought desirable for them to do so. With the transformation of the jury from a body of fact-knowers to one of fact-finders, however, came a corresponding concern that jurors be impartial. In common-law England the property qualifications for jury service (discussed in Chapter 4) were thought to provide a useful, albeit rough, dividing line between those who had the qualities of intellect, temperament and character to be jurors and those who did not. Nonetheless, it was recognized that individuals who might be acceptable jurors in some trials might be unacceptable in others. The parties, accordingly, were permitted to challenge jurors for cause, and the court would excuse those who were shown to be biased in respect to the particular case under consideration. Challenges for cause could be lodged by either side, and there were no limits on the number of such challenges which could be made.

In addition to challenges for cause, parties were allowed to challenge jurors peremptorily. A peremptory challenge could be made, without explanation, on any basis that a party saw fit. It was the peremptory challenge which allowed prospective jurors whose impartiality was suspect but not sufficiently obvious to justify a challenge for cause to be removed from the jury. Although initially both the Crown and the defendant were permitted to exercise peremptory challenges, the Crown's prerogative was withdrawn by statute in 1305 and replaced by a right to ask jurors to stand by. This had much the same effect as the peremptory challenge because, unless the panel of prospective jurors was completely exhausted, jurors asked to stand by would not serve. As in the case of a peremptory challenge, no reason for a stand-by request had to be provided.

While the Crown's ability to challenge jurors peremptorily was abrogated by statute, the defendant's right remained. However, over the years the number of peremptory challenges permitted the defendant has been gradually whittled away. At common law the defendant was allowed 35 peremptory challenges. This number was subsequently reduced, first to 20, then to seven, and finally to three.[10] In 1988 the defendant's right of peremptory challenge was repealed altogether.[11] The justifications advanced in support of abolition reveal a sea change in the government's concept of a criminal trial.

According to Blackstone, the peremptory challenge reflected that 'tenderness and humanity for which English laws [were] justly famous' (Blackstone, 1765, p. 352). But why would the law wish to exhibit tenderness and humanity to those who were accused of having committed, in some cases, heinous crimes? Blackstone offered two reasons. The first is the desirability that the defendant have a good opinion of the jury that is to try him. Blackstone did not elaborate, but arguably a defendant is more likely to accept the verdict of such a jury than that of one imposed upon him. If convicted by the latter, the defendant might enter prison focusing on the unfairness of the trial rather than on the wrongfulness of his crime, and be correspondingly less amenable to rehabilitation. The peremptory challenge thus furthered the interest of the state in having the verdict of the jury accepted by the defendant. The second justification for the peremptory challenge offered by Blackstone was so that a defendant could remove jurors against whom a challenge for cause has been rejected by the court. Consequently, the defendant would not have to fear that the juror who perceived in the challenge an attack on his character might take his resentment out in the verdict. Taking these two justifications together, the peremptory challenge assured a defendant that he would be tried, if not by a jury of his peers, by at least a jury in whose selection he had a voice.

There are other advantages to the peremptory challenge. Because the basis for a challenge does not have to be explained, it allows 'the covert expression of what we dare not say but know is true more often than not'

(Babcock, 1975, p. 553). A wealth of psychological studies confirm what common sense and experience tell us – that certain individuals have deep-seated biases which hinder their ability to be impartial in certain kinds of cases or in cases involving certain kinds of defendants. To acknowledge this publicly, however, might be politically divisive.[12] Most jurors prefer to consider themselves to be bias-free. Indeed, they may honestly believe this and be unaware of any bias. To expose a juror's prejudices in open court or to manoeuvre the juror into admitting to bias is likely to stimulate resentment and may further exacerbate the polarization between the juror and the group that is the object of his or her dislike. The peremptory challenge allows the integrity of the jury to be preserved while avoiding the undesirable social and political consequences of publicly labelling jurors as biased.

The peremptory challenge also benefits the lawyers who are trying the case. Experienced barristers believe that they can identify, even if they cannot prove to a court's satisfaction, jurors who are biased. The peremptory challenge allows the barrister's intuition, judgement and courtroom experience to be put to advantage. Although one might decry reliance on such substitutes for proof, it must be borne in mind that the English barrister has never been in a strong position from which to make truly informed jury selection decisions. The practical effect of not being allowed to investigate or question prospective jurors is that the barrister is deprived of the basis for making a meaningful assessment of a juror's impartiality. There is an additional strategic advantage of the peremptory challenge to the barrister. One of the byproducts of having tried a large number of cases is that the barrister develops a sensitivity to the characteristics of jurors who will react positively and negatively to his or her style. The peremptory challenge allows the removal of jurors who are likely to react negatively. This benefits the court and the jury as well, for barristers are likely to be more effective in presenting their case to a panel perceived to be friendly than one seen as hostile. It is obviously unfair to saddle a defendant with jurors whose opposition is not to the merits of the defendant's cause but to the defendant's lawyer.

Peremptory challenges also benefit the judiciary. They spare the trial judge from having to assess the truthfulness of a juror's denial of bias when challenged for cause. Thus the legal system is able to preserve the socially desirable shibboleth that jurors will not lie about their impartiality. A judge can also rule against a marginal challenge for cause knowing that if the objection to the juror is strongly felt, the defendant can still excuse the juror peremptorily. In the same vein the peremptory challenge reduces the burden on appellate courts. The defendant who believes that a trial judge has made an incorrect ruling on a challenge for cause has a readily available corrective in the form of the peremptory challenge. Its exercise will in turn obviate the need for an appeal on the correctness of the judge's ruling.

Finally, in instances where the luck of the draw has yielded an unrepresentative panel, peremptory challenges can be used to restore balance to the jury. If, for example, there are no women among the first twelve persons called to the jury box, the exercise of peremptory challenges will open the door for additional jurors, some of whom might be female.

The beginning of the end for the peremptory challenge in Britain can be traced to a 1986 White Paper.[13] The government's stated concern was that the challenge was being used against qualified jurors whose appearance suggested that they might be unsympathetic to the claims of criminal defendants. A second articulated concern was that, in trials involving multiple defendants, peremptory challenges were being pooled to eliminate so significant a number of jurors as to undermine the principle of random selection. Many suspected, however, that the government's real concern was its perception that juries were becoming too defence-oriented. This fear was fuelled by a highly publicized speech by Sir Robert Mark, the then Police Commissioner (1973), in which he equated jury acquittals with failures. Implicit but unproven was an assumption that there had been an increase in the number of not guilty verdicts. Whether or not this was true, a subsequently commissioned government survey revealed a higher conviction rate in cases where the defence had exercised its peremptory challenges than in cases where it had not.[14] The survey also revealed that the White Paper's claim of widespread pooling of challenges in multi-defendant cases was very much exaggerated. Before parliament the Home Secretary conceded that the statistical case for abolition of the peremptory challenge was weak but continued to argue that abolition was supported by 'logic and common sense'.

It is submitted that neither logic nor common sense justified the abolition. The logic which equates a higher acquittal rate with a malfunctioning of the criminal justice system rests on a fundamental misconception about the purpose of a criminal trial. It implies that the jury's role is simply to place the community's imprimatur on the government's decision to prosecute. That position would deprive the jury of its independence. It was held in *Bushell's Case* (discussed in Chapter 2, pp. 35–9) that a jury could not be obliged to return the verdict that the judge thought correct. The trial would become a mockery if jurors were required to return the verdict that the prosecution thought correct.

The reasoning that attributed an increase in the acquittal rate to the defence's exercise of its peremptory challenges was also flawed. As an empirical matter, it might be pointed out that the alleged increase in the acquittal rate occurred during a period when the number of peremptory challenges was gradually being reduced, exactly the opposite of what one would have predicted if the government's thesis had been correct. The logic of the government's position was also suspect in that it seemed to assume that the exercise of a peremptory challenge would lead to the replacement of a neutral juror with one who favoured an acquittal. The more probable scenario is that a juror who favoured conviction would have been replaced by one who was neutral. The reason why is that a defendant had far more to lose than to gain by peremptorily challenging a neutral juror. If the neutral juror were replaced by a juror perceived to be favourable to the accused, the Crown could be expected to ask the juror to stand by; if the neutral juror were replaced by a juror who was inclined to favour a conviction, the defendant was in a worse position and with one less peremptory challenge. In short, peremptory challenges were too valuable a commodity to squander on neutral jurors.

Another of the concerns cited in the 1986 White Paper was that barristers in multi-defendant trials were combining their peremptory challenges in order to skew the composition of the jury. It is, however, the Crown's decision to try more than one defendant in a single trial that creates the potential for this deviation from a randomly selected jury. If the Crown fears that the threat to random selection is too great, the remedy lies within its control: it can simply bring separate trials. In practice, however, it is usually the defendants who are opposed to joint trials because of the risk of guilt by association. Even assuming that the Crown was correct in its claim that the pooling of peremptory challenges was too greatly distorting the composition of the jury, the problem hardly justified so drastic a solution as that of abolishing the challenge. A more measured response would have been to require defendants to share the number of peremptory challenges normally available to a single defendant, at least where the interests of the various defendants were not antagonistic.[15] Such an approach would have addressed the alleged abuse from cumulated peremptory challenges without forfeiting the constructive benefits of the challenge.

Many believed that the loss of the peremptory challenge would have little impact because biased jurors could still be excused for cause. But on what foundations is a challenge for cause to be constructed? As has already been noted, a barrister has virtually no information about jurors on which to base such a challenge. Even the juror's occupation is no longer listed on the jury form. Although there may be instances where a juror voluntarily discloses a ground for disqualification or where the lawyer or defendant is aware of such a ground, these will be comparatively rare. Unlike their American counterparts, English barristers are generally not permitted to investigate or question jurors for the purpose of discovering bias. Questioning of jurors is allowed after a *prima facie* case of bias is established,[16] but this exception serves to create a classic Catch-22 situation: a barrister can question a juror if the barrister can establish a *prima facie* case of bias, but without being able to question the juror, the barrister is poorly placed to establish this *prima facie* case. More generally, without the tools to make challenges for cause effective, they can only be of limited assistance in the search for an impartial jury.

The abolition of the peremptory challenge could have other undesirable ramifications. A challenge for cause requires the judge to make a ruling either upholding or denying the challenge. With the demise of the peremptory challenge, judges could be expected to be called upon to make many more such rulings. The ground for the challenge for cause would have to be stated for the record and, in some instances, a probing of the alleged ground would be necessary. The result would be more frequent, more time-consuming, and, to the jurors, more embarrassing questioning of their fairness. Ultimately, the judge would have to rule on whether or not to excuse the juror. A judge's decision to remove a juror for cause, however, carries a quite different message than a lawyer's peremptory challenge of the juror. When the court dismisses a juror, it in effect declares that the juror is unfit to sit in judgement in that case. When the court discounts the juror's declaration that he or she can be impartial, it implies that the juror is mistaken or, worse, a liar. A juror is understandably likely to resent these insinuations. In contrast, a juror removed by a peremptory challenge can rationalize the challenge as the product of the defence counsel's acknowledged partisanship. No in-court proclamations concerning the juror's fairness are necessary and any resentment that is felt will be directed against the party exercising the peremptory challenge and not the court.

Traditionally, challenges for cause have been limited to fairly narrow grounds. This was tolerable so long as the back-up of the peremptory challenge existed to allow the removal of jurors on the borderline of unacceptable bias. With this option no longer available, courts might be expected to come under pressure to expand the grounds for challenges for cause. To date such pressure has not materialized. In part this may be due to the fact that the peremptory challenge was never that valuable to English barristers to begin with, as without the ability to investigate or question jurors, there was little basis for exercising it in an intelligent manner. The loss occasioned by its withdrawal may therefore have been minimal in practice. Nonetheless, it is symbolically significant, as it marks an acceptance of the position that equates a randomly selected jury with an impartial jury. It constitutes the turning of a blind eye to the lessons of both common sense and social science research regarding the nature of bias.

Scientific Jury Selection in America

There is no lack of opportunity for lawyers in the United States to identify biased jurors.[17] In its widest sense, 'jury selection' includes the selection of the district in which the trial will be held, for it is from this district that the jury pool will be compiled. In cases where there has been significant pre-trial publicity, a lawyer may attempt to assess the extent of prejudice against the defendant within the community in which the trial is scheduled by conducting a survey to determine the attitude of local residents towards the crime and the defendant. The lawyer might commission an opinion poll or meet with 'focus groups' to discuss the pending case. The data generated can then be analysed by trained social scientists and, where appropriate, used to support a motion for a change in venue.[18] In a case which has been widely reported, however, a change in venue to a neighbouring district may have little effect since the prospective jurors in the new locale will have been exposed to similar, if not identical, news coverage. Accordingly, the defence may wish to investigate a number of possible venues within a more extensive geographical area, the objective being to identify the one in which the accused is most likely to receive a fair trial. The defendant will then be in a position not only to argue for a change in venue but also to propose a particular alternative with empirical data to support that choice.

Along with their views on the pending case, demographic, socioeconomic and psychological data about the participants in the survey or focal group can be collected. This demographic information may be of value in establishing that a subsequently compiled jury pool is not representative of the community. The data can also be used as part of a strategy of jury selection. Demographic information from survey and focus group participants can be correlated with the participants' attitudes towards the issues and parties in the case. Using this information, it becomes possible to construct profiles of favourable and unfavourable jurors. During *voir dire* questioning (see below), the lawyer will attempt to match prospective jurors against the profiles. Those predicted by the profile to be unfavourable can be challenged peremptorily if there is no ground for excusing them for cause.

Mock trials can be used in a strategically similar manner, although they serve more conventional purposes as well.[19] A mock trial will typically be held well in advance of the actual trial. The lawyer will convene a group of randomly selected individuals to hear the evidence and arguments that are likely to be presented in court. A legal colleague might play the role of the lawyer on the opposing side. The mock jury, having listened to the witnesses[20] and the arguments of counsel, is allowed to deliberate. Some lawyers have constructed 'mock jury rooms' with one-way mirrors which allow them to observe the deliberations without being seen. Positions taken by mock jurors during deliberations can be correlated with previously obtained demographic information, and the resulting data incorporated into the profiles of favourable and unfavourable jurors. The lawyer might also use the mock jurors as a focal group, discussing with them their reactions to various aspects of the case. Statutory restrictions on communicating with jurors obviously do not apply to mock jurors who are under no obligation to participate.

Community surveys, focus groups and mock trials tell a lawyer what a representative sample of the community may think about the case. What the lawyer really wants to know, however, is what the prospective jurors who will hear the case think. It is out of this specific pool, and not the community in the abstract, that the lawyer must fashion an impartial jury. With the publication of the names of those in the jury pool, a second phase of jury selection begins. The defence lawyer may investigate or hire a private detective to investigate prospective jurors. The investigation may consist of nothing more than a drive past the juror's home, with notes being made of such readily observable items as the socioeconomic neighbourhood in which the juror lives, the appearance of the juror's home, and the age and make of the juror's automobile, as well as any bumper stickers that might be attached to it. The inquiries may extend to an examination of public records, such as those relating to the juror's marital history, land purchases and employment. Investigators have also been known to attempt to interview a prospective juror's neighbours and co-workers.

It is not only defence counsel that has adopted this strategy. Prosecutors have also used the police to investigate prospective jurors.[21] These investigations may be even more invasive of a juror's privacy than those conducted by the defence, as they may extend to records not accessible to the general public, such as criminal and tax records. In addition, the juror's neighbours, associates and employers are likely to feel more compelled to answer the questions of police than those of private investigators. Because the prosecutor may be able to draw upon the state's entire civil service there is a serious problem of disparity of resources. The state has theoretically unlimited investigative reserves under its control; the defence is usually restricted by the defendant's financial means (although, in some high-profile cases, volunteers may be prepared to assist). However, it is arguably the demands of the case and not the wealth of the defendant that should dictate the extent of juror investigation. Although the problem of resource imbalance could be addressed by judicially-ordered sharing of juror information, there is little enthusiasm for this remedy. To some extent this may reflect a philosophical commitment to an adversarial system but it may also be based on a fear on the part of diligent lawyers that their opponents will piggy-back on their hard work and industry.

Investigations of jurors, whether by the prosecutor or the defence, are inherently troubling (Okun, 1968). American Bar Association rules suggest that discreet investigations of prospective jurors are permissible, but those which are vexatious or harassing are not.[22] The line between the two is often murky. Legal ethics aside, there is the more fundamental issue of juror privacy. The US Supreme Court has identified a right of privacy within the framework of the Constitution,[23] and has held that this right is not forfeited by virtue of becoming a juror.[24] This is sound policy: the willingness of citizens to undertake jury duty could be drastically reduced if the perceived price were the loss of one's privacy. In cases where there is a perceived threat to juror safety, a court may withhold the publication of juror names.[25] Such restrictions are typically imposed in cases involving defendants who might be inclined to threaten the jurors. The courts have not shown a comparable willingness to protect juror privacy in less extreme circumstances.

The final stage of the jury selection process occurs at trial. In American courts each side is permitted to ask questions of prospective jurors – a process known as *voir dire*. The questioning can extend to any subject matter that might lead a court to conclude that a juror is not impartial. From the responses to the *voir dire* questions, the lawyers attempt to assess each juror's impartiality. Jurors may then be excused for cause if the questioning reveals a bias that will prevent the juror from fairly deciding the case. Most judges, however, are reluctant to dismiss jurors who claim to be able to be impartial, thus leaving the lawyer with the option of challenging the juror peremptorily. Unlike in Britain, peremptory challenges are regarded as an integral part of the jury selection process. The number of peremptory challenges allotted to each party will be limited (and will vary between jurisdictions and with the nature of the case). Counsel will usually attempt to rank order jurors on their degree of acceptability and exercise peremptory challenges against those who are lowest on their list. It is not sound strategy to challenge any juror whose impartiality is slightly suspect, for the excused juror could be replaced by one who was less favourable, while the number of peremptory challenges remaining will have been reduced.

Voir dire can be quite time-consuming, and there have been cases where this phase of the trial has taken longer than the presentation of the evidence. In part this is because intensive questioning may be required to probe a juror's innermost biases. In a less sophisticated age lawyers would ask a perfunctory question to the effect of whether any member of the jury knew of any reason why he or she could not serve impartially in the case at bar, and would receive the perfunctory negative answer. Lawyers now appreciate that a more subtle approach is required if an accurate gauge of a juror's impartiality is to be obtained. Instead of asking whether any of the jurors are prejudiced against blacks, for example, counsel will ask each juror to describe his or her experiences with persons of other races. Instead of a *pro forma* denial of racism, the lawyer will receive what may be a quite lengthy disquisition on the juror's encounters with racial minorities. The open-ended question will have elicited a more meaningful answer, but at the expense of valuable court time. Parties who have prepared profiles of favourable and unfavourable jurors may also engage in lengthy background questioning of each juror simply to ascertain the demographic and socioeconomic information that will allow a preliminary evaluation of the juror's suitability as measured by the profile. This, of course, is only a rough guide and not the end to the inquiry, and counsel will still want to probe the particular juror's views on the issues raised by the case.

In theory, peremptory challenges facilitate the impanelling of an impartial jury. In practice, however, lawyers are not so much looking for impartial jurors as for jurors partial to their own side. That this should be so should come as no surprise. Lawyers would do their clients a not easily explained disservice if they were to reject a juror perceived to be predisposed to their position in favour of one thought to be neutral. In an adversarial system it is each side's responsibility to discover and challenge jurors who are biased in favour of the opposition; there is no obligation to challenge jurors believed to favour one's own position. As a result, lawyers are attuned for indications of partiality for or against their case, but not necessarily for the character traits that make for an impartial juror. Indeed, prosecutors may challenge jurors perceived to be ideological or political liberals, while defence lawyers will challenge those who embrace conservative values. Both sides may exercise peremptory challenges against intelligent and discerning jurors, preferring to try their case to persons with more malleable minds. These challenges will distort the representativeness of the jury and, if one subscribes to the Supreme Court's view that a jury representative of a cross-section of the community will produce a 'diffused impartiality', will also undermine the jury's impartiality.

The thesis that an impartial jury will emerge from the elimination of partial jurors is based on a questionable equation of impartiality with the absence of partiality. As has previously been suggested, additional qualities may be required of the impartial juror. Although it may not be accurate to refer to these as qualities of impartiality, they are personality characteristics and orientations which contribute to impartial decision-making. Even the modest goal of eliminating partial jurors encounters practical obstacles since it assumes equal access to information about jurors and equally adept lawyers on each side. These assumptions have always been suspect and have become more so as a consequence of the trend to enlist behavioural scientists to identify jurors with subconscious predispositions. By conducting demographic studies and background investigations of jurors, analysing their psychological profiles and observing paralinguistic cues and body language during *voir dire*, these experts are able to predict which jurors will favour which side. In one sense this is not new. Lawyers have always sought, usually on the basis of hunch or intuition, to choose favourably disposed jurors. What is different is that the social scientists, with their more sophisticated techniques and more rigorous methodologies, are more likely to succeed. By converting what was an 'art' into a 'science', the social scientist increases the risk of a jury composed of persons with subconscious prejudices that will undermine the impartiality of the jury (Etzioni, 1974).

Sceptics maintain that jury selection is not an exact science and that it is impossible to predict all of the variables that may affect a juror's thinking (Abramson, 1994; Berman and Sales, 1977). As Saks (1976) puts it, 'social scientists can't rig juries'. He and his fellow sceptics are no doubt correct but they may be missing the point. However slight the advantage, the side that uses scientific selection techniques will be better placed to make jury selection decisions than the side that does not. Where the reason for the imbalance is more related to the financial resources of the parties than to the merits of the case, there is cause for concern since in a finely balanced case, the extra edge can make the difference between a favourable and an unfavourable verdict. There may also be certain types of cases, usually disregarded in the sceptic's global rejection of scientific jury selection, where these methodologies may be particularly effective. Cases involving widespread publicity, or sensitive racial or political issues, may fall into this category.

The Role of the Court in Jury Selection

The American legal system is prepared to acknowledge, in a way the British system is not, that all persons have biases and that some of these may interfere with a juror's ability to be impartial. The American legal system, again unlike its British counterpart, provides parties with the tools needed to discover juror prejudices and the means for removing prejudiced jurors from the panel. It has broken down because lawyers have subverted those tools to serve their own partisan ends. The lesson to be learned is that, in an adversarial system, the responsibility for selecting an impartial jury cannot be entrusted to lawyers alone. Lawyers have an obligation to their clients and an interest in seeking jurors who will return a verdict favourable to that client. Both the state and the public, however, also have a stake in jury selection. The state wants to preserve the appearance of fairness (as well as the actual fairness) of a criminal justice system which entrusts the responsibility for determining guilt and innocence to ordinary citizens. It is essential that the public has confidence in the integrity of that system and the impartiality of the jurors. The public has an interest in avoiding wrongful acquittals and, worse still, wrongful convictions. It looks to the jury to prevent injustice and to provide fair and just verdicts.

For the reasons indicated, lawyers should not be entrusted with the sole responsibility for jury selection. The court should share in this responsibility, and not just by ruling on challenges initiated by the parties, as is usually the case. Trial judges have a residual power to excuse jurors who are unfit or incompetent[26] but rarely exercise it. A more proactive approach is required. Judges should assume the responsibility for protecting the state's and society's interest in an impartial jury and, on their own motion, excuse those jurors who lack the qualities of character and mind to be fair and impartial jurors.

With the assistance of trained social scientists, judges should develop a 'Juror Aptitude Test' to help them identify the desired jurors (Note, 1968). Devising the specific questions to be asked would obviously be a challenge but seemingly not beyond the capabilities of modern social scientists. The key is first to be clear about what qualities are being sought and then to develop questions which will indicate the presence or absence of these qualities. Robert Redmount, a psychologist turned lawyer, has outlined the types of qualities that such a test might seek to measure (Redmount, 1957). The purpose in setting these out below is not to endorse Redmount's specific criteria but to indicate the lines of possible inquiry:

> 1. *Critical Thinking Ability.* [The] prospective juror [needs to] be able to draw sound inferences from data and observations, to recognize implied assumptions, to reason logically by deduction and interpolation, and to evaluate strength and relevance of argument.
>
> 2. *Personality Status.* The prospective juror should be free of such mental disorder and emotional instability as would produce an undue preoccupation with his own problems of adjustment, and a significant distortion of reality.
>
> 3. *Attitudinal Orientation.* The prospective juror should not be insensitive or opposed to the generally accepted values and conditions surrounding human propensities and human frailty, social order and the requirements of discipline, charity and compassionate understanding, justice, equality and integrity. He should be free of any morbid preoccupation or attitude which would materially color his perceptions and understanding of people and events.
>
> 4. *Social Perception.* The prospective juror's observation and interpretation of behavior should not be so faulty as to be thoroughly inaccurate, and his judgment in social situations should not reflect marked naiveté or gullibility.
>
> 5. *General Information.* The prospective juror should not lack such a fund of general information as would prevent a minimal awareness of things and events in society necessary for an elemental adjustment.
>
> 6. *General Information About the Institution of Law.* The prospective juror should not be totally ignorant or grossly misinformed as to the character and function of generally known legal processes and legal personnel.

When prospective jurors arrive on the appointed day of their service, they would be administered a questionnaire which would consist of the Juror Aptitude Test augmented with case-specific questions submitted by the parties in the trials scheduled during the juror's service.[27] This pre-trial questionnaire would replace *voir dire*. It would be more efficient, for the questionnaire would not have to be completed in open court. It would provide more accurate information, for jurors would be able to consider their answers. Under the current system of *voir dire* jurors are under pressure to respond promptly to a lawyer's in-court questions and sometimes will fail to express their views accurately. Admittedly, lawyers would lose the opportunity to take into account a juror's body language and non-verbal cues while responding to particular questions, as well as the opportunity to probe ambiguous responses. Despite these losses, it is submitted that the questionnaire, perhaps supplemented by the opportunity for limited follow-up questions when the court deemed it appropriate, would strike a reasonable balance between the need for a sound basis upon which to make informed jury selection decisions and the need for a manageable and efficient procedure. Since challenges would be 'blind', claims that parties were using challenges on race or on other improper grounds would be virtually eliminated, particularly if jurors were identified by number rather than by name. Jurors would be assigned to cases, based on their ability to judge the particular case impartially. Those who were deemed by the court to be lacking the basic character traits required to be impartial in any case would be excused on the court's motion. After the court had exercised its power to excuse jurors, the parties would be allowed to raise challenges for cause. As presently required, these would have to be supported by a legally cognizable ground for dismissal. The moving party, however, would have the benefit of being able to cite specific answers in the questionnaire to support the challenge. Finally, the parties would be allowed to exercise however many peremptory challenges were allowed by law. If only to preserve the defendant's confidence in the fairness of the proceedings, a limited number of peremptory challenges should be permitted.

All rulings would be made outside the jury's presence. Challenged jurors would, as a result, never learn whether it was the court or one of the parties which had caused them to be excused. Other jurors who were friendly with those who had been excused would likewise not know against which side to take out their displeasure, even if tempted to do so. Dismissed jurors, however, might still feel slighted as a result of having been denied the opportunity to serve, and the trial judge, as most already do, should reassure them that their excusal should not be interpreted as a general declaration of unfitness. The judge should explain that a challenge often represents nothing more than a 'best guess' that the individuals in question may not be the most appropriate jurors for the particular case.

Juror Training

A Juror Aptitude Test is not proposed with the aim of excluding a large swathe of prospective jurors. Most persons are capable of being competent jurors with appropriate training, and the courts should take responsibility for providing such training. At present, prospective jurors typically receive, along with their summons to jury duty, a booklet which describes the mechanics of the legal system and the jury's role in it.[28] At the trial, the judge will usually make a few welcoming remarks, and a short introductory film describing the role of the jury may also be shown. What the jurors are not likely to receive, on the other hand, is any practical advice on how to conduct their deliberations. The judge may exhort them to consider the evidence carefully and listen to the views of others, but the judge's advice is likely to end there.

As a result, juror deliberations tend to be an exercise in improvization. Some juries take a straw poll on a verdict before beginning to discuss the evidence, while others engage in a lengthy exchange of views before taking any vote. One of the lessons of social science research, however, is that premature voting tends to harden positions and can have an inhibiting effect on the discussion of issues perceived to be beyond the scope of the preliminary vote (Hastie *et al.*, 1983). The problem is that nobody warns the jurors of those undesirable effects.

Even if a jury begins by engaging in a general exchange of views, at what point should a vote be taken? And how should the deliberations proceed up to that point? Should there be a round wherein each juror in turn gives his or her opinion without interruption, or is it preferable for there to be a general discussion during which jurors are free to interrupt whenever they wish to take issue with a point being made by another juror. To maintain a semblance of order, is it desirable to agree on a moderator (the foreperson?) who will be responsible for determining in what order the jurors will speak, or would this give the individual in question too much power? Should the timing of any vote be preset or a natural outgrowth of the point which the deliberations have reached? If the latter, who makes this determination? Is this too the responsibility of the foreperson, or should any member of the jury be allowed to call for a vote at any time? May different types of cases call for different approaches? These questions and others, extending to even such mundane matters as the shape of the table in the jury room (traditionally rectangular, but circular might better emphasize the jurors' equality) are susceptible to empirical research, and such research should be encouraged. Social scientists – particularly those with an expertise in learning theory and group dynamics – as well as seasoned trial lawyers and courtroom observers, may be able to contribute valuable insights. An impetus would no doubt be provided if the judges were to indicate that these contributions would be taken seriously in the formulation of a juror training programme.

Indeed, jurors may themselves be eminently capable of establishing the necessary ground rules to cover their deliberations, if only they were encouraged to put their minds to the task. After all, such rules are usually little more than the dictates of common sense. Chapter 7 will examine the topic of 'citizens juries', but, briefly, a citizens jury consists of a group of randomly selected individuals who are brought together to examine an issue of social or political importance, presented with evidence, and allowed to deliberate to a verdict. Rather than deciding guilt or innocence, citizens juries will typically make recommendations relating to public policy. A citizens jury will usually last from three to five days, and the evening before the first session may be devoted to preparing the jurors for their task. In this session the jurors, with the assistance of trained facilitators, will explore their goals and concerns, and establish the ground rules that will govern their deliberations. Various citizens juries have compiled the following dos and don'ts:

Do...	**Don't...**
• listen to and respect your fellow jurors • allow everybody to feel comfortable	• make personal attacks on other jurors or laugh at (rather than with) them
• accept that different people proceed at different paces	• rush others who may seem slower than you to grasp a point • move on prematurely
• allow each juror to say what is on his/her mind; share thoughts • stick to the merits	• interrupt or 'cross-talk'
• help others develop their ideas	• 'put down' ideas with which you disagree but do indicate the difficulties you are having with the idea
• keep to the point	• bring up clear irrelevancies
• feel free to brainstorm	• be critical of seemingly 'way-out' ideas; consider all ideas on their merits

- recognize the value of cross-fertilization
- speak up if you do not follow an argument or disagree with something somebody says

- take dogmatic positions
- attempt to railroad those who do not agree with your positions
- 'give in' if not persuaded
- feel compelled to join the majority purely for the sake of preserving harmony

These guidelines are not exhaustive and may need adjusting to fit the demands of the particular case. They are presented simply to demonstrate that jurors, if given the chance, are capable of coming up with sensible rules to govern their deliberations. Legal jurors also possess this capacity, but never receive any indication that there would be value in establishing procedural ground rules before turning to the substance of their deliberations.

As noted, prospective jurors in Britain and some American states may be shown a short film that describes the legal system and the jury's role within it. Although a film holds considerable potential, those currently in use tend to be anodyne and unambitious. They sketch the jury's role in matter-of-fact terms and rarely underscore the challenge facing the jurors or the satisfaction that comes from successfully meeting that challenge. A worthwhile training film should excite the jurors' imagination and appeal to their aspirational selves. The movie classic *Twelve Angry Men*, where a lone initial hold-out ultimately persuades his eleven conviction-minded colleagues to return a not guilty verdict, is, despite its theatricality, both inspirational and instructive. It brings out the need to distinguish between the substance of testimony and the personality of the witness. It shows how bias can be combated in the jury room. Most importantly, it reveals the synergistic and dialectic forces at work within the jury and illustrates how a principled verdict will emerge from democratic deliberations.

The proposal here is not that all jurors be compelled to sit through *Twelve Angry Men*. The legal system should produce its own film (or, if current restrictions were to be relaxed, a videotape of an actual jury deliberation) that illustrates what goes on in a jury room. The film should bring out both the potential and the pitfalls of the deliberations. Following its screening, the jurors, assisted by a court-appointed facilitator would review the film. Selected portions could be replayed to clarify or highlight key points. The objective of the exercise would be to identify – or, better still, get the jurors to identify for themselves – good decision-making practices. This session would itself serve as an example of how a group discussion might proceed. It would also provide the jurors with the opportunity to get to know each other and to become comfortable with speaking in each other's presence. It is important that members of a jury – or any decisional group – develop a mutual regard and respect that will allow them to disagree with each other without becoming destructively confrontational. Jurors must have the confidence to speak frankly without having to fear being the subject of personal attack. The facilitator should strive to create an environment in which jurors will subsequently be able to work together.

Both the deliberations depicted in the film and the discussion following it will provide jurors with insight into ways in which they might conduct their own deliberations. It makes sense, however, to provide the jurors with the opportunity to test these new-found skills in a setting that will not have major repercussions for the liberty of a defendant should they get it wrong. In a second phase of juror training jurors would engage in a simulated exercise involving a hypothetical fact situation which would be presented through videotaped testimony. After viewing the tape, the jurors would deliberate to a verdict. The deliberations would be observed through a one-way mirror by qualified experts. Following the verdict, the court-appointed facilitator would review the deliberations with the jurors, not for substance but for process. Again, however, a secondary agenda could be to promote the types of group dynamics and interactions that will ease the jury's subsequent deliberations, while pointing out practices that may interfere with, or undermine, those deliberations.

Thus the jurors, before hearing a live case, will have been exposed to the introductory film, a critical discussion of that film and a simulated jury deliberation. They will have discussed and established ground rules governing their deliberations. In addition, specific techniques that will help the jurors can be taught. For example, instruction in note-taking would relieve jurors of having to rely on their memories when recalling witness testimony. In a lengthy trial, note-taking can be particularly valuable. Empirical research indicates that taking notes increases the note-taker's attentiveness and promotes long-term memory (Kiewra, 1987). However, jurors should not be left with the impression that the object of the exercise is to produce a verbatim transcript of a witness's testimony. The goal rather is to record the salient points. Jurors should also be encouraged to write down their subjective impressions of witnesses and any potentially significant non-verbal cues that they might observe. Other techniques that might be pointed out to the jurors include the value of diagrams and flowcharts in reconstructing the chronological and causational sequence of events. The jurors should also be alerted to the kinds of emotions and traumas that might affect them during the course of the trial.[29]

Sound and sensible decision-making requires attention not only to logic but to intuition. Jurors need to be reassured that they should not automatically discount their feelings about how a case should be decided, the natural tendency being to overvalue logic and undervalue intuition (perhaps because the latter seems less rigorous or scientific). Both logic and intuition have a role to play in the decision-making process, but each has to be approached critically. Jurors need to put their intuitions about a case under a microscope to assure themselves that they are based on legitimate concerns and not irrational prejudices. The dialectics of the jury room will facilitate this critical analysis, but during the testimony the jurors should also be monitoring their reactions to witnesses and asking themselves, when they feel hostile towards a witness, why they are having that reaction. In the pretrial training sessions, psychologists can teach ways to achieve this self-monitoring.

It might be thought that the training of jurors constitutes a relatively large investment in time and resources for a task that juries already seem to be doing tolerably well. I would not wish to be seen to be disputing the fact that the jury system already functions fairly effectively. Indeed, what is remarkable is that functions as well as it does without juror training and with only minimal guidance from the court. It would be both surprising and disappointing, however, if the overall effectiveness of the system could not be improved through instruction. Studies have demonstrated that problem-solving skills can be learned (Bloom and Broder, 1950; Polya, 1965) and that the closer the relationship between the training exercises and the task that must subsequently be undertaken, the more effective is the training. (Mansfield *et al.*, 1978). The experience of citizens juries is that preliminary sessions devoted to 'process' issues promote mutual respect among the jurors and allow for the recognition of stumbling blocks that might otherwise interfere with the deliberations. The pay-off for the legal system in the investment in juror training is likely to be a superior quality of jury decision-making and the elimination (or at least reduction) of those aberrational cases where jury room deliberations are infected by bias. In turn, the community would be able to have even greater confidence than it already has in jury verdicts. The 'democratic dividend' (see Chapter 4) to the jurors, as well as to the state, would also be enhanced.

The time spent in the training of jurors, it should be remembered, is not court time, as the training can proceed while the court goes about its other business. One of the most common complaints from jurors relates to the idle time that they spend waiting for their case to be called. This waiting period can be put to constructive use in juror training. If one were to assume a standard jury term of three to four weeks – somewhat longer than at present but justified by the fact that jurors gain in confidence with experience – then the investment of one or two days in preparing the jurors for their service would be neither disproportionate nor unreasonable. On citizens juries the equivalent of a half-day of a four-day programme is spent in such preparation, with demonstrably good effect.

Conclusion

Without specifically referring to the jury, philosophers, from Aristotle to John Stuart Mill and John Rawls in our present age, have extolled the type of intellectual challenge that is involved in jury duty. Grappling with a knotty problem and achieving a fair and just resolution provides a special kind of satisfaction. Jury deliberations force jurors to piece together conflicting testimony and give concrete form to intuitions which may well be correct but which need to be supported by sound reasons. In this chapter I have advocated juror training as a means of better preparing jurors for their task. Arguably, however, this preparation should begin long before the summons for jury duty arrives.

The temperament and character traits required of the responsible citizen and juror should be taught and reinforced from an early age. Children need to learn about justice and fairness as much as they need to learn about science and mathematics. Teaching students to think critically should be part and parcel of every academic course. It should be regarded not as a sterile classroom exercise, but as instruction in an indispensable life skill. It is an integral component of responsible citizenship, which of course includes jury service. Children should be taught to respect the opinions of others, not simply because tolerance and open-mindedness are virtues in themselves but because having to listen to the viewpoints of others help to contribute to the better understanding of one's own position. A course such as 'Justice, Fairness and Impartiality' should be an integral component of every school's curriculum.

In addition to formal tuition, young adults should be provided with the opportunity to acquire hands-on experience with the challenges that face a decision-making body. Practical problems, whose resolution has real-world consequences, focus the mind in the same way as the facts of a case focus the minds of legal jurors. Like legal jurors, the participants would learn that they have to make the hard decision and take responsibility for that decision. The school would provide a natural environment in which this practical experience could be gained. Students should serve, alongside their elders, on school boards and committees. They should have a voice and a vote on educational policies that, after all, will affect their lives. Although some might doubt whether students possess the maturity to be included on these bodies, the lesson to be learned from legal juries is that entrusting individuals with the responsibility for important decisions generates its own sense of responsibility. Just as serving on a jury teaches decision-making skills that can be put to subsequent use, so too will active involvement on decision-making bodies help to develop the maturity and self-confidence of the young. The parents and teachers on these bodies will serve as role models, and the fact that they will be looked to in this capacity is likely to elevate the quality of their own contributions to the decision-making process.

The feasibility of including children on educational committees is borne out by the experience in Austria where a conscious decision has been made to involve students in the setting of educational policy (Kisser, 1996). Individual students may raise concerns and make suggestions regarding the content and organization of their lessons. They may propose alternatives or additional teaching materials. On an institutional level, they are accorded a voice on policy decisions, such as those relating to the content of school magazines and the selection of outside speakers. They play an active part in determining the school's involvement in civic, political and cultural activities and hold seats on consultative bodies that shape general education policy. Another area in which students might be given a place is on disciplinary tribunals. These quasi-judicial bodies require their members to perform in a jury-like capacity, listening to evidence, deliberating and reaching a fair and just decision. That decision, for which the students – like jurors – will have to take responsibility, can affect the course of another student's educational career.

The Austrian experience of involving students in the making of educational policy has had many benefits. Students feel as though they are a part of the process and are keen to be engaged. As indicated by the number of Austrian students who participate in school elections, student apathy is not the problem it is in other countries (Kisser, 1996). This, in turn, has encouraged the Austrian Federal Ministry of Education and Cultural Affairs to provide ever-increasing amounts of information to students, with the aim of reaching and engaging as many students as possible. While the long-term effect of these initiatives is difficult to assess, it would be no surprise if the children grew up to be more civic-minded, more self-assured and more mature citizens as a result of their student experiences. The benefit of these experiences would also no doubt be felt if these students were later to be called to serve on a jury.

Notes

1 See, for example, Lord Lane, CJ, in *R.* v. *Ford* [1989] QB 868.
2 366 US 717 (1961).
3 Ibid. at pp. 722–3.
4 Ibid. at p. 728.
5 373 US 723 (1963).
6 Ibid. at p. 726.
7 421 US 794 (1975).
8 Ibid. at pp. 802–3.
9 *United States* v. *Burr*, 25 F. Cas. 49, 50–51 (CCD Va. 1807) (No. 14 x 692g).
10 Criminal Justice Act 1977.
11 Criminal Justice Act 1988, s.118.
12 See *Rostaino* v. *Ross*, 424 US 589, 596 (1976).
13 Home Office, Criminal Justice Plans for Legislation (HMSO 1986).
14 *The Times*, 7 January 1987.
15 In cases where multiple defendants are seeking to vindicate distinct interests, each defendant might be allowed the full complement of peremptory challenges. For in-between cases, a compromise solution could be fashioned by the court.
16 See *R.* v. *Kray* (1969) 53 Crim. App. R. 142.
17 See, generally, Gobert and Jordan (1990); National Jury Project (1987).
18 In some instances the pre-trial investigation may indicate that it is to the defendant's advantage to waive his or her right to a jury trial and have the case tried by a judge sitting alone.
19 For example, a mock trial permits a lawyer to try out various lines of argument. Those which are not well received by the mock jurors can be expected to be equally unsuccessful in front of the real jury. Counsel may decide either to sharpen the argument or discard it completely. Another advantage to mock trials is their value in assisting lawyers (particularly inexperienced lawyers) to improve their own presentations. In a similar vein mock trials allow the witnesses for the side conducting the mock trial to gain a foretaste of what it will be like to be subjected to direct and cross-examination, and the types of questions that they are likely to be asked.
20 Witnesses for the opposing side, of course, would not be required to participate in a mock trial or, indeed, to speak to the opposing side's lawyer except in formally prescribed settings.
21 In Chapter 4 it was noted that, in Britain, the comparable practice of jury vetting by police can occur.
22 See American Bar Association Code of Professional Responsibility DR 7–29, 7–30, and 7–108 (1980).
23 See *Griswold* v. *Connecticut*, 381 US 479 (1965).
24 *Press-Enterprise Co.* v. *Superior Court*, 464 US 501 (1984).
25 See, for example, *United States* v. *Barnes*, 604 F2d 121 (2d Cir. 1979), *cert. denied*, 446 US 907 (1980); *United States* v. *Eufrasio*, 935 F2d 553 (3d Cir. 1991); *United States* v. *Crockett*, 979 F2d 1204 (7th Cir. 1992). See generally King (1995).
26 See *R.* v. *Ford* [1989] QB 868.
27 The two sets of questions might be intermixed or form separate sections of the questionnaire. Each party to a case would be given the opportunity to submit questions and to object to questions submitted by the other side, and the court would prune the questions to eliminate duplicates or those that it deemed to be improper.
28 See, for example, *You and Your Jury Service* (HMSO).

29 Where jurors are forced to relive a horrific crime, such as rape or a particularly gruesome murder, they often suffer emotionally. In addition to pre-trial training, there should be post-trial counselling for jurors who are having difficulty in getting over the effects of what they have seen and heard.

7 From the World of Law to the World at Large

It is customary to conclude books about the jury with a look into the future, and this book is no exception. The future that I wish to examine, however, is only in part that of the legal jury. Despite criticism of the occasional verdict, the role of the jury in criminal trials seems relatively secure for the moment. Certainly this is so in the United States. The British critics are more vocal and the future of the jury in Britain perhaps more clouded. The highly respected Royal Commission on Criminal Justice, however, exonerated the jury of responsibility for the miscarriages of justice which had occurred during the 1980s and gave its unequivocal endorsement to the continuation of the jury system (Runciman Committee, 1993). Its report seems, at least temporarily, to have silenced the critics.

This is rightly so, for the benefits of jury trial are many. At the same time as the jury provides an efficacious means of resolving disputed issues of fact, it also stands guard against official abuses of power by legislatures, police, prosecutors and courts. By infusing the administration of the criminal justice system with the values of the community, the jury brings the law closer to the ordinary person's sense of justice and thereby keeps the law in touch with the people whose lives it is intended to govern. In addition, the jury provides a valuable check against the dangers of a judicial bureaucracy by combating legal formalism with common sense and practical reason. The fact that a verdict has been returned by ordinary citizens gives it a legitimacy that might be lacking if it were seen to be the product of a professional judiciary appointed and paid by the very state in whose name the criminal prosecution is brought. Yet judge and jury complement each other – the judge sets the legal parameters, the boundaries in which the jury operates, while the jury tempers the law with mercy and justice.

While the future that I wish to look at is in part that of the jury, in greater part it is that of political democracy. As both Britain and the United States prepare for the millenium, their centuries-old democratic institutions are creaking. Opinion poll after opinion polls suggests that the people have lost confidence in the government's ability to solve social problems. There is a growing sense that important decisions can no longer be left to the politicians and that the people themselves have to assume a greater share of the responsibility for decision-making. But how are the people to become involved? The answer does not lie in the proliferation of opinion polls or demagogic 'talk radio' programmes. A more effective means needs to be created to obtain the informed and reflective judgements of responsible citizens. The jury offers a model that has proved effective in the legal context and which, with appropriate modifications, can be put to use in a social and political context.

This chapter begins with a review of those features that distinguish the jury from other decision-making bodies. To a large extent this is an exercise in bringing together points that have already been made, as well as advancing proposals for ways in which the jury system could be improved. Following this review I discuss what I see as the growing problems in Anglo-American democracy – how and why governments have lost touch with their people. Finally, I proceed to examine how the processes of the jury can be adapted and put to work in the revival of democratic traditions which are under threat.

The Jury as Process

The jury system is unique. It is a system that relies on amateurs rather than professionals, and on generalists rather than specialists. It is a system in which information seeks out the decision-makers rather than the other way around, and where the decision-makers are given as much time as they need to arrive at a judgement. It is a system that takes one case at a time, giving each its individual attention. Its processes encourage rationality, but in its hierarchy of values justice trumps law. I have attempted to identify the key features of the jury: democratic selection; political equality; impartiality; informed decision-making; an opportunity for critical reflection; a synergistic and dialectic process of deliberation; and collective accountability. It might, however, prove useful briefly to review these here, along with proposed reforms, before attempting to take the discussion further afield. Suggestions for reform are offered in the spirit of fine-tuning a basically sound product rather than finding a replacement for a defective product.

Democratic selection and political equality

The modern jury is an independent, non-partisan institution whose membership crosses racial, religious, class, ethnic and gender lines. Jurors are selected without regard to political affiliation. Whereas few citizens may ever hold public office, any citizen may be summoned to serve on a jury. On that jury there is complete political equality. Each juror has one, and only one, vote, and each vote counts equally. All jurors are equal – in status and in voting power. Jurors make a difference, not just by their votes but also by their contributions to the democratic deliberations which take place in the jury room. It is on the basis of these contributions, and not on their curriculum vitae, that jurors ultimately judge each other. On the jury everybody is reduced – or, more accurately, elevated – to the political status of juror.

The democratic premise that underlies the jury system is that all citizens, regardless of rank, are competent to serve. Of course there may be some who lack the maturity or mental capacity to be effective, and they will be excused, but the general assumption is that these are few in number and that they should be identified on an individual basis. Blanket disqualifications and exemptions are to be avoided whenever possible. One of the challenges facing both the British and American legal systems is to develop additional sources of juror names beyond the electoral register in order to cast the juror net as wide as possible. At the same time the categories of juror exemptions and exclusions need to be pruned so that they extend no further than is absolutely necessary.

The jury's verdict is the judgement of the people. It is said, quite correctly, that the jury is the conscience of the community – the whole community. But the value of a jury that includes all segments of the community is not to allow each constituency to have its particular political agenda represented. This would convert the jurors to ciphers, and reduce the particular case to a mere backdrop against which social issues were debated. The particular case and its merits always take priority. The value of diversity is rather that it brings to the decision-making process the broadest possible range of perspectives so that jurors are forced to consider viewpoints which they may not have previously encountered or with which they may be relatively unfamiliar. This diversity of perspective forces jurors to think about facts and events in ways that might not otherwise have occurred to them. It is only by looking at a problem from all possible angles that a full understanding of its nature can be gained. A democratically selected jury is best able to provide that breadth of perspective.

Impartiality

For the community to have confidence in a jury's verdict, it must have confidence in the jurors. It is therefore critical that the responsibility for the verdict be given to persons whose impartiality has somehow been vouchsafed. Although jurors may be chosen at random, they ought to be screened for impartiality. Not only should jurors have no personal interest in the outcome of a case, they should possess those qualities of character and temperament that will allow them to judge the case in a fair and unbiased manner. These traits can be taught, however, and the legal system must take responsibility for providing the necessary training.

Democracy and impartiality, as has been emphasized, are not unrelated. The heterogeneous jury that is likely to be produced by the democratic selection of jurors will itself fight bias on the jury. Jurors challenge each other's prejudices. Theories of a case which are rooted in bias against the defendant or a victim will not be persuasive to members of the panel who do not share the juror's bias. This is why a heterogeneous jury is more likely to be impartial than one which is homogeneous. Whereas conflicting prejudices confront each other on a heterogeneous jury, shared prejudices reinforce each other on a homogeneous jury. A conscious effort should accordingly be made to impanel a heterogeneous jury.

Although a heterogenous jury will combat prejudice, there should also be an effort to identify those jurors whose prejudices are so fixed that they will prove impervious to reason. The responsibility for this screening cannot be left solely to lawyers whose partisanship is endemic to an adversary system. As guardian of the public interest, the court must share in the responsibility. The judiciary's role, moreover, should extend beyond taking a hand in the selection of jurors who have the potential to be fair and impartial. The court should also assume the responsibility for bringing out that potential so that it can be used to best advantage in the deliberations. Training sessions can be invaluable to the large majority of prospective jurors who are not so blatantly biased to be excusable for cause but whose decision-making abilities have not been fully developed either (in other words, the overwhelming majority of those in the jury pool).

The institution of pre-trial training sessions will allow the democratic base of the jury pool to be expanded, while reducing the need for intrusive and time-consuming questioning of jurors. Rather than excusing jurors whose fairness might be borderline, the courts would bring them to the requisite level of impartiality. Summing up, the judge should openly and frankly discuss with the jurors the importance of impartiality, as well as the dangers of prejudice and the nature of justice. The dialectic forces of the jury room will then keep the jurors on the tracks that have been laid.

Informed Decision-making

That most everyday decisions are based on incomplete information is not surprising. Opportunities can be lost by engaging in a prolonged effort to discover all of the information needed to make an optimal decision. An individual inclined to such thoroughness may be stymied by the obstacles in obtaining the desired information. In some instances the opposing problem can occur – too much rather than too little information. A decision-maker can often be overwhelmed by the abundance of reports and analyses available, and frustrated by the prospect of having to digest it all. Nor can the decision-maker ever be certain that all the relevant data has been discovered or that which has been discovered is complete and accurate.

Prior to being summoned, modern-day jurors, unlike their ancestors, will usually have little knowledge of the facts or issues in the case which is to be tried. It is obviously important that the jurors become familiar with these facts and issues, but it is also important that they should not be buried under an excess of information or misled by information of dubious quality. The Anglo-American legal system attempts to surmount these hurdles through an adversarial system which relies on lawyers representing the respective sides to locate witnesses and present the facts in a form that the jurors can understand. Overreaching is, to some extent, prevented by rules of evidence, but more by the fact that each side is given the opportunity to expose – through cross-examination and argument – the flaws and inconsistencies in the opposing side's case. In their closing speeches the lawyers for each side will present a narrative account of the facts, as they see them, for the jury to consider. The jurors may choose between these accounts or, more likely, construct their own story based on the evidence.

The trial judge has the responsibility for ensuring that the trial is conducted in accord with established rules of procedure and in an orderly manner. The judge's relationship with the jury is particularly critical, for it is the judge who is responsible for instructing the jury in the law which it is to apply to the case. This should be set out not in legalistic jargon but in language that will be comprehensible to the non-lawyers who sit on the jury. The judge should also indicate, where necessary, the reasoning behind the law and why it has taken the course it has. In addition, the trial judge should discuss with the jurors the importance of achieving justice and the types of consideration that might bear on this issue in the particular case.

Thus in a well run adversarial system the jury is provided with all the information – both legal and factual – that it needs to decide the case. It is not required to conduct its own investigations, although it should be encouraged, far more than it typically is, to ask questions of witnesses to clarify areas of confusion. It should also be encouraged to indicate witnesses for the court to call, who would seem to have relevant information to contribute. In cases where earlier testimony has been called into question by later testimony, the jury should be allowed to propose the recall of previous witnesses.

An Opportunity for Reflection

There is no rush to judgement on a jury. Jurors are excused from their jobs for the duration of their service and are compensated for their time. Unfortunately, the compensation is often rather low. In Britain the maximum payment for jurors is currently £44 per day plus expenses, although if the trial lasts longer than two weeks, this figure is doubled. This, however, seems a princely sum compared to the $5 per day paid to jurors in California.[1] Despite the economic implications, the compensation provided to jurors is in urgent need of review. Derisory payments undoubtedly deter many otherwise public-spirited citizens from serving on a jury. They also demean the critical role which jurors play in the administration of the criminal justice system. One way to ensure that jurors are not financially disadvantaged by their service is to require companies to continue to pay employees during their term of service. Some companies already do so on a voluntary basis, but this practice should be made obligatory by statute. Relieving jurors of job-related responsibilities and undue financial worries is essential if they are to be expected to give their undivided attention to the case before them and to consider that case properly. For jurors who are unemployed or self-employed, the state should recognize their contribution by the provision of reasonable compensation.

Jurors are allowed to conduct their deliberations in a jury room that is closed to third parties. The deliberations may not be taped or videorecorded, thereby insulating jurors from the unnerving effect that comes from knowing that one's every word is being scrutinized by outside observers. Jurors are also protected from third-party pressures during breaks in the trial by marshals. Historically, jurors in criminal cases were not permitted to separate, although this safeguard has now to some extent been relaxed.[2] This structured environment helps to maintain reasoned and rational dialogue, as well as insulating jurors from external pressures and intimidation.

Finally, there are no time constraints on the jury's deliberations. It is not unknown for a jury to take longer to decide a case than it took to present the evidence. Although there is no necessary correlation between the length and quality of the deliberations, and although the length of deliberations does not by itself guarantee a fair and just verdict, it does indicate that jurors take their responsibilities seriously. They are not, as some would suggest, eager to embrace the first verdict that might be proposed in order to return to their homes and families. Although it would be naive to suggest that such considerations may never enter a juror's mind, a combination of peer pressure and the jury's collective sense of responsibility will help to resist any such inclinations. As a result, the verdict is likely to be a carefully thought through and reflective judgement – one in which the community can have confidence.

Dynamic Deliberations

The verdict of a jury is not simply the sum of the twelve individual opinions that the jurors might have at the close of the evidence but rather the product of an intense, interactive process of deliberation. During the deliberation each juror can be expected to express his or her opinion of the case. Each opinion is subject to challenge by eleven others who have been exposed to the same testimony, arguments and instructions. Jurors who take unprincipled stances will have to justify their position and a failure to do so will lead to a rejection of the juror's position. Faulty reasoning will be exposed, as will analyses rooted in prejudice. Other jurors' comments may cause a juror to reconsider or abandon previously held positions. Analyses that are not well reasoned will be displaced by other analyses which will also be critically scrutinized. From this cauldron of dialogue and debate will ultimately emerge the theory of the case that best fits the facts, the law and the demands of justice. The process allows the community to have confidence that the right verdict has been reached.

The dynamics of the jury room are not dictated by statute or the directions of the judge but are inherent in the operation of the jury system. The requirement of a unanimous or at least super-majority verdict stimulates these dynamics. Requiring the jurors to reach a unanimous verdict is to be preferred, for it forces the jury to take seriously the arguments of each and every juror. No juror's concerns can be ignored if he or she is expected to join in the verdict. The problem of the irrational or eccentric juror, which the reform of a consensus verdict was designed to obviate, would have been better addressed by greater care in the selection and training of jurors.

Even if a unanimous/super-majority verdict were not required, there would be sound practical reasons for jurors to take other jurors seriously. If a juror did not, the others might respond in kind and pay no attention to the juror in question. Even without this practical constraint it can be maintained, with good reason, that jurors would listen to each other anyway. Few individuals are so certain of their opinions that they will brook no opposition, and most will be open to persuasion. This open-mindedness will be even more characteristic of a jury whose members have received the recommended juror training. Jurors who disagree with positions contrary to their own will at least want to demonstrate why the position with which they disagree is misguided. Peer pressure will also demand a response. The discourse will continue until a consensus is forged, which, as Kalvin and Zeisel (1966) discovered, occurs in the overwhelming majority of cases. But perhaps this should come as no surprise. The processes of the jury room, although rooted in contention, ultimately promote consensus.

Collective accountability

Jurors are ordinary citizens who are asked to undertake an extraordinary task – that of sitting in judgement of a fellow human being. This is a daunting challenge, and one that few persons would want to take on by themselves. Part of the reason that judges – who might be expected to resent the intrusion of laypersons into their professional domain – may not be opposed to the jury is that it relieves the judge of having to take sole responsibility for the verdict. Nor are the jurors expected to take on this assignment as individuals. Theirs is a collective enterprise. In an era in which citizens are increasingly less dependent upon their neighbours than in the past, jury service is one of the few remaining examples of a shared community responsibility.[3]

Jurors work together in many ways by compensating for any lapses in concentration on the part of any of their members during the testimony, by pooling their recollections of the evidence in order to construct an accurate picture of the facts and by challenging each other to think critically about the case. Although they may argue heatedly during the deliberations, by so doing, they help each other see the case more clearly.

While jurors contribute their individual opinions and insights during the deliberations, the final verdict will be that of the jury as a whole. Of whatever parts it is composed, the verdict represents a decision for which all the jurors must take collective responsibility. Unlike appellate court judges, individual jurors are not permitted to file dissenting opinions. That there should be collective accountability is inappropriate. No juror should concur in a verdict to which he or she is opposed in conscience and the trial court should make that clear in its directions.

Democracy in Decline

Given the advantages of the jury system, it might be wondered why similar bodies are not employed in other decision-making contexts. My contention is that they should. More particularly, I plan to show how the model of the jury can be adapted to revitalize Anglo-American democratic traditions that have fallen into decline. But, first, a case must be made that such revitalization is needed. What, if anything, is wrong with the system of representative government which today passes for political democracy in the United States and the United Kingdom? In its favour is the fact that it has operated reasonably successfully for centuries. As Edmund Burke once warned, caution should be exercised in tampering with institutions that have a long history of adequately serving society's needs.

In both Britain and the United States, there is unprecedented social equality and freedom of opportunity. But *social* democracy is not *political* democracy. Political democracy envisages self-government by the people. Its roots can be traced to ancient Athens, where up to 6000 citizens would regularly gather to debate the political questions of the day (Hornblower, 1992). In the US town meetings were frequently held in the small villages of New England. At such meetings every individual who wished to speak was allowed to do so, and all present were permitted to vote. The ancient Greek and colonial New England practices represented models of participatory democracy.

The nineteenth and twentieth centuries, however, witnessed a population explosion which made participatory democracy something of an anachronism. On national issues it was clearly impossible to bring together the millions of people who might be affected by pending legislation. Of necessity if not choice, society was forced to trade in its model of participatory democracy for one of representative government. In place of direct citizen involvement in government was substituted elections in which the people were permitted to choose legislators to represent their interests in the national assembly. The practical effect, however, was to rob the citizenry of their democratic right to be involved in the operation of the government and replace it with a periodic opportunity to choose between preselected, and often unattractive, candidates.

It is questionable whether elected officials do in fact represent the interests of their constituents. Most legislators vote as they are directed by their party leadership, especially in Britain where party discipline seems to be more effectively exercised than it is in the United States. It should not be assumed, however, that political parties reflect the views of the people. In modern British politics there are three major parties and the successful candidate in an election often receives only a minority of the vote. Third parties are less frequently encountered in the United States, but the winner of the election may still receive less or perhaps only slightly more than a bare majority of the votes cast. There is the further complicating factor of the inferences to be drawn from the not insignificant portion of the electorate (particularly in the United States) who choose not to vote. Is it fair to assume that these non-voters are equally comfortable with the positions of all of the major parties – or equally disenchanted? Taking into account all of these factors, it becomes difficult to maintain that the official position of a party, and legislative votes along party lines, reflect the wishes of the people, even when the legislative votes accord with the party's electoral manifesto.

It is even an error to assume that the positions of successful candidates in an election are endorsed by those who vote for the candidates. For one thing, in most elections, candidates are chosen by political parties and not the people. The people's choice may be limited to two or three unpalatable alternatives. Furthermore, except in the relatively rare case of a referendum, voters are not afforded the opportunity to express an opinion on particular issues. Elections tend to turn more on personalities and general philosophy than on specific issues. Party manifestos and platforms may be deliberately vague in order to attract as many supporters as possible. Those who do vote for candidates because of their stated positions will typically agree with some but not all of those positions. They cast their ballots for the candidates with whom they share the most common ground on the issues which most matter to them. This is quite different from saying that they support a given party on the entirety of its manifesto. Victorious candidates like to claim mandates when, more often than they would care to admit, their success is attributable to the fact that they were perceived as the lesser of evils.

When legislators are not directed by party, they may fall under the sway of lobbyists representing special interest groups within society. It is not the job of such a lobbyist to represent the public interest and the one-sided arguments made by the lobbyist may give a distorted view of the issues. There may well be no 'public interest' representative to correct the distortions. While capitalist enterprises are able to afford lobbyists, the poor, not surprisingly, cannot. Of course, they can vote out a representative who fails to support their interests, but an election may be in the distant future. By the time of the election the issue, or the legislator's vote on it, may be a distant memory, or have been displaced by more pressing concerns. Elections are also expensive to run, and candidates may be financially dependent on the same corporate sponsors that lobby them. This incestuous relationship further exarcerbates the strong influence of the lobbyist.

Let us hypothesize, however, a legislator who genuinely seeks to represent the views of his or her constituents. How is the legislator to ascertain those views? There are few formal mechanisms through which the people can make their opinions know. Referendums are infrequent,[4] expensive and rarely enlightening. It is often difficult to capture complex issues in a question suitable for a referendum, and a poorly worded question can yield misleading results. At best the vote in a referendum will reflect majority preferences; it may more realistically reflect only the preferences of the organizations that were most successful in getting their supporters to the polls. As there is rarely a provision on a referendum for a voter to suggest alternatives, an analyst who wished to make sense of the vote will not discover an option that might have received greater public support had it been on the ballot. There is also the same problem that exists in respect to elections of the inferences to be drawn in regard to those who do not vote.

Public opinion polls, in contrast to referendums, proliferate. New polls replace old polls before there has been time to digest the implications of the previous poll. The results may seem to be a reflection of public opinion, but the opinions that they measure are usually those of an uninformed public. This factor could be taken into account if those polled were prepared to concede their lack of knowledge but many respondents apparently prefer to express opinions on subjects about which they know little rather than to admit to ignorance.[5] Even those who genuinely believe themselves to be well informed have rarely been the recipients of a full and balanced presentation of the arguments on both sides of an issue. Their knowledge tends to be culled from the views of a few outspoken legislators and the editorials of their favoured newspaper. The political rhetoric that passes for information is often aimed at exploiting the public's fears and base instincts. Consequently, opinion polls tend to measure emotional rather than intellectual/rational responses, and off-the-top-of-the-head opinions rather than reflective judgements. They do not tell the legislator what the views of the people would be if they were better informed and given the opportunity to think seriously about the issues (Fishkin, 1995). A vicious cycle is created wherein political soundbites form the basis of the public opinion which is measured in the polls, and the poll results are incorporated into the speeches of politicians eager to cater to the popular mood (ibid.).

It often appears that the premise under which politicians proceed is that the people either are not interested in government or do not have an opinion worth listening to. Whether these assumptions are correct is difficult to assess. The reason that many citizens may not make the effort to become informed on political affairs is because they despair of having an impact on government policy. The average voter practises what Downs (1957) called 'rational ignorance' – he or she rationally concludes that, given the limited impact of their single vote in an election, a major investment in learning about the issues is not warranted. The lack of an effective mechanism whereby the people can make their views known encourages an undesirable passivity which is then equated by the politicians with apathy. Negative campaigning has come to dominate election campaigns, with personal attacks on opposition candidates being favoured over discussions of the issues. When issues are discussed, the objective appears to be to distort the opposing party's position out of all recognition rather than to clarify one's own or articulate the differences between the parties. Face-to-face televised debates between the candidates are avoided in the United Kingdom and, in the American presidential elections, where they do take place, serious questions are met with barely responsive set speeches. Voters are provided few opportunities to question the candidates. On the rare occasion when they are, there is usually no opportunity given to follow up on the answers to a question.

Those who wish to become more actively involved in public affairs are left with few, and not particularly attractive, options. They can write to their legislator, but those who have taken this path usually receive only a standard response thanking them for their interest and soliciting their continued support. Rarely does the reply, typically written by an aide, address the points made in the constituent's letter. Face-to face meetings with the legislator – for example, in a local surgery – hold more potential but, even then, the constituent may receive little more than a polite audience. When a subsequent vote is taken in the legislative, the constituent's analysis is easily dismissed as the viewpoint of a disgruntled minority if it disagrees with that of the legislator.

Individuals who feel strongly about issues of public policy may have to mobilize themselves into an effective lobbying force if they expect to be heard. This can be both time-consuming and expensive, however. Only the zealots seem to have the hours and the energy to persist, and these 'professional citizens' may be as unrepresentative of the general public as the lobbyists who represent corporate interests. The selective information supplied by the citizens' lobby seems to be shaped by political ideology, while that of the corporate lobby is shaped by financial self-interest but neither may reflect the real concerns of the people. A people's lobby, in any event, would be hard-pressed to compete effectively with better financed corporate lobbies. The remaining alternatives for those who wish to express their views are even less promising. Callers who seek to be heard on talk-radio programmes typically become fodder for the host's insults. Protesters who take to the streets find that their actions engender fear rather than support, with politicians and the public alike seeming to take a jaundiced view of protesters regardless of the merits of their cause. There is the basic problem that protests are essentially negative when what is needed is a way for citizens to make a positive contribution to government (Stewart, 1997).

The effect of the obstacles placed in the way of the citizen who wishes to become involved in the political process is to induce a sense of powerlessness, frustration and, ultimately, alienation. Many simply give up on the effort to influence the political discourse. Lacking input from the people, the politicians see themselves as free to do as they like. Except perhaps for a brief period before the quadrennial or quinquennial national election, little serious attempt is made to discover the views of the people. It is no wonder that most individuals, when questioned, state that the government is unresponsive to their concerns. The disintegration of meaningful democratic government seems almost inexorable: the hurdles in the way of citizen participation discourage efforts to become involved; the absence of involvement is equated with apathy, or, worse still, approval; the politicians then feel justified in doing as they please, at which point powerful interest groups, both political and economic, step in to bend government to their own ends. Elected officials who, in theory, owe a duty to their constituents in practice give their allegiance to their party or special interests. Representatives tend to be far removed – psychologically, if not physically – from the voters who put them in office. Stripped of the rhetoric which so often surrounds it, modern representative government is little more than the oligarchic rule of a small clique of professional politicians.

Recapturing Democracy

The ideal of political democracy envisages a citizenry which is actively engaged in the affairs of government. It does not assume an altruistic or infallible populace and accepts that the people can be shortsighted and foolish. The guiding principle is rather that the people are the best judges of what is in their collective best interest. The challenge lies in finding a way to involve the public in the operation of the government.

We have seen in the jury a decision-making model in which members of the community are informed on controversies which they are then responsible for adjudicating. Can this model be adapted to decisions on social and political issues? The term 'citizens jury'[6] will be used to refer to a group of citizens, drawn at random and representative of society, who are brought together, informed on an issue through the oral and written testimony of witnesses, whom they are allowed to question, provided with the opportunity to deliberate and then asked to give their conclusions and recommendations. The goal is to discover what a fair and impartial cross-section of the public would think about an issue if they were to become truly informed about the issue and were given the opportunity to reflect and discuss the issue with equally informed others.

Citizens juries may be modelled on the legal jury, but there is no reason why the two need be identical in all respects. Those features of the legal jury that are little more than the residue of tradition and custom need not be preserved. There is little reason, for example, why the advocates and moderator (the counterparts to the lawyers and the judge) should have to wear robes and wigs, or use archaic forms of address. There are sound reasons for dispensing with rules of evidence which prevent the decision-makers from obtaining a complete picture of all relevant considerations. There is, properly, less indulgence of forensic tactics whose purpose is to mislead the jurors or obscure the issues. Indeed, many citizens juries have dispensed with advocates altogether and simply allow witnesses to make a statement to the jury, with the jurors then being allowed to question witnesses. Even when advocates are involved, citizens juries are actively encouraged to set questions and propose additional witnesses (sometimes only by generic description) from whom they wish to hear. Usually citizens juries, unlike their legal counterparts, will give a statement of reasons for their 'verdict', so that other citizens can evaluate the merits of their decision. Finally, there is no requirement of unanimity, the thinking being that juror divisions in themselves convey an important message. Rather than the all-or-nothing – guilty or not guilty – verdict of the legal jury, the verdict of the citizens jury can identify shades and nuances of opinion, as well as differences among the jurors.

Service on a citizens jury should be voluntary. One of the long-term objectives is to promote a culture wherein the opportunity to serve is welcomed. Motivation level is inevitably higher on tasks which are voluntarily undertaken than it is on those which are compulsory. This is not to say that reasonable steps should not be taken to encourage service on a citizens jury. Jurors should be fairly, if not liberally, compensated for their time and efforts. Where needed, transportation should be provided, and creche and childcare facilities made available. While service on a citizens jury ought to remain voluntary, prospective citizen jurors, like legal jurors, should not be able to volunteer themselves.

The opening chapters of this book explored the considerations of legal and moral justice that arise in criminal cases. Comparable issues can arise on a citizens jury that is convened to address a specific controversy. But citizens juries may also be convened to obtain general guidance on issues of public policy (as will be seen, this is in fact where they have most commonly been employed). Now the issues of justice that arise will focus not on justice in the individual case but on justice within society as a whole.

Rawls (1972) has written extensively on the topic of distributive justice, and he too sees it as emerging from process. His 'process', which was examined in Chapter 1, consisted of the creation of a hypothetical 'original position'. Citizens juries might be seen as an attempt to give life to this artificial construct. There are critical differences, of course – most notably that citizen jurors, unlike the members of Rawls' congress, are aware of their individual characteristics and therefore able to visualize the impact that their decisions will have on their personal lives. However, for the lack of knowledge of where one's personal best interests lie – the characteristic feature of those in the 'original position' – is substituted, as will be discussed subsequently, a communitarian perspective. Both frameworks arguably lead to fair and just decision-making. Before examining in detail the processes at work on a citizens jury, however, it may prove useful to look at some examples of citizens juries in practice.

In Germany, Professor Peter Dienel of the University of Wuppertal runs the Research Institute for Citizen Participation and Planning Procedures (*Forschungsstelle Burgerbeteiligung und Planungsverfahren*). It employs 'planning cells' (*planungszelle*), similar in function, if not in name, to citizens juries, to assist local and national planning bodies. The counterpart to the Institute in the United States is the Jefferson Center, a non-profit organization based in Minneapolis. Indeed, it was the Center's founding director, Dr Ned Crosby, who first coined and has since trademarked the term 'citizens jury'. Both Crosby's citizens juries and Dienel's planning cells have been operational for approximately 25 years. Citizens juries are a more recent innovation in Britain but, in the past two years, the Institute for Public Policy Research (IPPR), Opinion Leader Research (OLR), the King's Fund, the Economic and Social Research Council (ESRC) and the Local Government Management Board have all experimented with the format.

Dienel's planning cells typically consist of 25 or more members who are divided into panels of five at the deliberation stage. There is the risk in a five-member body that it might be dominated by a single individual, or that it might break down if one or two of its members were unavailable. Absenteeism, however, has not proved to be a problem,[7] and the impact of a domineering juror is limited to the one sub-cell of which the juror is a member. More troubling, on the other hand, is the potential lack of diversity in so small a unit as five. Any given cell may be highly unrepresentative, and each unrepresentative in its own way. By contrast, the Jefferson Center deliberately sets out to ensure that its citizens juries consist equally of men and women who mirror the racial, educational, and socioeconomic composition of the community. To this end, it employs a fairly strict quota system in selecting juries. A half-way position is taken in the British citizens juries, with a conscious effort being made to achieve balance but without the rigour of a quota system. Cross-sectional representation is important if the goal is to assess what the community would think about an issue if it were informed and given the opportunity to deliberate, but less so if the aim is to see if opinion will change when exposed to the dialectics of jury debate.

Citizen jurors have consistently demonstrated both independence and a willingness to consider innovative solutions to problems. In Britain, the Lewisham citizens jury, convened to examine drug abuse, went against the prevailing tide of political and public opinion by favouring treatment rather than punishment of offenders. Decriminalization of 'soft' drugs also attracted strong support, as did education and an end to the hypocrisy over legal/illegal drugs (Druglink, 1997). The opinions of professionals will also be closely scrutinized. When planning cells were asked to evaluate designs for a new town hall in Cologne, they came out in favour of more open space and greenery in front of the proposed hall than allowed for in any of the designs (Stewart *et al.*, 1994). The city council overruled the objection of the architects and accepted this recommendation. A similar iconoclasm was demonstrated when the West German Ministry of Research and Technology enlisted planning cells to study the future energy directions of the country, putting 56 distinct proposals before 24 cells. The cells favoured renewable energy sources and were particularly cautious in respect to nuclear options, stressing the need to develop an adequate system of waste management before embarking on any nuclear energy programme.

Dienel's planning cells have had considerable impact. They are usually commissioned by governmental bodies, which thereby become psychologically, even if not contractually, committed to making use of their findings. In fact, the standard agreement between Dienel's Institute and the commissioning body stipulates that the latter will adopt the recommendations of the planning cells or publicly state the reasons for not doing so. A similar provision has been incorporated into the contracts for citizens juries which have been held in Britain. In contrast, the citizens juries of the Jefferson Center are usually convened at the behest of private (often charitable) organizations or are initiated by the Center itself. This allows for greater freedom in choosing the topic and the format, but means that the jury's verdict will have less practical impact. Among the many subjects that the Jefferson Center has tackled are healthcare priorities, welfare reform, the federal budget, arts in the schools, traffic congestion, agriculture and water policy, juvenile crime, and the relative merits of electoral candidates.

An example may serve to illustrate the nature of the Center's activities, and how a typical citizens jury is conducted. In October 1993 a jury was convened to consider the issue of national healthcare reform (Jefferson Center, 1993). The jury consisted of 24 members selected by a professional sampling organization. It was deliberately balanced in respect to age, race, gender, education, geographical residence, political affiliation and source of healthcare financing of its members. The jury's task was to consider the desirability and direction of healthcare reform generally and, specifically, the merits of President Clinton's then pending healthcare proposals. Over a five-day period the jurors heard testimony from two dozen witnesses, including White House aides who testified in favour of the Clinton plan, and Republican opponents who presented alternative plans. Two former members of Congress were responsible for the management of each side's case, including the selection and questioning of witnesses. As is typical of citizens juries, the jurors played an active role in the evidentiary phase, asking many probing questions of the witnesses. How much would the various plans cost and how would they be funded? Would they reduce or increase the amount of healthcare bureaucracy? How susceptible would they be to fraud, waste and abuse? What quality controls and means of maintaining ethical standards were envisaged? Would the plans lead to more primary care providers and fewer specialists? What would be the effect on the funding of medical research?

In what might be described as a split verdict, the jury unanimously favoured healthcare reform, but rejected the Clinton plan by a vote of nineteen to five. It was not that the jurors were more impressed by the Republican alternatives, although they did believe that these deserved further study.[8] The one idea that did capture their imagination was for a single-payer plan based on a Canadian model, and the jurors twice requested its sponsor to return and provide more information. (This is not atypical of citizens juries, which often will strike off in directions not envisaged by the commissioning body.)The final verdict, however, did not endorse any specific proposals but identified criteria against which any healthcare plan should be evaluated. Among the criteria identified by the healthcare jury were:

- universal and comprehensive coverage
- affordability
- equitable cost for all
- non-cancellability
- portability (so that coverage would not be lost when one changed jobs)
- coverage of pre-existing conditions
- consumer choice
- an emphasis on preventive care
- provisions for accountability (Jefferson Center, 1993, p. 11).

The jurors also stressed the need for a bipartisan approach to healthcare reform and were particularly insistent that whatever plan was adopted should be applicable to everybody regardless of wealth, position or status.

Healthcare issues have also been the subject of many of the citizens juries in Britain, particularly those initiated by the IPRR and the King's Fund. In one of these, sponsored by the Cambridge and Huntington Health Authority, jurors were asked to consider the extent to which the public should be involved in decisions relating to healthcare rationing and what criteria should be used in making rationing decisions. They were further asked how quality of care should be balanced against quantity and how uncertain treatments for serious conditions should be balanced against effective treatments for less serious conditions. After hearing from doctors, patients and healthcare professionals, the jury concluded that the public should be actively involved in establishing rationing criteria and that, in general terms, quantity should be preferred to quality and proven treatments for minor conditions should be preferred to speculative treatments for more serious conditions. However, the jurors were by no means unanimous, and the strength of those who favoured different options varied considerably. Perhaps for this reason, the jurors also recognized the value of maintaining some flexibility within any scheme adopted.

Having the views of the citizen jurors not only provides healthcare administrators with insight into the community's priorities but also gives them a democratic justification, when the subsequent real-life case inevitably arises, for a decision to deny a patient an expensive high-risk treatment for a serious condition. This prioritizing in the abstract, which is done by the citizens jury, is similar to the distributive justice decisions made by Rawls's settlers in the 'original position' (see Chapter 1) – in each case the decision-makers are called upon to determine their priorities without knowing how their choices might subsequently affect them personally. After all, one of the jurors on the Cambridge and Huntington Health Authority's jury might later have been the patient who was denied the speculative treatment. The decision of the jury might then be regretted, but the juror/patient, having been part of the decision process, would be able to appreciate the rationale.

Similar in conception to planning cells and citizens juries is the 'deliberative opinion poll' designed by Professor James Fishkin of the University of Texas. His aim also is to bring together a random sample of ordinary citizens and provide them with the opportunity to deliberate among themselves. In 1994, with the sponsorship of Granada Television and *The Independent* newspaper, Fishkin conducted a deliberative poll on the topic of crime in Britain (Fishkin, 1995). Three hundred participants were selected from 40 randomly chosen constituencies to meet over the course of a weekend and examine the problem of crime and what could be done about it. Despite some initial fears that women, youths, the elderly and parents with young children might be underrepresented among those who volunteered, the group turned out to be a virtual microcosm of the national population (ibid., pp. 166–7). Advance briefing papers were sent to the participants. Various experts, including national politicians, addressed the group as a whole and were questioned by its members. Periodically, the participants broke into subgroups to discuss what they had heard and to formulate questions for future witnesses. At the close of proceedings each participant was asked to complete a questionnaire which enquired as to their individual views. This questionnaire was identical to one that had been administered prior to the presentation of any evidence or formal group discussion. The two sets of questionnaires were then compared in an attempt to assess the effect of the process. The results are discussed in the next section.

Planning cells, citizens juries and deliberative opinion polls – the names may differ but the concepts are the same. The variations are in detail – the length of time allotted to the 'trial', the number of jurors,[9] the format for selecting witnesses and presenting evidence – but all seek to determine what an informal and representative sample of the people, given the opportunity to reflect and deliberate on an issue of public importance, would think about the issue. The critical common denominators are cross-section representation, informed decision-making and democratic deliberation. All aspire to a jury sample that matches the greater community, defined in terms not only of geographical location but also of demographic characteristics and socio-economic interests. Each takes responsibility for educating the participants through the oral and written testimony of witnesses. The witnesses are selected with the goal of providing a comprehensive and balanced picture of the issue being examined.[10] The problem of 'rational ignorance' disappears as information is brought directly to the jurors, who are also able to question the witnesses. The jurors are thus engaged in the process, as well as being responsible for the decision – another key common characteristic of the three models.

Following presentation of the evidence, the participants retire into small groups where they discuss and debate the issues and address whatever questions have been put to them. Usually only group members are present at these deliberations but, in some formats, facilitators have been recruited to lead the discussions. There are advantages and disadvantages to facilitators. On the plus side, they are able to encourage shy or quiescent members of the group to participate; they can exercise a degree of control over dominant individuals who threaten to dominate the deliberations; they can mediate inter-juror disagreements; they can keep the deliberations focused and on track; and they can construct a written record (to be subsequently reviewed by the jurors for accuracy) which includes group decisions/recommendations as well as dissenting positions.

However, there are also dangers: facilitators may inhibit candour, wield disproportionate influence (particularly if they appear knowledgeable on the subject) and distort the natural course of the deliberations. For example, in attempting to keep the deliberations 'on track', the facilitator may be subconsciously influenced by his or her own view of the merits. Similarly a facilitator may encourage those with whose opinions the facilitator agrees to take a more active role in the deliberations while discouraging those with whom he or she disagrees. Encouragement and discouragement may take such subtle and non-observable forms as a slight nodding of the head or a frown. There is also a question of what a facilitator should be facilitating: some facilitators seem more concerned with promoting participation and having the jurors feel good about themselves than in encouraging critical thinking about the problem at hand. All in all, the jury is still out on the value of facilitators. More experience will be required to determine whether the advantages outweigh the disadvantages, but it might be noted that legal juries have functioned effectively for centuries without their assistance – although whether they would be even more effective with such help is open to question.

One of the key differences between legal and citizens juries is that, in the latter, no attempt is made to bring the group to a consensus or unanimous decision. This difference is both explained and justified by the nature of the questions being addressed. On public policy issues the judgement of the group should capture the spectrum of opinion within the group. It would be misleading to suggest that there are no disagreements when there are, and there would be no advantage in so doing. In a criminal trial, on the other hand, a defendant should not have to leave the courtroom under a cloud of suspicion created by a split verdict, and a legal jury is pressed to avoid such a result. The manner in which the criminal justice system weights the burden of proof – jurors must be persuaded of guilt beyond a reasonable doubt – dictates the resolution of cases where the evidence is equivocal. Moreover, the all-or-nothing – guilty or not guilty – legal verdict, will also mask the strength of feeling among the jurors regarding a defendant's culpability. The jurors may be convinced that the charges against a defendant are utterly without foundation or they might believe that the defendant was *probably guilty* but that there remained a slight but reasonable doubt. In both instances a legal jury is obliged to return a verdict of not guilty. On a citizens jury there is no need for definitive answers, and the final report can attempt to capture both the range and intensity of juror opinion.

Learning from Citizens Juries

The shroud of secrecy which surrounds the deliberations of a legal jury has repeatedly been noted. Statutory restrictions prevent the recording or videotaping of the deliberations, third parties are not allowed to be present in the jury room, and jurors may be prohibited from disclosing the substance of their discussions. However, the restrictions that frustrate attempts to learn about the deliberations of legal juries do not apply to citizens juries, and the observation and study of the latter can be used to enrich our understanding of the former.[11] Legal juries and citizens juries are mutually beneficial – the legal jury provides a model for the citizens jury, and the citizens jury sheds light on the processes at work on a legal jury. Whereas the procedures in a legal case are fixed, different formats can be experimented with on citizens juries to see which are the most effective and in which type of cases. Unlike in mock jury experiments, where the artificiality of the exercise can induce a lack of seriousness, citizen jurors will be aware that their decisions can alter the course of the political debate, even if they might have no formal status.

Much has been learned about citizens juries from the work of Dienel, Crosby and Fishkin. In Britain as previously noted, citizens juries are a more recent phenomenon, but already lessons are emerging. After examining the pilot studies the Institute for Public Policy Research and Opinion Leader Research concluded that, in general terms, citizen jurors are able to grasp complex issues, ask pertinent questions and reach sensible conclusions (IPPR and OLR, 1996). They also discovered that citizen jurors see themselves as representatives of the community, rather than as individuals – the reasons for which will be examined more closely later in this section. The jury experience is well received, and jurors are both willing to become involved and able to make a meaningful contribution.

American courts that allow challenges for cause to jurors who have been exposed to inflammatory publicity seem to proceed on the assumption that, when exposed to media hype, the public will form opinions that will prove impervious to the force of reason or evidence.[12] Perhaps the courts are just being overcautious, but it is difficult to know for certain the psychological effects of initial impressions. What, if anything, can we learn from citizens juries on this issue? The topic of a citizens jury is often one that has generated much press coverage. Editorials and columnists will generally take forceful and sometimes strident positions, and their readers will no doubt have been influenced by these. It would be surprising, for example, if those who took part in Fishkin's deliberative poll on crime or the Lewisham citizens jury on drugs did not have opinions – in many instances strongly held opinions – on the subject. If changes of opinion were to occur as a result of the evidence and the deliberations, it would support the thesis that legal jurors too are capable of overcoming the effects of previously formed opinions.

The participants in Fishkin's deliberative poll on crime, completed 'before' and 'after' questionnaires. Unlike the situation on a legal jury where, if questioned on *voir dire*, a juror might be tempted to misstate his or her opinions in order to be selected, there was no reason for participants to lie on the 'before' questionnaires since idiosyncratic views did not disqualify a respondent from participating. Comparison of the before and after answers to Fishkin's questionnaires is revealing (Fishkin, 1995, Appendix). The percentage of respondents who agreed with the statement that sending more offenders to prison is an effective way of preventing crime dropped from 57 to 38 per cent, while the percentage of those who agreed with the statement that the courts should send fewer people to prison rose from 29 to 44 per cent. Along with this decreased confidence in the deterrent effect of prison came an increased interest in alternatives to imprisonment, particularly for juvenile offenders. The percentage of those who favoured giving a first offender a stern warning while placing the responsibility on the parents to sort the juvenile out increased from 49 to 63 per cent. Rehabilitative options also attracted greater support: compulsory training and counselling for non-dangerous criminals was favoured by 75 per cent in the 'after' questionnaire compared with 66 per cent in the 'before' questionnaire. The percentage of the respondents who saw the need for maintaining procedural protections for those accused of crime and who objected to 'cutting corners' to secure a conviction also rose. Consistent with this theme was the increase from 36 to 50 per cent of the respondents who would preserve the right to silence (the right not to answer police questions without having one's failure to respond being commented on in court) and the decrease from 58 to 41 per cent of those who thought the invocation of the right should count against a defendant.

A similar evolution of views occurred on the Lewisham citizens jury on drugs. Of the jurors who participated, only five remained fixed in their views (Druglink, 1983). Treatment and education emerged as the dominant themes and, by the close of proceedings, 15 of the 16 jurors agreed with the statement that 'young people will try drugs. The best we can do is teach them about the real dangers' (ibid.).

These results are not only interesting in their own right but also because they run so counter to the politicians' view of public opinion. In both the 1996 American and the 1997 British elections the major political parties espoused a strong anti-crime package featuring a crackdown on criminals, 'Three strikes and you're out' (a baseball metaphor), reflecting the idea that after three convictions an offender should be sentenced to life imprisonment, became the catchphrase of American politicians, while in Britain a tough government sentencing bill, incorporating similar principles, attracted broad bipartisan support. The politicians seemed to assume that the public wanted criminals to be dealt with harshly. The Lewisham citizens jury and Fishkin's deliberative poll, on the other hand, appear to indicate that an *informed* public is prepared to be more understanding and less draconian in its approach to those convicted of crime.

The sceptic might argue that these results are attributable to a liberal bias in the selection of witnesses and evidence. There can be no question that the choice of witnesses can have a bearing on the outcome. Because of this factor, it may make sense to assign partisan 'case advocates' for each side, who are responsible for selecting witnesses, as opposed to having a 'neutral' steering committee, select the witnesses (the most common approach utilized, particularly in Britain). Advocates, of course, can be expected to select witnesses who will be able effectively to present their point of view. While the choices of a steering committee might appear objective, they can be influenced by the subconscious biases of its members. In any event, the results of Fishkin's deliberative poll on crime were not one-sided. There was no significant change in the number of respondents who favoured the death penalty or who thought that 'prison life should be made tougher and more unpleasant'. This suggests that the respondents did not get swept up in an anti-prison current, as the sceptics insinuated, but rather considered each issue on its individual merits.[13]

Consider also the results of the citizens jury convened by the Jefferson Center to examine the federal budget. One of the issues before the jurors was whether national taxes were too low. The question of taxation, like that of crime and drugs, is one that few adults will not have considered. Most people have strong views on the subject, with most being opposed to higher taxes. This predictable position was reflected in an initial poll of the citizen jurors. Fully half indicated that they favoured cutting taxes, while only 17 per cent were even open to the possibiity of raising them. Yet, after hearing expert witnesses and engaging in small group deliberations the jury recommended an increase in taxes of US $70 billion (Stewart *et al.*, 1994). Obviously, juror minds had changed.

The citizens jury on the federal budget also serves to dispel one of the myths that has grown up about the legal jury, which is that it is incapable of understanding the evidence in complex cases, such as those involving commercial fraud. It might be recalled that it was concerns of this sort that led the Roskill Committee (1986) to recommend replacing jurors in complex fraud trials with an expert panel. Yet unravelling the federal budget may be every bit as difficult as unravelling the financial machinations in a complex fraud case. More recently, the Jefferson Center asked citizen jurors to consider how the state of Minnesota's expenditures might be trimmed to meet a $1.5 billion shortfall anticipated in the year 2001. The Center's staff, in evaluating this project, concluded that:

> ... the jurors clearly were able to grasp the big picture of the problems which may face the state in 2001... [and] came up with a package approach for dealing with the fiscal problems that was at once ... responsible and thoughtful ... . (Jefferson Center, 1996)

This evaluation was concurred in by nontrial observers. The jurors were prepared – more prepared than most politicians – to make touch choices and consider courses of action that might prove unpopular.

The Center's citizens juries on the federal and state budgets are instructive for yet another reason. They demonstrate that jurors are prepared to place the common good above their own personal interests. Of course, the verdict of the juries was hypothetical, in that no one's taxes would actually be raised because of them. Nonetheless, there was no incentive for the jurors to lie. On the contrary, there was the possibility that the legislature might have taken the verdict, which the jurors were aware was to be reported and publicized, as reflective of public opinion generally. Legislators who might have previously shied away from tax increases because of fear of a public backlash might, as a result, have become less hesitant after the verdicts. By being disingenuous about their true preferences on taxes, the jurors could have financially disadvantaged themselves.

But why do citizens juries have this communitarian orientation? As it does in respect to legal juries, the answer seems to lie in the dynamics of the deliberations. Talking with others both brings out the full implications of policy choices and clarifies one's own thoughts on the issue. A further effect of face-to-face debate is to force those involved to see issues from the perspective of others. On a citizens jury, those jurors who believe they would be disadvantaged by a particular proposal will ask the others to see the proposal from their perspective. In a face-to-face exchange it is impossible to avoid the challenge. Engaging in such a process sensitizes the participants to the needs of others. It heightens one's sense of empathy.

That citizens juries do generate a communitarian perspective is confirmed by the findings of those who have examined jury deliberations (IPPR and OLR, 1996, Stewart, 1997). A consistent, identifiable thread which characterizes these deliberations is that jurors are prepared to put aside their own interests and think in terms of the public good. Nor is the public good, as some economists might have it, seen as something which is achieved by each individual pursuing his or her own self-interest. Rather, the jurors appear to grasp that the public good entails responding to the concerns and needs of others. Just as justice trumps strict adherence to law on a legal jury, so communitarian interests seem to trump selfish interests on a citizens' jury.

A striking example of the empathy that can be generated occurred in Fishkin's deliberative poll on crime. One female member of the group challenged a senior Conservative Party spokesperson on the government's then pending bill to abolish the right of silence. The official had maintained that the right of silence was the refuge of the professional criminal. The woman countered that retarded citizens – like herself – would be at risk if the right were to be withdrawn, as they might easily be manipulated into making a legally damaging admission. It was apparent that the other members of the deliberative poll (as well as the national television audience) were moved by her passion and appeal to fair play, even though the overwhelming majority of them were not themselves retarded. Her intervention may in no small measure have accounted for the opposition in the final poll to any weakening of the right of silence.

Crosby refers to the willingness of citizen jurors to look beyond their own well-being and adopt policies that will help others, particularly those with the greatest need, as a form of 'negative utilitarianism' (Crosby, 1991). Whereas utilitarianism (in crude terms) envisages the greatest happiness for the greatest number, negative utilitarianism entails a preparedness to sacrifice one's own happiness in order to benefit the least well-off members of society (see also Rawls, 1972). Whether jurors see themselves personally better off living in a fair and just society, thereby explaining their apparent altruism in less altruistic terms, may be a nice point for debate, but it should not be allowed to obscure the fact that jurors are willing to look at issues from a broader societal perspective, no matter what the reason. To repeat a point made in respect of legal juries, the concern for others that characterizes the deliberations is the natural outgrowth of process, and does not have to be – and, indeed, is usually not – mandated by formal rule or the instructions of a judge/moderator.

Do citizen jurors become better informed citizens as a result of their experience? Witnesses bring their knowledge to the jurors and must reduce that knowledge to terms that will be understood by those who are not experts in their field. To explain a complicated theory in simple terms is undoubtedly as salutary an exercise for the expert as it is an instructive one for the jurors. The experience of the participants in the Jefferson Center's national health reform jury bears out the educational gain for the jurors. At the outset, when the jurors were asked whether they understood the major points in President Clinton's healthcare package, only 33 per cent of the jurors felt that they understood the proposals and 54 per cent confessed to ignorance or confusion. By the conclusion, however, 88 per cent claimed to understand the issues, while only 4 per cent still felt confused. Likewise, on the Lewisham citizens jury on drugs, only a handful of the 16 jurors thought that they were well informed at the outset, but by the end 15 did. Levels of sophistication also increase. Crosby's healthcare jurors came to appreciate that trade-offs in priorities would be inevitable and that taxes would have to rise to meet national healthcare costs. Fishkin similarly concluded that the participants in his deliberative poll on crime developed a more sophisticated understanding of the complexity of the issues (Fishkin, 1995).

Participation in a citizens jury can lead to a gain not only in knowledge but in self-confidence. Initially jurors tend to be deferential to expert witnesses. As they became better informed, however, they became more willing to challenge the experts. Their questions became more probing, and, in their deliberations, jurors are openly critical of the experts.[14] On the Sunderland Health Authority's citizens jury, half of the jurors initially indicated that they thought that the public should *frequently* be involved in decisions regarding health services, while the remaining jurors divided evenly between the public *occasionally* being involved and *always* being involved. By the close of proceedings, however, these percentages were turned around, with 50 per cent of the jurors having the view that the public should *always* be involved (Sunderland Health Authority, 1997).

A final question worth asking is how the jury experience is regarded by the jurors themselves. Anecdotal evidence from legal jurors is mixed, but more systematic feedback from those who have served on citizens juries is encouraging. When the 24 jurors who sat on the Jefferson Center's Health Care Reform Jury were asked to assess the experience, for example, 17 indicated that they were 'very satisfied', while seven described themselves as 'satisfied'. Not a single juror chose the 'neutral', 'dissatisfied', or 'very dissatisfied' categories to describe the experience. This is not atypical. Dienel reports planning cells that have dispensed with scheduled coffee breaks of their own accord in order to continue their discussions.[15] Similarly, Crosby tells of citizens juries where the participants requested additional meetings in order to take their deliberations forward (Crosby, 1980). The IPPR King's Fund and ESRC citizen jurors almost uniformly stated that they found the experience educational and rewarding.

This combination of anecdotal and empirical evidence serves to refute the intimations of politicians that ordinary people are not interested in public affairs or are unwilling to become involved. The effect of serving on a citizens jury actually seems to whet the appetite of jurors. Crosby tells of previously apolitical jurors who were so enthused by the experience that they became political activists. One spouse of a participant in Fishkin's deliberative poll on crime confided that whereas her husband had not previously read newspapers, he had subsequently developed the habit of reading 'every newspaper every day' (Fishkin, 1995, p. 168). She added that he was going to be a much more interesting person to live with in retirement. Such effects demonstrate how the citizens jury experience can help to foster an informed and engaged citizenry.

Reinventing Representative Government

The number of participants in most citizens juries is usually between 12 and 16. Fishkin's deliberative polls are the exception. Although the number of participants is far larger, it is still a minute percentage of the population at large. The verdict of a planning cell, citizens jury or deliberative poll should of course be reported, but it would be more meaningful if ways could be developed to enable a greater proportion of the public to become directly rather than vicariously involved in the process. How might this be done?

Modern developments in communications technology may hold the key to unlocking the potential of citizens juries. Both Fishkin and Crosby have been successful in persuading television networks to broadcast their proceedings.[16] This allows the public to share in the informational benefits of the trial. A Web site on the Internet would allow those with computer access to become involved in the deliberations. The King's Fund, working together with the Science Museum, set up an 'electronic citizens jury' in conjunction with the citizens jury held in Buckinghamshire on the topic of back pain treatment.[17] A summary of each day's evidence was entered into the site, and the jury's recommendations were also reported. The users of the site were able to acquaint themselves with the evidence presented to the jury (and a tracking of the sub-sites visited by those who accessed the main site indicated that this in fact occurred); make comments; ask questions; contribute opinions, thoughts and ideas; and, ultimately, vote on whether they agreed or disagreed with the jury's recommendations. Interestingly, there was strong agreement between the citizens jury which heard the 'live' testimony and the electronic citizens jury. Approval by the latter of the former's recommendations ranged from 88 to 100 per cent.

Of course, not everybody has a PC or access to the Internet, so the electronic citizen jurors may not have been as representative of the public as the actual citizens jury, which was selected to match the demographic profile of the community. The broad consensus between the views of the two juries, on the other hand, suggests that heterogeneity and diversity may not be as important as previously thought – at least in respect to issues that do not touch on sensitive subjects such as race. In the long term, in any event, the electronic citizens jury will become more representative as computers become more common and available in public access sites such as libraries, and the general population becomes more computer literate. Nonetheless, there are dangers in giving members of an electronic citizens jury a 'vote that counts'. It is all too easy for an organization that feels strongly about an issue or has a vested interest in the outcome to hijack the results by mobilizing its members to register their votes – even if they have not followed the evidence or listened to the arguments. The comments of the Internet users may be of greater value. They often raise issues and perspectives that might not have been considered, thereby taking the deliberations in new directions and stimulating the thinking of other participants in a positive way. In terms that have been used previously, the electronic jury adds to the dialectics and synergism of the deliberations. All this, moreover, can be achieved in respect to a worldwide audience, and more economically and efficiently (participants need not take time off from their jobs), than a citizens jury where all the jurors are assembled in the same place.

The willingness of prospective jurors to devote time and energy to a citizens jury is likely to be in direct proportion to the reception given to their verdict. One member of the Hertfordshire citizens jury on waste management, when asked whether the investment in the jury had been well spent, commented that it depended on whether its proposals were taken seriously (Kuper, 1996). It is also noteworthy that information/voting sites on the Web typically attract a significant number of browsers who do not vote, perhaps because they see the vote as more of an opinion poll than something that will be given serious consideration in the decision-making process. Even if jurors are liberally compensated for their efforts, the experience may prove frustrating if the fruits of their labours are summarily brushed aside by those in authority. Although there is every indication that citizen jurors approach their service consientiously, the seriousness of purpose which surrounds the endeavour would be enhanced if the jurors knew for sure that their recommendations would enter into the decision-making calculus. This obviously already occurs in respect to a legal jury by virtue of the fact that the jury's verdict will have significant repercussions for the defendant. In many of the citizens juries held in Britain, as well as in respect to Dienel's planning cells, there is a 'contract' between the sponsoring authority and the jury that, if the latter's recommendations are not adopted, then the sponsoring authority will make the recommendations public and explain the reasons why they are being rejected.

To achieve a comparable impact on a national level may be more difficult, but the way forward was demonstrated by the Reform Party of Canada. When the issue of physician-assisted suicide arose, the party decided to hold an 'electronic town meeting' (Becker, 1994). Voters in the parliamentary districts represented by the party were contacted at random and asked to serve as members of a panel. Those who agreed were sent literature setting out the arguments for and against physician-assisted suicide. A televised debate was then held, after which the respondents registered their opinions. The party had previously committed itself to be bound by a 70 per cent vote in either direction. In the event, the verdict of the electronic town meeting in favour of physician-assisted suicide was contrary to the party's previous official stand, and it was required to change its position accordingly.

The Canadian experiment suggests a brave new world where citizens juries help to transform the face of representative government. In this new world important questions of national policy would be submitted to one or more citizens juries in each legislative district. Legislators with strongly held views of their own would be allowed to appear as witnesses before the jury but would not be permitted to be present during its deliberations. Because their recommendations will represent the views of an informed cross-section of the community which has had the opportunity to reflect on the issues, the citizen jurors have a strong claim to be taken seriously, and a substantial consensus jury vote should presumptively bind the constituency legislator. If there was not a substantial consensus, the legislator would be free to exercise his or her best judgement on the issue but, even then, the legislator will have been the beneficiary of the informed views of the citizens jurors. If the legislator decided to vote contrary to a consensus recommendation of the jury, he or she should be required to publicly explain the vote.

An even braver new world can be envisaged. The democratic premise underlying citizens juries is that ordinary people, when provided with the needed information to make a decision and given the opportunity to reflect and deliberate, are as, if not more, competent decision-makers than politicans. Unlike politicians, they are not beholden to political parties or lobbyists. Starting from these premises a system of government that did away with professional politicians and political parties altogether can be envisaged. Rather than simply having citizen juries in each district which fed their verdicts into a national legislature, the legislature itself would be transformed into a mega-citizens jury whose membership would be chosen at random.

The idea is not as radical as it might seem. In ancient Greece the holders of many public offices were chosen by lot, the operating principle being that all citizens were capable of fulfilling the duties of public office (Dunn, 1992). Kleisthenes introduced a Council of Five Hundred whose rotating membership served for a period of a year. No citizen could serve more than twice during his lifetime (the male adjective is deliberate as women were not citizens and thus not eligible). The Council was advised by an assembly which included all citizens who wished to be members. In the legal sphere, Solon established a court of the people which heard appeals of magistrates' decisions – a concept which was subsequently extended to the trial itself. In both of these 'people courts' the jurors were randomly selected.

A modern-day version of the Athenian model was predicted by the British historian and MP James Bryce (Bryce, 1888). Bryce identified four forms of political democracy. The first, characterized by the Greek experience, consisted of 'primary assemblies' in which the whole of the people met, debated and decided issues of public importance. Bryce believed, however, that such a mode of government was only possible in small communities. Bryce's second form of government was the representative assembly. Here representatives of the people, elected at periodic intervals, were left relatively unfettered to pursue those policies that they thought were in the national interest. This Bryce perceived to be the prevailing system in his native England.[18] In the third form of government, legislators were elected for a more limited term than in the second and were kept in greater check. They were conceived of as delegates of the people rather than as leaders chosen because of their superior wisdom and vision. The legislature was likely to be under constitutional restrictions and power in theory rested with the people. This was Bryce's impression of the government in the United States.

Finally, Bryce forecast a fourth stage of government – the evolutionary product of the third – where the elected representatives would become superfluous and the people would rule directly. It would be a government, in short, of the people. But Bryce saw major obstacles in the way of such a government: the difficulty of accurately ascertaining the views of the public; the fact that public opinion often consists of nothing more substantial than impressionistic judgements fuelled by newspaper editorials and political rhetoric; and the danger of a tyranny of the majority that would not give due consideration to minority interests. These hurdles would be overcome in the proposed national citizens assembly where hearings would precede votes on controversial issues, thereby allowing the views of the citizen legislators to be informed by experts as well as by those who would be affected by the policy under consideration. The communitarian perspective promoted by face-to-face dialogue could be expected to serve as a check on any tyranny of the majority. A further check that could be adopted would be a requirement of a substantial consensus (of, say, 75 per cent) before any new policy could become law. This super-majority requirement (not unlike that on a modern-day legal jury) would not only provide protection to minority interests, but would also help guard against overly frequent and potentially destabilizing shifts in policy.

Random selection of citizen legislators in the national assembly would also ensure that the legislators are truly representative of the people. Under the existing political system, it can only be wondered what representatives represent. The composition of neither the British Parliament nor the US Congress is representative of the racial, ethnic and gender composition of their respective nations. Nor, in the absence of proportional representation, is it representative of the prevailing range of political ideologies. It is perhaps representative of geographical divisions, but in Britain, at least, candidates often run for parliament in districts other than those in which they reside.

Terms of service in the national citizens' assembly, as they were in Athens, would be limited, perhaps to one or two years, as it is desirable to allow as high a percentage of the population as possible to serve. Before embarking on a term of service, there would be training sessions conducted by the outgoing representatives in order to brief the new members on the nature of their duties and on pending legislation. After completion of a citizen's terms of service, there would be a period, of, say, 15 years, when reselection would not be permitted. Despite this moratorium, the benefits of service could be anticipated to have a carry-over effect. As in Fishkin's anecdote about the previous non-reader of newspapers who became a news addict after having participated in a deliberative poll, so too the habit of active citizenship, once tasted, is likely to become a staple part of the citizen's diet. Ex-assembly members can be expected to continue to take an active interest in public affairs and to communicate their opinions to those who take their place in the assembly. Because a citizen might be drafted to serve at any time, there would be a strong incentive to keep informed on issues of public concern.

There are obviously many details that would need to be fleshed out before such a radical proposal as a national citizens assembly might be considered seriously.[19] Indeed, until considerably more momentum were to be generated for the concept, it would not be worth the effort required to work out the details. It is presented here simply to illustrate the potential of the citizens jury movement.

Conclusion

We have seen that democracy has fallen into decline, partly as a consequence of natural forces and partly as the result of the cynical manipulation of the people by politicians. In a more complex and fast-moving society, irregular general elections are no longer an adequate means – if they ever were – for the people to make themselves heard. In any event, a consultative role is not the aspiration. For a democracy to thrive, the people must become actively involved in its operation. The opposite has in fact occurred. Lacking direct input into the operation of government, the people have become passive. The jury provides a model for allowing them to reclaim their democratic heritage and play a more constructive role in government. Citizens juries, like legal juries, are empowering. For the 'rational ignorance' which characterizes the public's general approach to elections is substituted a methodology that takes responsibility for educating citizens before they are called upon to express an opinion. In place of the rhetorical excesses of the politicians there is a balanced presentation of all sides of an issue through the testimony of knowledgeable witnesses whom the jurors are able to question. Rather than having no structured opportunity to discuss the issues with knowledgeable others, citizen jurors are able to debate matters of common concern with persons who are as well informed as themselves. The integrity of the process gives legitimacy to the result.

Citizens juries provide a viable forum wherein the insights and experiences of ordinary people can be brought to bear on the decision-making processes of government. The deliberations allow differences of opinion to be openly discussed, critically examined and fairly resolved. Deliberations transcend the narrow and sterile application of rules-for-rules-sake and create a bigger picture where considerations of fairness and justice become paramount. Face-to-face dialogue promotes empathy and forces jurors to see issues from a communitarian perspective. Even if minds are not changed, jurors come to better understand both the opposing point of view and their own position. If there is merit in Aristotle's dictum that human beings are political by nature, then citizens juries can be seen as the means whereby that natural inclination is allowed to flourish.

Citizens juries not only provide a forum in which ordinary people can examine social and political issues, but also help to give concrete definition to what it means to be a citizen. Citizenship, arguably, entails more than voting in a periodic election or contributing one's views to an opinion poll. It envisages direct engagement in the decision-making processes of government and taking responsibility for decisions that will affect the society. This is what legal and citizens juries are all about. As a by product, the jurors become more mature and responsible decision-makers in their own lives. The jury experience demonstrates that, when ordinary people are given the responsibility for important decisions, they take their task seriously, carry it out conscientiously, and for the most part do it well. The jury stands proudly at the crossroads of legal method, moral philosophy and democratic theory.

Notes

1 California Civ. Proc. Code, s.215 (West 1982).
2 See, for example, Criminal Justice and Public Order Act of 1994 (UK). Jurors are routinely instructed, however, to inform the court of any attempt to approach them or influence their decision.
3 *Williams* v. *Florida*, 399 US 78 (1970).
4 Adonis and Mulgan (1994, p. 2) report that since the rise of modern constitutional politics, around 1000 national referenda have been held, half in Switzerland, and less than a quarter in other western liberal democracies.
5 In a 1976 poll respondents were asked to comment on 'The Public Affairs Act of 1975'. Although no such Act existed, this did not prevent one-third of the respondents from expressing an opinion of the Act (Bishop, *et al.*, 1980).
6 The term has been granted a service mark by the US government. The application was made by Dr Ned Crosby, an American political theorist who is the director of the Jefferson Center. When the term is used in this book, it is intended to refer to a generic

concept and not to the specific model of a citizens jury that is promulgated by Dr Crosby.

7 Of the 1900 people who took part in planning cells since their inception, there have been only two or three absences (Stewart, *et al.*, 1994, p. 30).

8 One recommendation that a citizens jury might make is that another citizens jury should be convened to examine an issue that the first jury did not have the time to explore.

9 Whereas the number of participants citizens juries is usually limited to 12–24, Fishkin brings together several hundred people for his deliberative poll. The size of planning cells usually falls womewhere in between.

10 There is an issue, to be discussed on p. 215, as to whether witnesses should be selected by partisan advocates or a neutral steering committee.

11 Although the possibility should not be ignored that the knowledge that they are being observed might distort the nature of the deliberations (by, for example, making jurors less candid, particularly when discussing personal experiences), those who have observed group deliberations tend to believe that this inhibiting effect is short-lived. As jurors become immersed in their deliberations they soon seem to forget that they are being watched.

12 See, for example, *Irvin* v. *Dowd*, 366 US 717 (1961).

13 It should be noted that the reported results described the 'net change' between the 'before' and 'after' questionnaires. A finding of 'no change' may indicate that no respondents changed their minds, but is equally consistent with wholesale changes of mind that cancelled each other out.

14 See Lenaghan and New, *Health Service Journal*, 11 April 1996 at p. 8.

15 Although this example is offered as proof of juror commitment, it may be that short periodic breaks serve a constructive purpose by providing an opportunity for participants both to digest what they have heard and to discuss with one another informally the testimony and the issues.

16 Fishkin's deliberative poll on crime was broadcast by Granada Television. The weekend's proceedings were compressed into a three-hour documentary. A more ambitious deliberative poll on the choices in the 1996 American presidential election was broadcast over a three-day period in January 1996 by the Public Broadcasting Service (PBS). Crosby's National Health Reform citizens jury was also the subject of a PBS documentary.

17 The discussion which follows is based on a paper presented at the University of Essex on 23 April 1997 by Colin Finney, who created the Web site.

18 Bryce had an advantage in this regard because he himself was an MP. His observations on the American political system, in contrast, were based on his visits to that country.

19 There would, for example, need to be provision for the 'casework' dimension of representative government (that is, looking after the interests of individual constituents). This responsibility might be allocated to an administrator conversant with the substantive area at issue.

Bibliography

Abramson, J. (1994), *We, the Jury*, Basic Books.

Adler, S. (1994), *The Jury*, Times Books.

Adler (1973), 'Socioeconomic factors influencing jury verdicts', *New York University Review of Law & Social Change*, **3**, (1).

Adonis and Mulgan (1994), 'Back to Greece: the scope for direct democracy', *Lean Democracy*, **2**.

Adorno, T., Frenkel-Brunswick, E., Levinson, D. and Sanford, R. (1950), *The Authoritarian Personality*, Harper.

Alexander, J. (1963), *A Brief Narration of the Case and Trial of John Peter Zenger*, Harvard University Press.

Allen, M. (1996), *Textbook on Criminal Law*, (3rd edn), Blackstone Press.

Altschuler (1989), 'The Supreme Court and the jury: Voir dire, peremptory challenges, and the review of jury verdicts', *University of Chicago Law Review*, **56**, p. 153.

Altschuler and Deiss (1994) 'A brief history of the criminal jury in the United States', *University of Chicago Law Review*, **61**, p. 867.

American Bar Association Advisory Committee on Fair Trial and Free Press (1968), *Standards Relating to Fair Trial and Free Press*, American Bar Association.

American Bar Association (1980), *Standards for Criminal Justice*, American Bar Association.

Andrews (1978), 'Uses and abuses of the jury' in P. Glazebrook, *Reshaping the Criminal Law*, Sweet and Maxwell.

Aristotle (1925), *The Nicomachean Ethics*, trans. W.D. Ross, Clarendon Press.

Arnold (1980), 'A historical inquiry into the right to trial by jury in complex civil litigation', *University of Pennsylvania Law Review*, **128**, p. 829.

Asch (1951), 'Effects of group pressure upon the modification and distortion of judgments', reprinted in H. Guetzkow (ed.), *Groups, Leadership and Men*, Carnegie Press.

Ashby (1978), 'Jury selection and the Sixth Amendment right to an impartial jury', *Creighton Law Review*, **11**, p. 1137.

Atiyah, P. and Summers, R. (1987), *Form and Substance in Anglo-American Law*, Oxford University Press.
Austin, J. (1955), *The Province of Jurisprudence Determined*, Weidenfeld and Nicolson.
Babcock (1975), 'Voir dire: preserving "Its Wonderful Power"', *Stanford Law Review*, **27**, p. 545.
Baker, J. (1979), *An Introduction to Legal History*, Butterworths.
Baldwin and McConville (1979), *Jury Trials*, Clarendon Press.
Bankowski (1988), 'The jury and reality' in M. Findlay and P. Duff (eds), *The Jury under Attack*, Butterworths, p. 80.
Baron, J. (1994), *Thinking and Deciding*, (2nd edn), Cambridge University Press.
Becker (1994), 'Electrifying democracy', *Lean Democracy*, **34**.
Bentham, J. (1821), *The Elements of the Art of Packing as Applied in Special Juries in Cases of Libel Law*, Wilson.
Berkowitz (1991), 'Breaking the silence: should jurors be allowed to question witnesses?', *Vanderbilt Law Review*, **44**, p. 117.
Berman and Sales (1977), 'A critical evaluation of the systematic approach to jury selection', *Criminal Justice and Behaviour*, **4**, p. 219.
Bishop, Oldendick, Tuchfarber and Bennett (1980), 'Pseudo-opinions on public affairs', *Public Opinion Quarterly*, **44**, p. 198.
Black, D. (1963), *Theory of Committee and Elections*, Cambridge University Press.
Blackstone, W. (1765), *Commentaries on the Laws of England of Public Wrongs* (1765).
Blanck, Rosenthal and Cordell (1985), 'The appearance of justice: judges' verbal and nonverbal behavior in criminal jury trials', *Stanford Law Review*, **38**, p. 89.
Bloom, B. and Broder, L. (1950), 'Problem-solving Processes of College Students. An Explanatory Investigation', University of Chicago Press.
Bloomstein, M. (1968), *Verdict: The Jury System*, Dodd, Mead and Co.
Blume (1944), 'The place of trial of criminal cases: constitutional vicinage and venue', *Michigan Law Review*, **43**, p. 59.
Boehm (1968), 'Mr. Prejudice, Miss Sympathy and the authoritarian personality: an application of psychological measuring techniques to the problem of jury bias', *Wisconsin Law Review*, p. 734.
Borchard, E. (1970), *Convicting the Innocent*, Plenum Publishing Co.
Bray and Noble (1987), 'Authoritarianism and decisions of mock juries: evidence of jury bias and group polarization', in L. Wrightsman, S. Kassin, and C. Willis, *In the Jury Box*, Sage Publications.
Bridgeman and Marlowe (1979), 'Jury decision making: An empirical study based on actual felony trials', *Journal of Applied Psychology*, **64**, p. 91.

Broeder (1965), 'The negro in court', *Duke Law Journal*, **19**.
Broeder (1954), 'The functions of the jury: facts or fictions?', *University of Chicago Law Review*, **21**, p. 386.
Broeder (1969), 'Occupational expertise and bias as affecting juror behavior: a preliminary look', *New York University Law Review*, **40**, p. 1079.
Broeder (1965), 'Voir dire examinations: an empirical study', *Southern California Law Review*, **38**, p. 503.
Bronson (1970), 'On the conviction proneness and representativeness of the death qualified jury: an empirical study of Colorado veniremen', *University of Colorado Law Review*, **42**, p. 1.
Bryce, J. (1888), *The American Commonwealth*, London.
Buckhout, Licker, Alexander, Gambardella, Eugenio, and Kakoullis (1979), 'Discretion in jury selection', in L. Abt and I. Stuart, *Social Psychology and Discretionary Law*, p. 176.
Burns, J. and Hart, H.L.A. (eds) (1970), *Complete Works of Jeremy Bentham*, Athlone Press.
Byrne (1988), 'Jury reform and the future', in M. Findlay and P. Duff (eds), *The Jury Under Attack*, Butterworths, p. 209.
Campbell and Le Poidwin(1980), 'Complex cases and jury trials: a reply to Professor Arnold', *University of Pennsylvania Law Review*, **128**, p. 965.
Card, R. (1992), *Card, Cross & Jones Criminal Law*, (12th edn), Butterworths.
Carlson, M., Halper, A. and Whitcomb, D. (1977), *One Day/One Trial Jury System*, National Institute of Law Enforcement and Criminal Justice.
Casper and Benedict (1994), 'The influence of outcome information and attitudes on juror decision making in search and seizure cases', in R. Hastie (ed.), *Inside the Juror*, Cambridge University Press.
Casper, Benedict and Perry (1989), 'Jury decision making, attitudes, and the hindsight bias', *Law and Human Behavior*, **13**, p. 291.
Charow and Charow (1978), 'Making legal language understandable: a psycholinguistic study of jury instructions', *Columbia Law Review*, **79**, p. 1306.
Cheng and Holyoak (1985), 'Pragmatic reasoning schemas', *Cognitive Psychology*, **17**, p. 391.
Christie (1974), 'Lawful departures from legal rules: "jury nullification" and legitimated disobedience', *California Law Review*, **62**, p. 1289.
Cicero (1928), *Laws*, Loeb Library edn.
Cohen (1977), 'The role of evidential weight in legal proof', *Boston University Law Review*, **66**, p. 635.
Cohen, J. (1977), *The Probable and the Provable*, Oxford University Press.
Coke, E. (1832), *Commentary Upon Littleton*, 9th edn, London.
Condorcet Marquis de (1785), *Essai sur l'application de l'analyse à la probabilité des decisions rendues à la pluralité des voix*, Paris.

Connor (1909), 'The constitutional right to a trial by a jury of the vicinage', *University of Pennsylvania Law Review*, **57**, p. 197.
Corboy, P. (1975), 'From the Bar', in R. Simon, (ed.), *The Jury System in America*, Sage Publications.
Cornish, W. (1968), *The Jury*, Penguin Books.
Cowan, Thompson and Ellsworth (1984), 'The effects of death qualification on jurors' predisposition to convict and on the quality of deliberation', *Law & Human Behavior*, **8**, p. 53.
Crosby (1992), 'A solution for difficult environmental questions', unpublished paper presented at the Humboldt Conference, 26 June 1992.
Crosby, E. (1991), *The Citizens Jury Process as a Basic Democratic Reform.*
Crosby, E. (1980), *Towards a New Democracy*, unpublished.
Cross (1967), 'The behaviour of the jury: a comment', *Criminal Law Review*, p. 575.
Dane and Wrightsman (1982), 'Effects of defendants' and victims' characteristics on jurors' verdicts', in N. Kerr and R. Bray (eds.), *The Psychology of the Courtroom*, Academic Press, p. 83.
Darbyshire (1991), 'The lamp that shows that freedom lives – is it worth the candle?', *Criminal Law Review*, p. 740.
Darrow (1936), 'Attorney for the defense', *Esquire*, **8**, p. 35.
Davis (1973), 'Black jurors', *Guild Practitioner*, **30**, p. 112.
de Tocqueville, A. (1960), *Democracy in America*, Vintage Books.
Demos (1994), *Lean Democracy.*
Denning, Lord (1981), *What's Next in the Law?*, Butterworths.
Devitt, E., Blackmar, C. and Wolff, M. (1987), *Federal Jury Practice and Instructions.*
Devlin, P. (1956), *Trial by Jury*, Stevens.
Devlin, P. (1979), *The Judge*, Oxford University Press.
Devlin, P. (1991), 'The conscience of the jury', *Law Quarterly Review* **107**, p. 398.
Devons (1965), 'Serving as a juryman in Britain', *Modern Law Review*, **28**, p. 561.
Dienel, P. (1992), *Die Manungszelle*, Westdeutsches Verlag.
Dienel, P. (1989), 'Contributing to social decision methodology: Citizen reports on technological projects', *Social Methodology for Technological Projects*, Kluwer, p. 133.
DiPerna, P. (1984), *Juries on Trial: Faces of American Justice*, Dembner Books.
Dooley (1991), 'Sounds of silence on the civil jury', *Valparaiso University Law Review*, p. 405.
Downs, A. (1957), *An Economic Theory of Democracy*, Harper and Row.

Druglink (1997), *Citizens Juries.*

Dubois (1962), 'Desirability of blue ribbon juries, *Hastings Law Journal*, **13**, p. 479.

Dunn, J. (1992), *Democracy, The Unfinished Journey*, Oxford University Press.

Dworkin, R. (1986), *Law's Empire*, Fontana Press.

Dworkin, R. (1978), *Taking Rights Seriously*, Duckworth.

Eastman (1945), 'The history of trial by jury', *National Bar Journal*, **3**, p. 87.

Ekman and Friesen (1967), 'Head and body cues in the judgment of emotion: a reformation', *Perceptual and Motor Skills*, **24**, p. 711.

Ekman and Friesen (1968), 'Nonverbal leakage and clues to deception', *Psychology*, **32**, p. 88.

Ekman (1968) 'Differential communication of affect by head and body cues', *Journal of Personality and Social Psychology*, **2**, p. 726.

Eldred and Price (1958), 'A linguistic evaluation of feeling states in psychotherapy, *Psychology*, **21**, p. 115.

Ellenberger, H. (1970), *The Discovery of the Unconscious.*

Ellsworth (1989), 'Are twelve heads better than one?', *Law and Contemporary Problems*, **52**, p. 205.

Elwork, A., Sales, B. and Alfini, J. (1982), *Making Jury Instructions Understandable*, Michie/Bobbs-Merrill.

Elwork, Alfini and Sales (1987), 'Towards understandable jury instructions', in L. Wrightsman, S. Kassin and C. Willis (eds), *In the Jury Box*, Sage Publications, p. 161.

Enright, S. and Morton, J. (1990), *Taking Liberties*, Weidenfeld and Nicolson.

Erlanger, H. (1970), 'Jury research in America: its past and future', *Law and Society Review*, **4**, p. 345.

Etzioni (1974), 'Creating an imbalance' *Trial*, **10**, p. 28.

Fahringer (1980), 'In the valley of the blind: a primer on jury selection in a criminal case', *Law and Contemporary Problems*, **43**, p. 116.

Farrar (1992), 'Ancient Greek political theory as a response to democracy', in J. Dunn, *Democracy, The Unfinished Journey*, Oxford University Press.

Findlay (1988), 'The role of a jury in a fair trial', in M. Findlay and P. Duff (eds), *The Jury Under Attack*, Butterworths, p. 161.

Findlay, M. and Duff, P. (eds) (1988), *The Jury Under Attack*, Butterworths.

Finkelstein (1966), 'The application of statistical decision theory to jury discrimination cases', *Harvard Law Review*, **80**, p. 338.

Fischoff (1975), 'Hindsight does not equal foresight: the effect of outcome knowledge on judgment under uncertainty', *Journal of Experimental Psychology, Human Perception and Performance*, **1**, p. 288.

Fishkin, J. (1995), *The Voice of the People: Public Opinion and Democracy*, Yale University Press.

Fletcher, G. (1988), *A Crime of Self-Defense: Bernhard Goetz and the Law on Trial.*
Forsyth, W. (1852), *The History of Trial by Jury*, London.
Frank, J. (1930), *Law and the Modern Jury*, Coward McCann Inc.
Frank, J. (1963), *Courts on Trial*, Atheneum.
Frank, J. and Frank, B. (1957), *Not Guilty*, Victor Gollancz.
Frankel (1990), 'A trial judge's perspective for providing tools for rational jury adjudication', *Northwestern University Law Review*, **85**, p. 221.
Frankfurter and Corcoran (1926), 'Petty federal offenses and the constitutional guaranty of trial by jury', *Harvard Law Review*, **39**, p. 917.
Frederick (1978), 'Jury behavior: a psychologist examines jury selection', *Ohio Northern University Law* Review, **5**, p. 571.
Freeman (1981), 'The jury on trial', *Current Legal Problems*, p. 65.
Freud, S. (1948), *The Psychotherapy of Everyday Life*, Brill edn.
Frey-Robin, L. (1950), *From Freud to Jung: A Comparative Study of the Psychology of the Unconscious*, Putnam.
Fried, Kaplan and Klein (1975), 'Jury selection: an analysis of voir dire', in R. Simon, *The Jury System in America*, Sage.
Friedland (1990), 'The competency and responsibility of jurors in deciding cases', *Northwestern University Law Review*, **85**, p. 190.
Friloux (1975), 'Another view from the bar', in R. Simon, *The Jury System in America*, Sage.
Fuller, L. (1958), 'Positivism and fidelity to law – a reply to Professor Hart', *Harvard Law Review*, **71**, p. 630.
Fuller, L. (1964), *The Morality of Law*, Yale University Press.
Galston (1994), 'Taking Aristotle seriously: republican-oriented legal theory and the moral foundation of deliberative democracy, *California Law Review* **82**, p. 331.
Gilligan, C. (1982), *In a Different Voice: Psychological Theory and Women's Development*, Harvard University Press.
Gobert, J. (1977), 'Victim precipitation', *Columbia Law Review*, **77**, p. 511.
Gobert, J. (1988), 'In search of the impartial jury', *Journal of Criminal Law and Criminology*, **79**, p. 269.
Gobert, J. (1989), 'The peremptory challenge – an obituary', *Criminal Law Review*, p. 528.
Gobert, J. and Jordan, W. (1990), *Jury Selection: The Law, Art, and Science of Selecting a Jury*, 2nd edn, Shepard's/McGraw-Hill.
Goldberg (1970), 'Toward expansion of *Witherspoon*: capital scruples, jury bias, and use of psychological data to raise presumptions in the law', *Harvard Civil Rights – Civil Liberties Law Review*, p. 53.
Goldstein (1985), 'Nothing is too complex', *American Bar Association Journal*, p. 39.

Goldwasser (1989), 'Limiting a criminal defendant's use of peremptory challenges: on symmetry and the jury in a criminal trial', *Harvard Law Review*, **102**, p. 808.

Gordan (1992), 'Juries as judges of the law: the American experience', *Law Quarterly* Review, **108**, p. 272.

Green, T. (1985), *Verdict According to Conscience: Perspectives on the English Criminal Trial Jury, 1200–1800*, University of Chicago Press.

Greer and White (1988), 'Restoring jury trial to terrorist offences in Northern Ireland', in M. Findlay and P. Duff (eds), *The Jury Under Attack*, Butterworths, p. 173.

Griew (1967), 'The behaviour of the jury – a review of the American evidence', *Criminal Law Review*, p. 555.

Griew (1985), 'Dishonesty: objections to *Feely* and *Ghosh*', *Criminal Law Review*, p. 341.

Grisham and Lawless (1973), 'Jurors judge justice: a survey of criminal jurors', *New Mexico Law Review*, **3**, p. 52.

Groddick, E. (1950), *Exploring the Unconscious*, Vision Press.

Harman, H. and Griffith, J. (1979), *Justice Deserted*, National Council for Civil Liberties.

Hart, H.L.A. (1958), 'Positivism and the separation of law and morals', *Harvard Law Review*, **71**, p. 593.

Hart, H.L.A. (1961), *The Concept of Law*, Oxford University Press.

Hassett (1958), 'A jury's pre-trial knowledge in historical perspective: the distinction between pre-trial publicity and "prejudicial" publicity', *Law and Contemporary Problems*, **43**, p. 155.

Hastie, R. (ed.) (1994), *Inside the Juror*, Cambridge University Press.

Hastie, R., Penrod, S. and Pennington, N. (1983), *Inside the Jury*, Harvard University Press.

Hegel, G. (1988), *Phenomenology of Spirit*, Indiana University Press.

Hepburn (1980), 'The objective reality of evidence and the utility of systematic jury selection', *Law and Human Behavior*, **43**, p. 889.

Hermann (1970), 'Occupations of jurors as an influence on their verdict', *Forum*, **5**, p. 150.

Heuer and Penrod (1991), 'Some suggestions for the critical appraisal of a more active jury, *Northwestern Law Review*, **85**, p. 226.

Hewstone, M. (1990), *Causal attribution: from cognitive processes to collective beliefs*, Basil Blackwell.

Hitchler (1931), 'Motive as an essential element of crime', *Dickinson Law Review* **35**, p. 105.

Hobbes, T. (1914), *Leviathan*, Everyman edn.

Holdsworth, W. (1966), *A History of English Law*, 7th edn.

Holmes, O.W. (1987), 'The path of the law', *Harvard Law Review*, **10**, p. 383.

Hornblower (1992), 'Creation and development of democratic institutions in Ancient Greece', in J. Dunn, *Democracy, The Unfinished Journey* Oxford University Press, p. 13.
Horowitz (1985), 'The effect of jury nullification instruction on verdicts and jury functioning in criminal trials', *Law and Human Behavior*, **9**, p. 25.
Horowitz (1988), 'Jury nullification: the impact of judicial instructions, arguments, and challenges on jury decision making', *Law and Human Behavior*, **12**, p. 439.
Howe (1939), 'Juries as judges of criminal law', *Harvard Law Review*, **52,** p. 582.
Huigens (1995), 'Virtue and inculpation', *Harvard Law Review*, **108**, p. 1423.
Hunt (1982), 'Putting juries on the couch', *NY Times*, (Magazine), November.
Hunter (1935), 'Law in the jury room', *Ohio State University Law Journal*, p. 1.
Hutcheson (1929), 'The judgment intuitive: the function of the "hunch" in judicial decision', *Cornell Law Quarterly*, **14**, p. 174.
IPPR and OLR (1996), *Citizens' Juries: Towards Best Practice*, Working Paper.
James Committee (1975), *The Distribution of Criminal Business between the Crown Court and the Magistrates' Court*, HMSO.
James (1959), 'Status and competence of jurors', *American Journal of Sociology*, **64**, p. 563.
James (1959), 'Jurors' assessment of criminal responsibility' *Social Problems* **7**, p. 58.
Jefferson Center (1993), *Citizens Jury on America's Tough Choices, Health Care Reform*, Final Report, Jefferson Center.
Jefferson Center (1996), *Citizens Jury on State and Local Fiscal Matters – Can We Afford the Future*?, Final Report, Jefferson Center.
Johnson (1985), 'Black innocence and the white jury', *Michigan Law Review*, **83**, p. 1611.
Joiner (1975), 'From the bench', in R. Simon (ed.), *The Jury System in America*, Sage Publications.
Jung, C. (1950), *Psychology of the Unconscious*, Dodd, Mead.
Jurow (1971), 'New data on the effect of a "death qualified jury" on the guilt determination process', *Harvard Law Review*, **84**, p. 567.
Kadish, M. (1967), The crisis of over-criminalization', *Annals*, **374**, p. 157.
Kadish, M. and Kadish, S. (1973), *Discretion to Disobey: A Study of Lawful Departures from Legal Rules*, Stanford University Press.
Kahn, A., Donnerstein, A. and Donnerstein, M. (eds) (1984), *Social Psychology*, Braun & Co.

Kairys, Kadane and Lehoczky (1977), Jury representativeness: a mandate for multiple source lists', *California Law Review*, **65**, p. 776.
Kalven, H. and Zeisel, H. (1966), *The American Jury*, Little Brown.
Kant, I. (1959), *Foundations of the Metaphysics of Morals*, Lewis Beck translation.
Kaplan (1968), 'Decision theory and the factfinding process', *Stanford Law Review*, **20**, p. 356.
Kassin (1990), 'The American jury: handicapped in the pursuit of justice', *Ohio State Law Journal*, **51**, p. 687.
Kaufman (1967), 'A fair jury – the essence of justice', *Judicature*, **51**, p. 88.
Kassin, S. and Wrightsman, L. (1987), 'On the requirements of proof: The basis of judicial instruction and mock juror verdicts' in L. Wrightsman, S. Kassin and C. Willis (eds), *In the Jury Box*, Sage Publications, p. 143.
Kennebeck (1975), 'From the jury box', in R. Simon (ed.), *The Jury System in America*, Sage Publications.
Kennedy, L. (1964), *The Trial of Stephen Ward*, Gollancz.
Kerr (1978), 'Severity of prescribed penalty and mock jurors' verdicts', *Journal of Personality and Social Psychology*, **36**, p. 1431.
Kerr, Atkin, Stasser, Meek, Holt and Davis (1976), 'Guilt beyond a reasonable doubt: effects of concept definition and assigned decision rule on the judgments of mock jurors, *Journal of Personality and Social Psychology*, **34**, p. 282.
Kerr, N. and Bray, R. (eds) (1982), *The Psychology of the Courtroom*, Academic Press.
Kerr and McCorn (1987), 'The effects of the jury size and polling method in the process and product of jury deliberations in L. Wrightsman, S. Kassin and C. Willis (eds), *In the Jury Box*, Sage, Publications.
Kessler (1973), 'An empirical study of six- and twelve- member jury decision-making processes', *University of Michigan Journal of Law Reform*, **6**, p. 712.
Kessler (1975), 'The social psychology of jury deliberations', in R. Simon (ed.), *The Jury System in America*, Sage Publications, p. 67.
Kiewra (1987), 'Notetaking and review: the research and its implications', *Instructional Science*, **16**, p. 233.
King, M. and May, C. (1985), *Black Magistrates*, Cobden Trust.
King (1986), 'Nameless justice: the case for the routine use of anonymous juries in criminal cases', *Vanderbilt Law Review*, **49**, p. 128.
Kisser (1996), 'Children exercise children's rights: participation of pupils in Austrian schools', *The International Journal of Children's Rights*, **4**, p. 407.
Knittel and Seiler (1972), 'The merits of trial by jury: some aspects of

English jury trial and continental modes of trial', *Cambridge Law Journal*, p. 316.

Kuhn (1968), 'Jury discrimination: the text phase', *Southern California Law Review*, **41**, p. 235.

Kuper (1996), 'Citizens juries: The Hertfordshire Experience', Working Paper Series, University of Hertfordshire.

LSE Jury Project (1973), 'Juries and the rules of evidence', *Criminal Law Review*, p. 208.

LaFave, W. and Israel, J. (1984), *Criminal Procedure*, West.

LaFave, W. and Scott, A. (1986), *Criminal Law*, (2d edn), West.

Langbein (1992), 'On the myth of written constitutions: the disappearance of criminal jury trial', *Harvard Journal of Law and Public Policy*, **16**, p. 119.

Larue (1976), 'A jury of one's peers', *Washington and Lee Law Review*, **33**, p. 841.

Lempert (1992), 'A Jury for Japan', *American Journal of Comparative Law*, p. 37.

Lenaghan and New (1996), 'Setting priorities: is there a role for citizens' juries?' *British Medical Journal*, **312**, p. 1581.

Lempert (1975), 'Uncovering "nondiscernible" differences: empirical research and jury-size cases', *Michigan Law Review*, **73**, p. 643.

Levi (1988), 'The role of the jury in complex cases', in M. Findlay and P. Duff (eds), *The Jury Under Attack*, Butterworths

Llewellyn, K. (1960), *The Common Law Tradition: Deciding Appeals*, Little Brown & Co.

Lloyd (1992), 'Democracy, philosophy, and science in Ancient Greece', in J. Dunn, *Democracy, The Unfinished Journey*, Oxford University Press.

Locke, J. (1952), *The Second Treatise of Government*, (T. Peardon edn.).

Loftus, E. (1979), *Eyewitness Testimony*, Harvard University Press.

Mack (1976), 'Full-time major criminals and the courts', *Modern Law Review*, **39**, p. 241.

Maher (1988), 'The verdict of the jury?', in M. Findlay and P. Duff (eds), *The Jury Under Attack*, Butterworths.

Mansfield, Busse and Krepelke (1978), 'The effectiveness of creativity training', *Review of Educational Research*, **48**, p. 517.

Marder (1987), 'Gender dynamics and jury deliberations', *Yale Law Journal*, **96**, p. 593.

Margolin (1973), 'The indigent criminal defendant and defense services: a search for constitutional standards', *Hastings Law Journal*, **64**, p. 24.

Mark, R. (1973), *Minority Verdict*, (Dimbleby Lecture), BBC Publications.

Marshall (1974), 'The judgement of one's peers: some aims and ideals of jury trial', in N. Walker (ed.), *The British Jury System*, Cambridge University Press.

Mayer, R. (1992), *Thinking, Problem Solving, Cognition*, (2nd edn), W.H. Freeman & Co.

McCabe, S. (1974), 'Jury research in England and the United States', *British Journal of Criminology*, **14**, p. 276.

McCabe, S. (1975), 'Discussions in the jury room: are they like this?', in N. Walker (ed.), *The British Jury System*, Cambridge University Press, p. 22.

McCabe, S. (1988), 'Is jury research dead?', in M. Findlay and P. Duff (eds), *The Jury Under Attack*, Butterworths, p. 27.

McCabe, S. and Purves, R. (1972), *The Jury at Work*, Basil Blackwell.

McCabe, S. and Purves, R. (1974), *The Shadow Jury at Work*, Basil Blackwell.

McConahy, Mullin and Frederick (1977), 'The uses of social science in trials with political overtones: the trial of Joan Little', *Law and Contemporary Problems*, **41**, p. 205.

McCormick (1986), 'The interest of the state and the rule of law', in P. Wallington and R. Merkin (eds), *Essays in Memory of E.H. Lawson*, Butterworths.

Mehrabian and Wiener (1967), 'Decoding of inconsistent communications', *Journal of Personality and Social Psychology*, **6**, p. 109.

Mill, J.S. (1859), *On Liberty*, London.

Mill, J.S. (1861), *Considerations on Representative Government*, London.

Mill, J.S. (1863), *Utilitarianism*, London.

Mitchell and Byrne (1973), 'Effects of jurors' attitudes and authoritarianism on judicial decisions', *Journal of Personality and Social Psychology*, **25**, p. 123.

Mitford, J. (1969), *The Trial of Dr Spock*, Alfred A. Knopf.

Montefiore, P. (ed.) (1975), *Neutrality and Impartiality*, Cambridge University Press.

Moore, L. (1973), *The Jury: Tool of Kings, Palladium of Liberty*, W.H. Anderson.

Morgan, 'A brief history of special verdicts and special interrogatories', *Yale Law Journal*, **32**, p. 575.

Morris Committee (1965), *Report of the Departmental Committee on Jury Service*, HMSO.

Morris, T. (1974), *Free Men All: The Personal Liberty Laws of the North, 1780–1861*, John Hopkins.

Mungham and Bankowski (1976), 'The jury in the legal system', in P. Carlen (ed.), *The Sociology of Law*, University of Keele.

Myers (1987), 'Rule departures and making law: juries to end their verdicts', in L. Wrightsman, S. Kassin and C. Willis (eds), *In the Jury Box*, Sage Publication, p. 95.

Nagel, S. and Neef, M. (1979), *Decision Theory and the Legal Process*, Lexington Books.

National Jury Project (1987), *Jurywork*, (2nd edn).
Nemeth (1977), 'Interactions between jurors as a function of majority vs. unanimity decision rules', *Journal of Applied Social Psychology*, **7**, p. 38.
Nemeth (1992), 'Minority dissent as a stimulant to group performance', in S. Worchel, W. Wood and J. Simpson, *Group Processes and Productivity*, Sage Publications, p. 95.
Nemeth and Sosis (1973), 'A simulated jury study: characteristics of the defendant and the jurors', *Journal of Social Psychology*, **90**, p. 221.
Newman (1955), 'Trial by jury: an outmoded relic?', *Journal of Criminal Law, Criminology and Police Science*, **46**, p. 512.
Note (1938), 'Should the jury fix the punishment for crimes?', *Virginia Law Review*, **24**, p. 462
Note (1947), 'The blue ribbon jury', *Harvard Law Review*, **60**, p. 613.
Note (1960), 'Change of venue in criminal cases: the defendant's right to specify the county of transfer', *Stanford Law Review*, **26**, p. 131.
Note (1960), 'Community hostility and the right to an impartial jury', *University of Colorado Law Review*, **60**, p. 349.
Note (1964), 'The changing role of the jury in the nineteenth century', *Yale Law Journal*, **74**, p. 170.
Note (1968), 'Personality tests for prospective jurors, *Kentucky Law Journal*, **56**, p. 832.
Note (1970), 'The case for black juries', *Yale Law Journal*, **79**, p. 531.
Note (1974), 'Toward principles of jury equity', *Yale Law Journal*, **83**, p. 1023.
Note (1976), 'The constitutional need for discovery of pre-voir dire juror studies', *Southern California Law Review*, **49**, p. 597.
Note (1977), 'Juror bias – a practical screening device and the case for permitting its use', *Minnesota Law Review*, **64**, p. 987.
Note (1977), 'Limiting the peremptory challenge: representation of groups on petit juries', *Yale Law Journal*, **86**, p. 1715.
Note (1982), 'The right of privacy of prospective jurors during voir dire', *California Law Review*, **70**, p. 708.
Note (1987), 'Batson v. Kentucky: the new and improved peremptory challenge', *Hastings Law Journal*, **38**, p. 1195.
Note (1988), 'Discrimination by the defense: peremptory challenges after Batson v. Kentucky', *Columbia Law Review*, **88**, p. 355.
O'Connell and Carpenter (1983), 'Psychology and trials: some disturbing insights, *Missouri Law Review*, **81**, p. 299.
Okun (1968), 'Investigation of jurors by counsel: its impact on the decisional process', *Georgetown Law Journal*, **56**, p. 839.
Packer, H. (1968), *The Limits of the Criminal Sanction*, Stanford University Press.

Padawar, Singer and Burton (1975), 'Impact of pretrial publicity on jurors' verdicts', in R. Simon (ed.), *The Jury System in America: A Critical Overview*, Sage Publications.
Padfield, N. (1995), *Criminal Justice Process*, Butterworths.
Phares and Wilson (1972), 'Responsibility attribution: role of outcome severity, situational ambiguity, and internal–external control', *Journal of Personality*, **40**, p. 392.
Polya, G. (1965), *On Understanding, Learning and Problem Solving*, Wiley.
Pound, R. (1908), 'Common law and legislation', *Harvard Law Review*, **21**, p. 383.
Pound, R. (1910), 'Law in books and law in action', *American Law Review*, **44**, p. 12.
Pound, R. (1966), *An Introduction to the Philosophy of Law*, Yale University Press.
Radzinowicz, L. (1948), *History of the English Criminal Law and its Administration from 1750*, Stevens & Sons.
Rawls, J. (1972), *A Theory of Justice*, Oxford University Press.
Redmount (1957), 'Psychological tests for selecting jurors', *Kansas Law Review*, **5**, p. 391.
Rhine (1969), 'The jury: a reflection of the prejudices of the community', *Hastings Law Journal*, **20**, p. 1417.
Robertson, Rich and Ross (1973), 'Jail sentences for driving while intoxicated in Chicago: a judicial policy that failed', *Law and Society Review*, **8**, p. 55.
Roskill Committee (1986), *Fraud Trials Committee Report*, HMSO.
Runciman Committee (1993), *Report of the Royal Commission on Criminal Justice*, HMSO.
Saks, M. (1976), 'Social scientists can't rig juries', *Psychology Today*, **9**, p. 48.
Saks, M. (1976), 'The limits of scientific jury selection: ethical and empirical', *Jurimetrics Journal*, **17**, p. 3.
Saks, M. (1977), *Jury Verdicts*, Lexington Books.
Sales, B. (ed.) (1977), *Psychology in the Legal Process*, Spectrum Publications.
Saltzburg and Powers (1982), 'Peremptory challenges and the clash between impartiality and group representation', *Maryland Law Review*, **14**, p. 337.
Sand and Reiss (1985), 'A report on seven experiments conducted by District Court judges in the second circuit', *New York University Law Review*, **60**, p. 423.
Scheflin (1972), 'Jury nullification: the right to say no', *Southern California Law Review*, **45**, p. 168.

Scheflin and Van Dyke (1980), 'Jury nullification: the contours of a controversy', *Law and Contemporary Problems*, **43**, p. 51.
Scheflin and Van Dyke, J. (1991), 'Merciful juries: the resilience of jury nullification', *Washington and Lee Law Review*, **48**, p. 165.
Schmidt (1983), 'Juries, jurisdiction, and race discrimination: the lost promise of *Strauder* v. *West Virginia*', *Texas Law Review*, **61**, p. 1401.
Schulman, Shaver, Colman, Emrich, and Christie (1973), 'Recipe for a jury', *Psychology Today*, May, p. 37.
Sealy (1975), 'What can be learned from the analysis of simulated juries?', in N. Walker (ed.), *The British Jury System*, Cambridge University Press, p. 12.
Sealy and Cornish (1973), 'Juries and their verdicts', *Modern Law Review*, **36**, p. 496.
Shaw (1932), 'Comparison of individuals and small groups in the rational solution of complex problems', *American Journal of Psychology*, **44**, p. 491.
Sidgwick, H. (1919), *Elements of Politics*, 4th edn.
Sigall and Ostrove (1995), 'Beautiful but dangerous: effects of offender attractiveness and nature of the crime on jurors judgement', *Journal of Personality and Social Psychology*, **31**, p. 410.
Simon, R. (1967), *The Jury and Defense of Insanity*, Little, Brown.
Simon, R. (ed.) (1975), *The Jury System in America*, Sage Publications.
Skinner, B.F. (1971), *Beyond Freedom and Dignity*, Pelican Books.
Slaton (1994), 'Democracy's quantum leap', *Lean Democracy*, p. 32.
Smith (1966), 'Percy Foreman: top trial lawyer', *Life*, p. 92.
Snyder (1971), 'Sex role differential and juror decisions', *Sociology and Social Research*, **55**, p. 442.
Sosis (1974), 'Internal–external control and the perception of responsibility of another for an accident', *Journal of Personality and Social Psychology*, **30**, p. 393.
Spencer, H. (1868), 'Representative government' in *Essays: Moral, Political, and Aesthetic*, p. 182.
Spencer, J. (1989), *Jackson's Machinery of Justice*, Cambridge University Press.
Sperlich (1982), 'The case for preserving trial by jury in complex civil litigation', *Judicature*, **65**, p. 397.
Squires (1994), 'The cracked mirror: the future for representation', *Lean Democracy*, p. 26.
Stephan (1974), 'Sex prejudice in jury simulation', *Journal of Psychology*, **88**, p. 305.
Stephan (1975), 'Selective characteristics of jurors and litigants: their influ-

ence on juries' verdicts', in R. Simon (ed.), *The Jury System in America: A Critical Overview*, Sage Publications.
Stephen, J. (1883), *History of the Criminal Law*, Macmillan 1883.
Stewart, J. (1995), *Innovations in Democratic Practice*, Institute of Local Government Studies.
Stewart, J. (1996), *Further Innovations in Democratic Practice*, Institute of Local Government Studies.
Stewart, J. (1997), *More Innovations in Democratic Practice*, Institute of Local Government Studies.
Stewart, J., Kendall, E. and Coote, A. (1994), *Citizens' Juries*, Institute for Public Policy Research.
Strodtbeck and Mann (1956), 'Sex role differentiation in jury deliberations', *Sociometry*, **19**, p. 3.
Strodtbeck, J. and Hawkins (1957), 'Social status in jury deliberations', *American Sociological Review*, **22**, p. 713.
Suggs and Sales (1978), 'Using communication cues to evaluate prospective jurors during the voir dire', *Arizona Law Review*, **20**, p. 629.
Suggs and Sales (1981), 'Juror self-disclosure in the voir dire: a social science analysis', *Indiana Law Journal*, **56**, p. 245.
Sunderland Health Authority (1997), *Sunderland Citizens' Jury Report*, Sunderland Health Authority.
Swett, D. (1969), 'Cultural bias in the American legal system', *Law and Society*, **4**, p. 79.
Tapper, C. (1995), *Cross and Tapper on Evidence*, 9th edn, Butterworths.
Thaman (1995), 'The resurrection of trial by jury in Russia', *Stanford Journal of International Law*, **31**, p. 61.
Thayer, J.B. (1892), 'The jury and its development', *Harvard Law Review*, **5**, p. 249.
Thayer, J.B. (1898), *A Preliminary Treatise on Evidence at the Common Law*, Little Brown.
Thompson, E.P. (1977), *Whigs and Hunters*, Peregrine Press.
Thompson, E.P. (1980), *Writing by Candlelight*, Merlin Press.
Thompson, Fong and Rosenhan (1981), 'Inadmissible evidence and juror verdicts', *Journal of Personality and Social Psychology*, **40**, p. 453.
Tribe, L. (1971), 'Trial by mathematics: precision and ritual in the legal process', *Harvard Law Review*, **84**, p. 1329.
Ugwuegbu, (1979), 'Racial and evidential factors in juror attributions of legal responsibility', *Journal of Experimental Social Psychology*, **15**, p. 133.
Uviller (1990), 'Acquitting the guilty: two case studies on jury misgivings and the misunderstood standard of proof', *Criminal law Forum*, **2**, p. 1.
Van Dyke (1970), 'The jury as a political institution', *Catholic Lawyer*, **16**, p. 224.

Van Dyke, J. (1977), *Jury Selection Procedures: Our Uncertain Commitment to Representative Panels*, Ballinger Publishing Co.
Walker, N. (ed.) (1974), *The British Jury System*, Cambridge University Press.
Walsh (1969), 'The American jury: a re-assessment', *Yale Law Journal*, **79**, p. 142.
Wanamaker (1937), 'Trial by jury', *University of Cincinnati Law Review*, **11**, p. 191.
Warner (1959), 'The development of trial by jury', *Tennessee Law Review*, **26**, p. 459.
Weinstein (1993), 'Considering jury "nullification": when may and should a jury reject the law to do justice?', *American Criminal Law Review*, **30**, p. 239.
Weld and Danzig (1940), 'A study of the way in which a verdict is reached by a jury', *American Journal of Psychology*, **53**, p. 518.
Wells (1990), 'Tort law as corrective: a pragmatic justification for jury adjudication', *Michigan Law Review*, **88**, p. 2348.
Wigmore, J. (1929), 'A program for the trial of a jury', *Journal of the American Judicature Society*, **12**, p. 166.
Wigmore, J. (1937), *The Science of Judicial Proof*, (3rd edn), Little Brown.
Williams, G. (1963), *The Proof of Guilt*, Stevens & Sons.
Wolff (1990), 'Juror questions: a survey of theory and use', *Missouri Law Review*, **55**, p. 817.
Worchel, S., Wood, W. and Simpson, J. (1992), *Group Processes and Productivity*, Sage Publications.
Wrightsman, L., Kassin, S. and Willis, C. (eds), *In the Jury Box*, Sage Publications.
Zander (1974), 'Acquittal rates and not guilty pleas: what do the statistics mean?', *Criminal Law Review*, p. 401.
Zander (1974), 'Are too many professional criminals avoiding conviction?', *Modern Law Review*, **37**, p. 28.
Zander (1975), 'Legal advice and criminal appeals: the new machinery', *Criminal Law Review*, p. 364.
Zander (1988), *Justice in Ferment*, I.B. Taurus.
Zeisel, N. (1971), '... And then there were none: the diminution of the federal jury', *University of Chicago Law Review*, **38**, p. 710.
Zeisel and Diamond (1978), 'The effect of peremptory challenges on jury verdict: an experiment in a federal district court', *Stanford Law Review*, **30**, p. 491.
Zeisel and Diamond (1987), 'Convincing empirical evidence on the six-member jury', in L. Wrightsman, S. Kassin and C. Willis (eds), *In the Jury Box*, Sage Publications, p. 193.

Index

Index of Authors Cited

For Product Safety Concerns and Information please contact our EU representative GPSR@taylorandfrancis.com Taylor & Francis Verlag GmbH, Kaufingerstraße 24, 80331 München, Germany

Batch number: 10725923

Printed by Printforce, the Netherlands